# BEYOND GERMS

# Amerind Studies in Anthropology

## Series Editor **John Ware**

# BEYOND GERMS

## Native Depopulation in North America

*Edited by*
CATHERINE M. CAMERON,
PAUL KELTON, *and*
ALAN C. SWEDLUND

THE UNIVERSITY OF
ARIZONA PRESS

TUCSON

The University of Arizona Press
www.uapress.arizona.edu

Printed in the United States of America
21   20   19   18   17   16      8   7   6   5   4   3

ISBN-13: 978-0-8165-0024-6 (cloth)
ISBN-13: 978-0-8165-3554-5 (paper)

Cover designed by Miriam Warren
Cover image: *Landing at Jamestown, 1607*, English School.
Private Collection/Bridgeman Images. The editors (Cameron,
Kelton, and Swedlund) requested this cover image, noting
that the indifferent over-the-shoulder look at the Natives as
more English colonists arrive at Jamestown speaks volumes
about the topic of this book.

Library of Congress Cataloging-in-Publication Data
Beyond germs : native depopulation in North America
/ edited by Catherine M. Cameron, Paul Kelton, and
Alan C. Swedlund.
    pages cm. — (Amerind studies in anthropology)
Includes bibliographical references and index.
  ISBN 978-0-8165-0024-6 (cloth : alk. paper)
 1. Indians of North America—Mortality. 2. Indians of
North America—Population. 3. Indians, Treatment of—
North America. 4. Indians of North America—History.
5. Indians of North America—Social conditions. 6. North
America—Ethnic relations. I. Cameron, Catherine M.,
editor. II. Kelton, Paul, editor. III. Swedlund, Alan C., editor.
IV. Series: Amerind studies in anthropology.
E98.P76B49 2015
970.004'97—dc23
                    2015005335

♾ This paper meets the requirements of ANSI/NISO
Z39.48–1992 (Permanence of Paper).

# CONTENTS

     Revolution                                                      198
     *Paul Kelton*

9.  Quality of Life: Native Communities Within and Beyond
     the Bounds of Colonial Institutions in California              222
     *Kathleen L. Hull*

10. The Pestilent Serpent: Colonialism, Health, and Indigenous
     Demographics                                                    249
     *James F. Brooks*

     *Contributors*                                                 263

     *Index*                                                        269

I'll never forget sitting in a college classroom more than forty years ago listening to anthropologist Henry Dobyns describe the effects of Old World diseases on "virgin soil" New World populations. Dobyns guessed that there were between 90 and 120 million American Indians living in the Western Hemisphere when Columbus landed in 1492. By the middle of the seventeenth century, 150 years later, that population had been reduced by some 90 percent. It was, Dobyns claimed, the greatest demographic catastrophe in human history, and most of the collapse went undocumented and was mostly unintended. It was not the sword and musket that killed so many American Indians but European-introduced diseases like smallpox, measles, and malaria.

The story should be familiar to anyone who has read Jared Diamond's blockbuster *Guns, Germs, and Steel* or Charles Mann's *1491*. Because of their long association with domestic animals that served as hosts for many of our species' most devastating epidemic diseases, Europeans brought a handful of exotic diseases with them when they landed on the shores of the New World. American Indians, who had few domestic animals, missed out on the immunity that centuries of natural selection had supposedly conferred on Euro-Asiatic-African populations and so were particularly susceptible to Old World pathogens. According to Diamond and others, germs were the main culprit in high American Indian mortality rates. For the most part, Europeans were innocent bystanders.

In February 2013, the Amerind Foundation hosted an advanced seminar for ten North American scholars whose research seeks to complicate this simple linear story. The symposium, entitled "Beyond Germs: The Impact of Colonialism on Indigenous Health in America," brought together historians, demographers, archaeologists, biological anthropologists, and epidemiologists who presented papers that challenged much of the received wisdom of American Indian mortality. We heard accounts of systematic genocide in New England and California, seventeenth-century slaving in the Southeast that decimated entire regions, and throughout the Americas, forced labor, population dislocations, and a wide range of other depredations. All of the scholars emphasized the same point: the structural violence of European colonization left New World populations more susceptible to Old World pathogens.

The seminar participants agreed that my old anthropology professor almost certainly overcounted the size of the precontact population of the Americas, and he probably overestimated the effects of "virgin soil" diseases as well. Epidemiologists and medical historians now question whether New World populations were particularly immunodeficient, since smallpox, malaria, yellow fever, and the like rarely discriminated between Native and colonial populations: the impacts of these diseases were devastating regardless of genetic inheritance. If Native mortality was higher, it was because Natives were subjected to so many additional stresses. In the words of one seminar participant, "It was the turbulence of colonization and not genetic liability that created Indians' devastating susceptibility to imported pathogens."

The arguments set out in this book will likely be challenged and scholarly debates will ensue that will perhaps lead to a more nuanced view of disease impacts in the New World. In the meantime, by challenging conventional wisdom, this book will likely have repercussions far beyond the narrow confines of paleoepidemiology. In my own field of Southwestern archaeology, extreme die-offs of Native populations from Old World diseases have been more or less assumed since at least the 1970s—despite the frequent lack of empirical evidence—and these assumptions have been used to prop up theories of historical disjunction between the pre-Hispanic past and the early colonial period. The collective angst surrounding the Columbian quincentenary produced some of the more extreme pronouncements about historical disjunction. Robert Dunnell, for example, took Dobyns's population estimates at face value to argue that "the general assumption of continuity between the ethnographic-historical accounts of Native Americans and the people responsible for the archaeological record is no longer valid" (1991:572). To avoid projecting a colonially distorted present into deep prehistory, many Southwestern archaeologists have abandoned the study of the historical Southwestern ethnographies, to the analytical impoverishment of our discipline. Research contained in this book will, one hopes, encourage scholars to reexamine some of these assumptions.

One of the greatest casualties of virgin soil disease theories has been the role of Native agency in colonial outcomes. Native peoples reduced by Old World diseases and crushed by vastly superior Old World technologies could offer only passive resistance to the colonial juggernaut. With colonial outcomes predetermined by germs as well as guns and steel, the actions and motivations of American Indians were irrelevant to historical outcomes. Again, the articles in this book challenge such overarching generalizations. The Iroquois remained active players in the politics of the Northeast at least until the late eighteenth century, on an equal footing with the various European colonial powers and the emergent American nation. The Pueblo Revolt of 1680, which evicted Spain from New Mexico for over a decade, had a profound impact on subsequent colonial policies in the years following the Spanish reconquest. The united Pueblo tribes and the various Native confederacies of the East were active agents in early colonial history, and their stories are an essential part of the complex narrative of American history.

This important book helps to restore American Indians as active agents in the history of colonial North America. It also helps to restore some moral balance to the story of the Columbian exchange. The immunological determinism of Dobyns, Diamond, Mann, and others lets European colonialism off the moral hook. But as history becomes less linear and more complicated, the moral consequences of colonialism shine more clearly through the haze of deep history.

## References

Diamond, Jared. 1997. Guns, Germs, and Steel: The Fates of Human Societies. New York: W. W. Norton.

Dunnell, Robert C. 1991. Methodological impacts of catastrophic depopulation on American archaeology and ethnology. *In* Columbian Consequences, vol. 3: The Spanish Borderlands in Pan-American Perspective, ed. D. H. Thomas, 561–80. Washington, DC: Smithsonian Institution Press.

Mann, Charles. 2005. 1491: New Revelations About the Americas Before Columbus. New York: Alfred A. Knopf.

Ware, John A. 2014. A Pueblo Social History: Kinship, Sodality, and Community in the Northern Southwest. Santa Fe, NM: School of Advanced Research Press.

# ACKNOWLEDGMENTS

We are extremely grateful for the opportunity to reconsider the causes of Native depopulation in the stimulating and hospitable atmosphere of the Amerind Foundation. Our lively discussions were interspersed with wonderful meals, scenic walks, and warm fires. John Ware encouraged the project early on and was an active participant in our deliberations. We thank him and his staff, especially the seminar coordinator, Barbara Hanson, for their efforts to make our seminar productive and enjoyable. Our thanks go also to the contributors to this volume, who were delightful companions in Dragoon and worked hard to meet every deadline we imposed as the book came together. Few editors are as lucky as we have been to have such a dedicated group of colleagues! At the University of Arizona Press, Allyson Carter, Scott De Herrera, and their staff were helpful at every step in the process, and we very much appreciate their efforts to smooth the publication process for us. We thank two anonymous reviewers whose comments were helpful in shaping the final manuscripts, Sally Bennett Boyington for expert copyediting, and Lindsay Johannson, University of Colorado, for editorial assistance.

# BEYOND GERMS

# Introduction

*Paul Kelton, Alan C. Swedlund,*
*and Catherine M. Cameron*

European colonization introduced smallpox, measles, and other infectious diseases to the Americas, causing considerable harm and death to indigenous peoples. There is no question that these diseases were devastating, but their impact has been exaggerated. Warfare, enslavement, land expropriation, removals, erasure of identity, and other non-disease factors also undermined Native populations. These factors in themselves had a more detrimental impact on some Native groups, and for the indigenous population as a whole, these factors worked in a deadly cabal with germs to cause epidemics, exacerbate mortality, and curtail population recovery. We may never know the full extent of Native depopulation, given the notoriously slim and problematic evidence that is available for indigenous communities during the colonial period, but what is certain is that a generation of scholars has significantly overemphasized disease as the cause of depopulation, downplaying the active role of Europeans in inciting wars, destroying livelihoods, and erasing identities. This scholarly misreading has given support to a variety of popular writers who have misled and are currently misleading the public.

The chapters in this volume build on a growing body of scholarship that goes beyond germ-centric explanations and collectively argue that many factors must be considered in understanding the fates of indigenous people after 1492. Written by archaeologists, biological anthropologists, and historians, the volume presents a novel, multidisciplinary approach to uncovering factors that resulted in the dramatic decline in Native populations. Using osteological and archaeological data, historic documents, oral records, government policies, and a rich mixture of other sources, the authors present detailed case studies from a number of regions of North America, including the Northeast, the Southeast, the Southwest, California, and Mexico. Although similar patterns of precipitous decline are evident among indigenous populations in other parts of the world, we have focused on regions with the most abundant and well-developed sources of data to provide the best possible understanding of this process. In these detailed studies, a variety of causes, in addition to germs, can be shown to have affected indigenous morbidity. These include overwork, destruction of resources and means of production, violence, enslavement, misunderstood or concocted narratives, erasure of indigenous identity, disruption of social nurturing, and the breakup and dispersal of communities.

The contributors take particular issue with a line of scholarly inquiry that has emphasized how biological forces outside of human control determined the outcome of Europe's attempt to colonize the Americas, with peoples from the former able to conquer the people of the latter continents with relative ease (e.g., Crosby 1972, 1986; Diamond 1997; Dobyns 1966, 1983). This deterministic scholarship promotes several problematic ideas. Among these is the "virgin soil" hypothesis. First, it argues that introduced diseases spread quickly throughout the American continents with little to no influence from other aspects of colonialism and, further, that the diseases were so deadly because Native Americans had no prior exposure to them. It argues that many Native groups, perhaps the majority of indigenous people, experienced infection and death from colonization's most notorious germ—smallpox—well before their few surviving descendants even saw a European. Second is the proposition that introduced diseases were the overriding cause of Native depopulation. Other aspects of colonialism are sometimes mentioned in this deterministic argument but only to emphasize that the colonizers' germs, not their brutality, bore the overwhelming responsibility for depopulation. The third contention is that population decline was linear and irreversible until a century or more after the first epidemics had erupted. Successive waves of disease meant that Natives would have little or no opportunity to recover.

Population estimates are critical to any arguments made about the effect of European intrusion on indigenous demography, yet the size of the precontact indigenous population has long been a subject of scholarly dispute. The earliest and most vociferous debate has been over Dobyns's population estimates (e.g., Henige 1998). Before the virgin soil hypothesis took hold in scholarship, numbers suggested for the North American population ranged as low as approximately 1 million (e.g., Mooney 1928). Dobyns revised them upward to as high as 18 million (Dobyns 1983). Thanks to the work of Douglas Ubelaker (e.g., 1992, 2000, 2006), Russell Thornton (e.g., 1987, 2000), and others, we now have broad estimates of the indigenous population size of North America before contact based on extensive archival research and modern estimation techniques. (North America is here defined as including the United States, northern Mexico, and Canada.) The estimates range between 2 and 7 million, with Ubelaker's tending toward the lower range of about 2 million (e.g., 2000:53; 2006) and Thornton favoring the higher figure (e.g., 2000:13). Most recently, Milner and Chaplin (2010), using spatial density models, have estimated the range as between 1.2 and 6.1 million. The numbers selected for pre- and postcontact population sizes will determine how steep the decline will be between zenith (or some precontact number) and nadir and how dramatically our representation of those changes will be affected (Johansson 1982; Meister 1976). A maximum precontact number coupled with a minimum postcontact number will result in an increase of many percentage points over what might actually have occurred. Much work is still needed to overcome limited demographic evidence and inadequate methods of calculating prehistoric and historic population sizes.

In the mid-1990s, several studies proved instrumental in refocusing our attention toward the complex history of European contact and disease. Two of the most important are Larsen's 1994 article in the *Yearbook of Physical Anthropology* and Waldram, Herring, and Young's 1995 book *Aboriginal Health in Canada*. Larsen, with his broad background in osteology and bioarchaeology, made a strong case that the skeletal biology of Native populations shows many classes of disease and trauma present in the prehistoric record and that, with the advent of agriculture and more-dense settlement, nutritional stress complicated the disease process prehistorically. Larsen also illustrated, through a comparison of regional studies, that while disease was an extremely significant factor throughout the protohistoric and early historic periods of contact, many groups and communities survived or even escaped the waves of extreme epidemics experienced in other areas. His research emphasized that the Americas were not lands free of disease before contact and that experiences in various regions could be quite different. He has expanded on this theme in subsequent publications and revisits the region of his primary research, La Florida, in chapter 3.

Waldram and colleagues made similar observations in *Aboriginal Health in Canada*, based on their work and that of their colleagues and collaborators researching First Nations populations in Canada. They challenged the idea that Natives lacked immunological competence to respond to novel pathogens and illustrated, through several regional examples in Canada, populations who did recover from epidemics, even the dreaded smallpox. Waldram and colleagues (1995, 2006) argued that while acute community infections were important in early contact experiences, the epidemiological impact of sustained European contact after the initial encounter, when the volume of settlers and intensity of interaction increased, created the greatest consequences. They also suggested, based on the Canadian experience, that no single depopulation model is adequate for the variety of cases observed. "The social history of each Aboriginal community must be evaluated to determine the extent to which infectious disease debilitated and depleted it" (Waldram et al. 2006:71). They pointed out that disruption of the social order and subsistence patterns, marginality to European settlement, and outright displacement are central to understanding the disease process.

Emerging from this recent scholarship are some more informed identifications of the likely causes of population transition and decline, more-reasonable estimates of magnitude of depopulation, if not precise numbers, and a more determined effort to use knowledge of contemporary case fatality rates and their variation for the relevant diseases introduced. Indeed, in a general sense, it was the apparent disparity between what we now refer to as *case fatality rates* among Europeans under ideal conditions and those reported for Native Americans in Mexico, Mesoamerica, Latin America, the American Southeast, and New England that gave rise to the virgin soil hypothesis in the first place. However, broad generalizations can be quite erroneous and misrepresent a great deal of regional and even intraregional variability. Disease is extremely important to what transpired, but it is not necessarily the dominant factor in all cases; second-wave settlement or later European occupation, rather than first contact, may have had the greatest impact on Native health (e.g., Kelton 2007; Waldram et al. 2006).

In 2003 two watershed publications on the virgin soil hypothesis appeared: David Jones's article in the *William and Mary Quarterly* and Suzanne Austin Alchon's book *A Pest in the Land*. While amplifying and elaborating on many of the points in earlier publications, Jones reviewed for readers what was currently known at the time of publication about the social history, epidemiology, and immunology of contact. He dissected the arguments for lack of disease resistance in Native Americans and showed the weaknesses of those arguments. Jones established a powerful platform by directly critiquing Jared Diamond's *Guns, Germs and Steel* (1997), illustrating how Diamond's critique of the racialized explanations of Native conquest and depopulation in the past was itself subtly reframed by claims that the "naïve" immune systems of the Natives were responsible for the massive loss from disease. Jones coupled background on this research with an analysis of why the virgin soil hypothesis could gain such traction and cachet with scholars and laypeople in the first place (e.g., Jones 2003:711–18).

Alchon's book provides an overview of the history of disease prior to 1492, reviewing the experience of colonialism and disease in Mexico, Brazil, the Caribbean, and major regions of North America. In it she makes important distinctions among the methods and purposes of Spanish, French, Portuguese, and English colonizers and argues that disease and mortality were very much entangled with patterns of European colonial processes, including military conquest, slavery and labor demands, and forced migrations. While lacking the detailed critique of the virgin soil hypothesis made by Jones, Alchon's book still provides a compelling argument for the complexity of indigenous depopulation in the Americas.

Mounting evidence in various regions has now established that while epidemics had devastating effects for tribal groups in several North American regions, they were not the sole or, in some cases, not even the major reason for indigenous population decline. Sheila Ryan Johansson's (1982) pioneering observation on the recovery times of premodern European populations and the expected recovery capabilities of many Native populations, reiterated by others (e.g., Larsen 1994; Thornton 2000; Waldram et al. 2006), bears repeating. European settlement, conflict, captivity, displacement, and destruction of indigenous means of subsistence, what Kelton (2007) identified as second-wave effects, typically had much greater impact. Massimo Livi-Bacci (2008) made a similar case for Latin America. He pointed out that colonialism was a shock to indigenous demography, and if epidemics had been the only factor involved, Native populations could have recovered within a few generations. What they could not overcome were aspects of colonialism that interfered with reproduction and fertility—enslavement, violence, and theft of resources (Livi-Bacci 2008).

These earlier critiques of the virgin soil hypothesis, while gaining some traction among some scientists and historians studying the history of disease, unfortunately have had little impact on the wider scientific community or in popular writing on Native American history. As David Jones illustrates in chapter 1 of this volume, many have been, and continue to be, seduced by the intuitive appeal of biological determinism. He brings his classic 2003 article up-to-date, delves deeply into the literature critiquing the virgin soil hypothesis, and provides a broad overview of the ongoing debates regarding the role of disease in depopulation and its association with the many other factors involved. He concludes that there are two parallel narratives—biological and social—and that each has a significant body of evidence supporting it. The subsequent chapters in the volume seek to break this intellectual logjam. They aim to strengthen the growing critique of the popular and pervasive deterministic models and bring multidisciplinary perspectives to bear on the subject matter. Contributors use in-depth analyses of regional case studies to offer keen insights into the dynamic nature of Native societies both before and after contact and show regional patterning that is easily lost in overgeneralizing the colonial/contact experience. The chapters collectively highlight the multiple aspects of colonialism that undermined Native societies, sometimes working independently and sometimes in conjunction with disease.

George Milner continues our critique in chapter 2 by bridging the precontact and protohistoric divide in the Eastern Woodlands of North America. He revisits his classic 1980 article, which was one of the first challenges to Dobyns's assertion of early and frequent pandemics to sweep the Eastern Woodlands of North America (Milner 1980). He brings new bioarchaeological and environmental evidence to his long-term study of Native populations in the Eastern Woodlands before and after European occupation. He notes that there was considerable population decline in the several centuries immediately prior to European contact. Across much of the midcontinent prominent chiefdoms lost significant population because of regional warfare and perhaps climatic change. By the fifteenth and sixteenth centuries, population had become widely dispersed into clusters of small villages. What followed were disparate scenarios of population loss and recovery that accompanied varying patterns of disease spread and intergroup conflict that do not readily fit the classic, single-explanation model of Native depopulation caused by widespread devastating epidemics. However, diseases, coupled with conflict and the economic and political agendas of Europeans and Euro-Americans, still took a heavy toll on the Native populations of the Eastern Woodlands.

In chapter 3, Clark Larsen moves the analysis to the scene of Europe's first sustained contact with Natives in what later became the United States, La Florida. He brings his considerable bioarchaeological background to an examination of the protohistoric conditions among Native populations in the region prior to contact. The region, with its agricultural chiefdoms, was already a place of social hierarchies and resource disparities among indigenous groups. Differential access to resources resulted in inequalities that could leave skeletal indicators on the human remains of the pre- and protohistoric residents. However, the Spanish occupation and exploitation of these populations raised the stresses of forced labor and nutritional deficiencies dramatically. Larsen presents extensive evidence that Spanish colonization exacerbated the impacts of disease, leading to devastating results that he terms the consequences of *structural violence.*

Debra Martin, focusing on the American Southwest, uses bioarchaeological and other evidence in chapter 4 to show "that life on the ground prior to contact was anything but a paradise." Episodic small-scale warfare and interpersonal violence compounded dietary and other health issues. Epidemics that followed in the wake of Spanish colonization presented an additional but not preeminent challenge. The larger challenge, she argues, was that of "creeping genocide." She regards epidemics as just one component of "an intertwined and systematic set of culturally and politically motivated practices that colonists implemented." These included a first wave of "massacres, enslavement, harsh taxation, and assimilation" that abated and then resumed in even harsher forms such as separation of children from families, forced assimilation, and the creation of reservations as marginalized dependent enclaves.

In chapter 5, Gerardo Gutiérrez explores the erasure of indigenous identities in Mexico through a detailed study of the history of the Spanish caste system from the contact period to recent times. He finds that the caste system was tightly intertwined with notions of degrees of racial purity and phenotypic traits that signaled Spanish ancestry or European features of "whiteness." For centuries, opportunity and economic success have been and, indeed, still are strongly associated with notions of whiteness and European ancestry, according to Gutiérrez. Over time this has diminished the number of people who are counted as indigenous, including Mestizos. Along with high rates of intermarriage between and among the various ethnic groups of Mexico, those of lighter complexion or with more-stereotypical European features have more easily moved up the social ladder, even though they may have a high proportion of Native ancestry. Gutiérrez also suggests that these social transformations have been influenced by the cosmetic and fashion industries, which allow indigenous people to alter their appearance to conform to socioeconomically dominant phenotypes. The powerful effect of these processes is that they have caused the "erasure" of the Native identity, even while indigenous genes live on.

Alan Swedlund's chapter focuses on New England and events tied most strongly to the interior along the Connecticut River valley. In this subregion, epidemics and colonial occupation were slightly delayed in comparison to coastal regions, and the impacts played out in somewhat different ways. Swedlund shows how conflict, captivity, and contagion all were involved in the colonial experience. The English themselves may have thought deaths from disease were much heavier than was actually the case, not fully recognizing Native movements and relocations to other communities. However, it was warfare, disruption, and the taking of productive homelands that had the greatest impacts. Drawing on the research and insights of others working in this region, Swedlund observes that Native persistence was obstructed by English occupation of Native farming and hunting lands, compounded by the gradual "erasure" of Natives through the popular histories and newspaper articles that portrayed New England's Indians as people of the past.

Catherine Cameron (in chapter 7) uses ethnohistorical and historical data from three regions—the Southeast, the Pays d'en Haut of New
France, and the Southwest—to explore the impact of warfare, captive-
taking, and enslavement on Native American health and mortality. She
argues that European intrusion changed indigenous warfare from a social practice to a commercial enterprise. While precontact warfare was
focused on male status striving, European demand for labor and the
opening of the New World to international markets that specialized
in human trafficking transformed the value of the indigenous captive.
Rather than serving as a prestige good, the captive became an item of
commercial trade. Europeans not only attacked their indigenous neighbors but also fomented warfare among them. Cameron shows that the
result in each area was many battlefield deaths and many more people
taken captive. Captives might be removed from indigenous rolls by
being sold off the continent, worked to death, or incorporated into
European or indigenous households, where their original identity was
obscured. Furthermore, social disruption, including the disruption
of subsistence practices, also took a toll on indigenous populations
through famine and the absence of curers and caregivers.

In chapter 8, Paul Kelton explores how narratives of disease became
constructed to obscure colonial violence against indigenous peoples.
His topic is the Cherokees' experience during what historian Elizabeth Fenn has called "the Great Smallpox Epidemic of 1775–82" (Fenn
2001). This epidemic spanned the North American continent and
brought much of its diverse human population into a single and deadly
event. Countless numbers of people from varied backgrounds, especially indigenous people, perished during this catastrophe. While other
scholars—both historians and anthropologists—have concluded that
smallpox struck the Cherokees during this time, Kelton demonstrates
that the evidence is sketchy at best. Frontier mythology records that
the disease did great damage to the Cherokees, but this Euro-American
account conflicts with the Cherokees' views of their experience during
the American Revolution, an experience largely characterized by the
scorched-earth strategy of marauding American armies rather than the
smallpox virus. Kelton thus cautions scholars to consider evidence more
carefully, contemplate how narratives are constructed and transmitted,

and look upon colonialism's deadly impact on indigenous peoples in a more nuanced way.

In contrast to most scholars, who look at the impact of epidemic disease at the small scale of the individual or at the large scale of the population, Kathleen Hull (in chapter 9) finds the community a fundamental analytical unit for understanding the impact of introduced disease. Observing that assessments of community health must consider both quality of life and sustainability, she explores responses to disease-related rapid population decline apparent in the small, fluid communities of Native California in the late eighteenth and early nineteenth centuries. In the remote Yosemite Valley, the indigenous Awahnichi people had developed a suite of responses to periodic population decline that they had apparently used over the centuries long before European contact. These included maintaining a distinct language and cultural identity even when they were forced to move outside the valley to live with other groups; accepting other people as members to build group size; and making a conscious effort to reform their identity in new circumstances in response to new diversity of membership. In contrast, indigenous people on California's coast were directly impacted by European colonization, were removed to missions, mingled in culturally and linguistically diverse groups, and were housed in prison-like dorms. These practices shattered indigenous communities, and they disappeared from view.

In a final chapter, James Brooks uses Mandan oral history, history, and archaeology to tell the broader story of Native American strength and endurance in both pre- and postcontact times. In one tale, the Mandan warrior Black Wolf triumphs over a pestilent and pox-ridden snake, and Brooks shows how the Mandans and their neighbors had similarly survived in the face of overwhelming population loss from disease in the late eighteenth and early nineteenth centuries. He takes the reader back to precontact times, exploring the fourteenth- and fifteenth-century "Vacant Quarter" in the Southeast and similar evidence of population decline and abandonment in the Southwest and shows how Native Americans had come back from each of these periods of deterioration. Moreover, Native American populations today are soaring after reaching a nadir in the early twentieth century. Brooks emphasizes that European colonization was devastating for Native Americans, but it was not the only challenge they have faced in their long history on the continent. Like Black Wolf's victory over the pestilent serpent, Native America finds ways to survive and overcome the challenges it faces.

Together the chapters suggest that colonial European states created what today might be termed "structural violence" that negatively affected the health and well-being of Native communities. This violence certainly increased Native vulnerability to germs, but it also led to long-term suffering from physical trauma and nutritional stress. As this group of interdisciplinary scholars demonstrates, the results of this trauma can be observed in the bones of the colonized but often cannot be seen in the documents of the colonizers and germ-centered narratives of European conquest. They also build on acknowledged associations between contact and depopulation by, for example, pointing out how fertility and reproduction are often ignored in deterministic models. Depopulation of particular Native groups would have been a linear process only if their respective members had lost their ability to reproduce. At times this certainly happened; forcible abduction of Native women from a group or ecological changes that decreased female fertility, for example, led to falling birth rates and disintegration of some communities. At other times, Natives did rebound by adopting captives, merging with other groups, and maintaining their dynamic patterns of subsistence that predated European contact. Unfortunately, such recovery remained invisible to their contemporaneous Europeans, who created systems of classification that obscured the actual number of people descended from indigenous ancestors and who concocted stories of inevitable Native decline.

These chapters, then, demonstrate that the story of European contact cannot be reduced to a tale of novel germs acting independently of colonizers in attacking Native populations lacking immunity. The fate of indigenous populations in regard to health was much more complex, involving, at the least, interactions among the environment, demography, disease ecology, cultural practices, and political-economic forces and power. Yet we cannot disregard the seductiveness of a simple, unicausal explanation. We also have learned that the narratives themselves, constructed from the late fifteenth century onward, have served a variety of interests, but certainly not accuracy or the integrity and well-being of indigenous peoples. We believe that scholars must free themselves from the overly simplistic explanations offered in the past. We offer this volume in an effort to bring new understanding to the complexity of indigenous depopulation in the Americas, provide further examples of how the colonial and postcontact experience transpired in various regions, and develop more complete and compelling explanations of the deep traumas of colonialism.

# References

Alchon, Suzanne Austin. 2003. A Pest in the Land: New World Epidemics in a Global Perspective. Albuquerque: University of New Mexico Press.

Crosby, Alfred W. 1972. The Columbian Exchange: Biological and Cultural Consequences of 1492. Westport, CT: Greenwood Publishing.

———. 1986. Ecological Imperialism: The Biological Expansion of Europe, 900–1900. New York: Cambridge University Press.

Diamond, Jared. 1997. Guns, Germs, and Steel: The Fates of Human Societies. New York: W. W. Norton.

Dobyns, Henry F. 1966. Estimating aboriginal American population, 1: An appraisal of techniques, with a new hemispheric estimate. Current Anthropology 7:395–449.

———. 1983. Their Number Become Thinned: Native American Population Dynamics in Eastern North America. Knoxville: University of Tennessee Press.

Fenn, Elizabeth A. 2001. Pox Americana: The Great Smallpox Epidemic of 1775–82. New York: Hill and Wang.

Henige, David. 1998. Numbers from Nowhere: The American Indian Contact Population Debate. Norman: University of Oklahoma Press.

Johansson, Sheila Ryan. 1982. The demographic history of the Native peoples of North America: A selected bibliography. Yearbook of Physical Anthropology 25:133–52.

Jones, David S. 2003. Virgin soils revisited. William and Mary Quarterly 60 (October):703–42.

Kelton, Paul. 2007. Epidemics and Enslavement: Biological Catastrophe in the Native Southeast, 1492–1715. Lincoln: University of Nebraska Press.

Larsen, Clark Spencer. 1994. In the wake of Columbus: Native population biology in the postcontact Americas. Yearbook of Physical Anthropology 37:109–54.

Livi-Bacci, Massimo. 2008. Conquest: The Destruction of the American Indios. Translated by Carl Ipsen. Malden, MA: Polity Press.

Meister, C. 1976. Demographic consequences of Euro-American contact on selected American Indian populations and their relationship to demographic transition. Ethnohistory 23(2):161–72.

Milner, George R. 1980. Epidemic disease in the postcontact Southeast: A reappraisal. Midcontinental Journal of Archaeology 5:39–56.

Milner, George R., and George Chaplin. 2010. Eastern North American population at AD 1500. American Antiquity 75:707–26.

Mooney, James. 1928. The aboriginal population of America north of Mexico. Smithsonian Miscellaneous Collections 80:1–40.

Thornton, Russell. 1987. American Indian Holocaust and Survival: A Population History Since 1492. Norman: University of Oklahoma Press.

————. 2000. Population history of Native North Americans. In A Population History of North America, edited by Michael R. Haines and Richard H. Steckel, 9–50. Cambridge: Cambridge University Press.

Ubelaker, Douglas H. 1992. North American Indian population size: Changing perspectives. In Disease and Demography in the Americas, edited by John W. Verano and Douglas H. Ubelaker, 169–76. Washington, DC: Smithsonian Institution Press.

————. 2000. Patterns of disease in early North American populations. In A Population History of North America, edited by Michael R. Haines and Richard H. Steckel, 51–98. Cambridge: Cambridge University Press.

————. 2006. Population size, contact to nadir. In Handbook of North American Indians, vol. 3: Environment, Origins, and Population, edited by Douglas H. Ubelaker, 694–701. Washington, DC: Smithsonian Institution.

Waldram, James B., D. Ann Herring, and T. Kue Young, eds. 1995. Aboriginal Health in Canada: Historical, Cultural, and Epidemiological Perspectives. Toronto: University of Toronto Press.

————, eds. 2006. Aboriginal Health in Canada: Historical, Cultural, and Epidemiological Perspectives. 2nd ed. Toronto: University of Toronto Press.

# Death, Uncertainty, and Rhetoric

# 1

*David S. Jones*

On Columbus Day, a Boston radio station replayed an interview with Charles Mann, author of the best-selling *1491* and *1493*. He explained how an epidemic, introduced by shipwrecked French sailors by 1616, had left the Massachusetts coast "suddenly, radically depopulated" (Mann 2012), facilitating English settlement. In a similar interview on NPR's *Fresh Air* (Mann 2011b), he told Terry Gross how Indians, who lacked domesticated animals, had missed out on animal-derived pathogens and the resultant natural selection experienced by Europeans, Asians, and Africans. The outcome was inevitable: "when the Europeans came over, started by Columbus, it was as if all the deaths over the millennia that have been caused by these diseases were compressed into 150 years in the Americas." Indians, ignorant of quarantine measures, accelerated the spread of epidemics, which "exploded like chains of firecrackers across the landscape." Mann retold a narrative familiar to most listeners. Native Americans, who had "no immunity" to Eurasian pathogens, had no chance. The outcome of the "Columbian Exchange" was awful, but it could not have been prevented. Europeans were innocent bystanders.

The familiarity of this narrative is vexing. Over the past several decades, fueled in part by the collective angst of the Columbian quincentenary, historians and archaeologists have conducted extensive research about the magnitude and causes of Native American mortality. Many have turned away from traditional explanations, which focused on natural selection, hemispheric immunodeficiency, and the inevitability of Indian demise. They have assembled a more complex portrait, with counternarratives that instead emphasize the contingency and social determinants of the epidemiological consequences of European arrival. It was the turbulence of colonization and not genetic liability that created Indians' devastating susceptibility to imported pathogens.

These new interpretations have not yet displaced theories of immunological determinism from academic or popular writing. Mann can cite ongoing scholarship and find many enthusiastic readers. Explanations of Indian depopulation are stuck in a standoff, with revisionist scholars unable to quash the familiar narratives. Why does the stalemate persist? Many factors contribute. First, the different narratives reflect choices between different worldviews. At the broadest level, they reflect a choice between styles of historical explanation: one biological and deterministic, the other social and contingent. At a narrower level, they reflect a choice between styles of epidemiological explanation. As Charles Rosenberg (1992) illustrated, observers of epidemics have swung between two poles: one that emphasizes configurations within the affected society and another that emphasizes contamination by outside influences. Second, it is difficult to synthesize what is known into simple narratives. Because of the complexity of post-1492 history, specific case studies can be found and deployed in defense of each perspective. Third, too much remains unknown about the timing, extent, and causes of mortality. In an ideal world, definitive demographic data would constrain the stories that historians tell about Indian mortality, but this does not happen. As a result, Indian demography remains a Rorschach test in which scholars and readers project their assumptions, interests, and biases. Historians, scientists, and journalists still pick and choose their stories of encounter and epidemics and craft them into narratives that support either inevitable decline or contingent outcomes. Rhetorical sleight of hand remains widespread by both sides.

Scholars interested in budging the conventional wisdom need to find new ways to channel the complexity of encounter and depopulation into persuasive narratives. They need to situate their work in broader projects to root out the stereotypes that still consume writing about American Indians (Merrell 2012; Usner 2009). This project will require scholars and activists to dismantle a pervasive ideological system.

## Competing Narratives of Susceptibility

Recognition of Indian mortality and speculation about its causes began soon after Europeans' arrival in the Americas. Peter Martyr d'Anghiera wrote one of the first histories of Spain's exploration of the Americas.

His work, which became one basis of the "Black Legend," placed blame squarely on the Spanish. He decried how the Indians, "simple poor men never brought up in labour, do dayly peryshe with intollerable travayle in the golde mynes" (d'Anghiera 1885 [1516]:172). Others, "brought to suche desperation" (d'Anghiera 1885 [1516]:172), killed themselves. Forced labor was compounded by war, famine, and then epidemics: "straunge diseases . . . consumed theym lyke rotton sheepe" (d'Anghiera 1885 [1516]:199). Bartolomé de Las Casas (1992 [1552]:29), who witnessed colonization firsthand, condemned his countrymen, who behaved "like ravening beasts, killing, terrorizing, afflicting, torturing, and destroying the native peoples." English colonists offered diverse explanations. Although providential explanations were widespread (such as one by John Smith [1986 (1631):275], "it seemes God hath provided this Country for our Nation, destroying the natives by the plague"), being good Aristotelians they saw multiple other causes at work simultaneously, including diet, living conditions, and behavior. The diversity of possible explanations allowed them to emphasize whichever ones were most expedient, a pattern that persisted over centuries of contact (Jones 2004, 2006).

In the nineteenth century, American historians began to rewrite the histories of European conquest. They moved away from narratives that praised divine providence and focused instead on heroic epics that celebrated the achievements of Spanish conquistadors. William Prescott's widely read *History of the Conquest of Mexico* (1843) and *History of the Conquest of Peru* (1847) defined this genre. As he explained in the preface to his Mexican history, "The subversion of a great empire by a handful of adventurers, taken with all its strange and picturesque accompaniments, has the air of romance rather than of sober history" (Prescott 2004 [1843]:xxii). The Aztecs, repeatedly described as primitive savages, were awed by Spanish horses and guns: "Castilian valor, or rather Castilian arms and discipline, proved triumphant" (Prescott 2004 [1843]:408). Prescott did not ignore disease. He explained how smallpox had struck Mexico, "sweeping over the land like fire over the prairies, smiting down prince and peasant, and adding another to the long train of woes that followed the march of the white men" (Prescott 2004 [1843]:361). But disease does not figure prominently in his account of European success. Prescott's epic set the tone for several generations of scholarship.

Disease began to make an increasing impression first on physicians, then on historians, in the late nineteenth century. A. B. Holder (1892:178), who worked as an agency physician on the Crow reservation in Montana in 1892, was impressed by the Crows' susceptibility to disease: "That their resistance to disease is much less than that of the civilized races, I have seen the evidence at the bedside, in watching them yield and die from diseases that I felt sure any stout white man had easily thrown off." William A. Jones, the commissioner of Indian affairs, noted in 1904 that American Indians had "not yet acquired any immunity" against measles and pneumonia (Jones 1905:36). Physician Woods Hutchinson (1907:199) concluded that they provided "a highly susceptible host" for tuberculosis. By 1920 the previously unexposed populations of American Indians had been described as "nearly 'virgin' so far as tuberculosis is concerned" (Bushnell 1920:35). Facing a parallel situation, medical authorities in South Africa similarly identified susceptible Africans as "virgin" populations (Packard 1989:4, 22–23).

The historiography took a dramatic turn in the mid-twentieth century, when writers backed away from their focus on European cultural superiority and turned instead to microbes. This move had several origins. Demographers, including Woodrow Borah, Sherburne Cook, and Henry Dobyns, used the potential impact of massive epidemics to justify their high estimates of precontact populations. Dobyns (1963:494), for instance, described Indians as "a virgin population of susceptible individuals lacking immunities." Historians, such as William McNeill and Alfred Crosby, collected examples of how disease had shaped the course of human history. Equipped with Crosby's concepts of Columbian exchanges and ecological imperialism, many historians welcomed epidemics into their narratives. As Pekka Hämäläinen (2010:173) described, "The result was what might be called a biological turn of American colonial history. Suddenly the conquest of Native America seemed a product not so much of Europe's techno-organizational superiority as of blind biogeographic luck."[1]

The narratives of this biological turn, especially its recurring refrain of "no immunity," have circulated widely. Consider three widely read examples: Alfred Crosby, Jared Diamond, and Charles Mann. Crosby offered a retelling of the Thanksgiving legend in *American Heritage* in the fall of 1978. English colonists did not carve Plymouth out of the wilderness. Instead, they built it atop the lonely ruins and overgrown fields of an abandoned Wampanoag village: "It was pestilence that had cleared the way for this tiny foothold in New England, and the shadow of death would be a major factor in giving the settlement form and substance in the months ahead" (Crosby 1978:39). Europe, as Crosby (1978:39) explained, had experienced a "golden age" of pathogens that left Europeans with "some kind of acquired immunity" that the Indians lacked. This contrast had tragic consequences: "Innocent of immunity or experience, the Indians were helpless" (Crosby 1978:39). Epidemics devastated "the tribes like an autumnal nor'easter raking leaves from the trees" and held the Indians at bay until the English were well established (Crosby 1978:39). Although Crosby's *American Heritage* essay focused on Plymouth, his other works, especially *The Columbian Exchange* (1972), provided the grand narratives. Native Americans, long isolated from other humans, fell victim to deep historical forces: "those creatures who have been longest in isolation suffer the most, for their genetic material has been least tempered by the variety of world diseases" (Crosby 1972:37). These ideas continue to be taught and cited decades later.

Crosby's impact has now been eclipsed by Jared Diamond's *Guns, Germs, and Steel* (1997). Winner of a Pulitzer prize, *Guns, Germs, and Steel* remained on the *New York Times* best-seller list for over two years and sold over 1.5 million copies. When President Clinton (2000) awarded Diamond a National Medal of Science, he cited, among other things, Diamond's "exceptionally creative scholarship." What drew this praise? Diamond offered an astonishingly simple explanation of how Europeans came to dominate so much of the world. Human history hinged on the shape of the continents. The east-west axis of Eurasia allowed easy sharing of domesticated crops and animals and new technologies, while the north-south axis of the Americas impeded such exchanges. Eurasians acquired a host of pathogens from their domesticated animals and "evolved substantial resistance to the new diseases" (Diamond 1997:92). When the two populations met, up to 99 percent of Americans died: "The main killers were Old World germs to which Indians had never been exposed, and against which they therefore had neither immune nor genetic resistance" (Diamond 1997:211–12). Astute readers will recognize that this is nonsense: American Indians have immune systems, encoded in their genes, that provide considerable resistance against pathogens. Yet Diamond makes this claim time and time again, not just in his popular writing but also in scientific journals. Rehashing the basic narrative in *Nature* in 2007, Diamond and his colleagues described how "previously unexposed Native American populations had no immunity or resistance" (Wolfe et al. 2007:282).[2]

The torch lit by Crosby and Diamond has been picked up by science journalist Charles Mann, whose *1491* (2005) won the National Academy of Science's Keck Award for the best book of the year. Jumping across time and place, he told familiar stories about New England in 1616, Hispaniola in 1493, and Peru in 1532. The Incas, as he described them, were a setup for disaster: "Smallpox radiated throughout the empire like ink spreading through tissue paper" (Mann 2005:87). Mortality was dire because "Indians had never been exposed to it—they were 'virgin soil,' in epidemiological jargon" (Mann 2005:87). Inspired by Borah and especially Dobyns, he described how epidemics spread farther and faster than colonists: "epidemics shot out like ghastly arrows from the limited areas they saw to every corner of the hemisphere, wreaking destruction in places that never appeared in the European historical record" (Mann 2005:93). As he explained in *1493*, thousands of years of European epidemics played out over just decades in the Americas (Mann 2011a:12). Trusting the highest estimates of precontact population, Mann (2005:94) astonished his reader: virgin soil epidemics might have "killed about one out of every five people on earth."

Although I have focused on these three widely read exemplars, claims of "no immunity" circulated far and wide. In the 1960s, for instance, Aidan Cockburn (1967:90) gave virgin soil theory the blessing of evolutionary biology, noting that the dramatic susceptibility of American Indians to European diseases was "the typical reaction of a 'herd' to a pathogen not previously exposed." Archaeologist Bruce Trigger (1966:440) described Indian mortality as a "cruel and fantastic example of natural selection." William McNeill (1976:180, 184), whose 1976 *Plagues and Peoples* did so much to put disease on historians' radar, described how Indians were "radically vulnerable to the disease organisms" while "the Spaniards were nearly immune." Crosby (1976:289) offered his own much-cited definition that same year: "Virgin soil epidemics are those in which the populations at risk have had no previous contact with the diseases that strike them and are therefore immunologically almost defenseless."

The idea even propagated in the work of the most careful and accomplished historians, those committed to writing Indian history that took Indians seriously. Francis Jennings (1975:22) mourned the Indians' lack of immunity: "Indeed, if there is any truth to biological distinctions between the great racial stocks of mankind, the Europeans' capacity to resist certain diseases made them superior, in the pure Darwinian sense, to the Indians who succumbed." James Axtell (1985:96–97) described how smallpox, measles, and all the others "careened unchecked through the 'virgin soil' populations of the New World." Richard White (1991:41) told how Indians, isolated from European pathogens, "had not been selected over time for resistance to such diseases," leaving them "doomed to die." Colin Calloway echoed this; with "no opportunity to build up immunological resistance," Indians "were doomed to die in one of the greatest biological catastrophes in human history" (Calloway 1997:33).

Counternarratives to virgin soil theory emerged almost immediately. As some physicians began writing about "virgin soil" populations in the 1920s, whether focused on American Indians or on South Africans, their colleagues began to express doubts. As Christian McMillen has shown, doctors of the Indian Medical Service became skeptical about the assumptions of virgin soils and racial inferiority in the 1920s. They increasingly turned to the problems of poverty and socioeconomic deprivation to explain the high prevalence of tuberculosis on the reservations. Louis Dublin, the famed statistician of the Metropolitan Life Insurance Company, reviewed the problem in 1942. He dismissed notions of inherent racial susceptibility and condemned researchers who blamed Indian bodies when the real cause was Indian poverty (McMillen 2008:637).

This sensibility slowly worked its way into the historical literature. Crosby provides perhaps the most interesting and important example. Even though he wrote evocatively about disease, evolution, and genetic susceptibility in *The Columbian Exchange* and *American Heritage*, he struck a different note in his classic 1976 essay in *William and Mary Quarterly*. He described the classic "no immunity" model and then disavowed it: "medical data on living American aborigines do not sustain it, and the scientific community inclines towards the view that Native Americans have no special susceptibility to Old World diseases that cannot be attributed to environmental influences, and probably never did have" (Crosby 1976:291). Noting that smallpox could cause terrible mortality in disease-experienced Europeans (for example, 38.5 percent case fatality rates during the Civil War), Crosby (1976:292) concluded that the "genetic weakness hypothesis may have some validity, but it is unproven and probably unprovable, and is therefore a weak reed to lean upon. What is more, we have no need of it." He instead emphasized the many environmental factors that might have contributed to American Indian susceptibility to Old World diseases, including lack of childhood exposure, malnutrition, and the social chaos generated by European colonization.[3]

Many scholars working on Indian depopulation in the 1980s and 1990s echoed this sense of contingency. Linda Newson (1985), struck by variations in the mortality experienced by different Central and South American populations, emphasized how the precontact structure of Indian populations and the nature of the Spanish colonial regime powerfully influenced what fraction died. Stephen Kunitz also compared the disparate outcomes experienced by similar groups. Why was mortality higher among the Hopis than among the Navajos or higher among Samoans than Hawaiians? Even though they were all supposedly "virgin," the different populations responded differently to introduced diseases: "The kind of colonial contact was of enormous importance" (Kunitz 1994:73).

By 2000 so much work had emerged about the complexity and contingency of the encounter that two works—Alchon's *A Pest in the Land* (2003) and my "Virgin Soils Revisited" (2003)—could offer synthetic reviews. Alchon argued that there was nothing fundamentally unique about the disease experience of Native Americans: all human populations have experienced devastating epidemics. What was unique for the Indians was European colonization. Had Indians simply experienced new pathogens, their populations would have declined and recovered, as happened in Athens (after its plague in 430 BCE), Rome (smallpox in the second and third century), and medieval Europe (bubonic plague). The burden of European colonization "explains the delayed or failed recovery of indigenous American populations" (Alchon 2003:3). Many writers in New Spain in the sixteenth century recognized that mortality rates varied from one place to another and that the outcomes depended on the timing, duration, and nature of the colonial encounter. Warfare and slavery put particular stress on Indian populations. In sum, "it was the disruption of day-to-day activities so crucial to the survival of any society that seriously undermined the demographic resilience of native American populations" (Alchon 2003:144).[4]

When I first encountered the literature on the Columbian Encounter as a medical student, I was startled by the ubiquitous—and impossible—assertions of "no immunity." Reading more, I found the work by scholars who emphasized contingency, as well as work in medical anthropology about social suffering and embodiment (Kleinman et al. 1996). When I returned to the medical literature on race, genetics, and immunology, I found more reasons to be skeptical of the simplistic claims made by Diamond and so many others. It became clear that virgin soil theory and its claims of "no immunity" had powerful and promiscuous appeal. They provided an alternative to human-centric histories, something that became increasingly attractive as environmental history rose to prominence. They shifted blame off Europeans and the Black Legend and onto morally neutral biohistorical forces. As Lawrence Summers, then president of Harvard University, described in 2004, "the vast majority of suffering that was visited on the Native American population as the Europeans came was not a plan or an attack, it was in many ways a coincidence" (Bombardieri 2005:B2). The narratives simultaneously shifted blame away from the failings of Indian societies and onto their inexperienced immune systems, something that was simply the result of quirky geography. Virgin soil theory resonated with powerful narrative tropes, telling how virgin Indians yielded to potent European pathogens. By representing Indian mortality as the product of a unique historical-immunological moment—the collision of two long isolated populations—it created a buffer between the horrors of the past and our present (Jones 2003).

It was not simply a question of getting the history right. Historical narratives inform how we think about health, inequality, and human agency. Alchon argued that virgin soil theory portrayed Indians as uniquely powerless victims of historical forces, a form of stereotyping that restricted their agency (Alchon 2003:3). It also obscured the impact of what Europeans actually did—the warfare, violence, forced labor, migrations, and disrupted social and political institutions. Massimo Livi-Bacci (2011:163) described how virgin soil theory "obscured other factors, and germs—instead of humans—became almost the sole agents of the American catastrophe. In its oversimplified and extreme version, the American catastrophe became a natural, ahistorical event, thus absolving the historian from further analysis." The crucial point for me was a simple one: Indians were not born vulnerable, they were made vulnerable, a distinction with great significance for contemporary health policy. Indian mortality "may have arisen from nothing more unique than the familiar forces of poverty, malnutrition, environmental stress, dislocation, and social disparity that cause epidemics among all other populations" (Jones 2003:742). Historians needed to move beyond "no immunity" and emphasize instead social and environmental contexts: "Only then can they overcome the widespread public and academic appeal of immunologic determinism and do justice to the crucial events of the encounter between Europeans and Americans" (Jones 2003:742).

## Advancing the Evidence Base

By 2003—a decade after the aborted celebrations of the Columbian quincentenary—two competing archetypal narratives offered explanations of Indian depopulation: one emphasized the biological and deterministic, the other the social and contingent. Over the next decade, work continued by scholars in many fields, especially in archaeology, to strengthen the case for contingent outcomes. These efforts take up four crucial topics: the high counters, the delayed introduction of new pathogens, the multiple causes of susceptibility, and the resilience of Native populations.

The popularity of virgin soil theory and its claims of "no immunity" have long been tied to the high estimates of precontact populations claimed by Borah, Dobyns, and others. In his 1998 *Numbers from Nowhere*, David Henige criticized these assumptions. In a 2008 review he renewed this criticism and castigated the continued circulation of high estimates of precontact populations, from Diamond to Mann, estimates for which "there is no evidence whatever" (Henige 2008:183).

He was especially vexed that "standards of proof in the debate have not changed during the past ten years" (Henige 2008:185). This was not hard to explain: "no further evidence has come to light to strengthen the hand of any of the combatants" (Henige 2008:185). Henige (2008:198) argued that the success of the high counters was "due in no small part to the high-octane capacity of numbers to convince, beguile, and deceive." Livi-Bacci, meanwhile, has offered a detailed reanalysis of one of the high counters' favorite exemplars: Hispaniola. While many writers have suggested a precontact population as high as 8 million, Livi-Bacci (2003, 2008) uses knowledge of Taino agriculture, gold production, social structure, and postcontact demography to show that the population was likely no higher than a few hundred thousand. These critiques do not deny that significant population loss occurred. Instead, they bring the losses into a range that can plausibly be explained without resort to fantastical assumptions about the state of Indian immunity.

Traditional virgin soil narratives also describe how European pathogens spread more quickly than Europeans, wiping out Indian populations that had not yet been colonized. The most extreme claim, made popular by Dobyns, argued that smallpox swept the hemisphere in the 1520s, decimating groups decades, even centuries, before close European contact. Careful work has now undermined this claim. For decades some scholars had acknowledged that certain pathogens actually spread slowly. Crosby (1972:46), for instance, noted in *The Columbian Exchange* that there was no smallpox in the Caribbean in the first twenty-five years after Columbus. Livi-Bacci (2003:38), who looked closely at records from Hispaniola, has shown that this was not limited to smallpox: "[B]efore 1518 there is no trace of major epidemics."

Other case studies have backed this up. In the conventional narratives of La Florida, for instance, Hernando de Soto led his expedition from Tampa Bay through northern Florida and into the interior of North America, introducing germs that wiped out Indian populations. When archaeologists have looked closely, however, they have not found evidence of this. Dale Hutchinson, for instance, participated in a detailed analysis of Tatham Mound, a burial site along de Soto's route. When the team looked at written records from Spanish explorations, they found "scant" evidence of early epidemics (Hutchinson 2007:169). Archaeological remains confirmed this: "the mass graves that are often associated with mass death (epidemics, warfare, mass disaster) are not present. Rather, an orderly placement of individuals into a mound with associated artifacts was found. The evidence supports the silence in the historic records regarding illness as an immediate and universal factor in depopulation" (Hutchinson 2007:172–73).

Epidemics were also slow to emerge in the Southwest. Although Spaniards encountered the Pueblo Indians in 1540, there is no evidence of major epidemics for nearly a century. As Elinore Barrett (2002:79) concluded, "The silence of records from the sixteenth-century Spanish exploring expeditions to New Mexico on the subject of disease and the apparent absence of large-scale reduction in the number of settlements during that time combine to reinforce the idea that the Pueblo population did not suffer epidemics of European diseases until the 1636–41 period."[5] More-remote groups avoided new epidemics even longer. Timothy Braatz (2003:67) shows that the Yavapais of the Colorado-Gila River region were likely spared smallpox until the eighteenth century.

Similar stories have emerged from detailed studies throughout North America. In contrast to Dobyns's claims of hemispheric smallpox in the 1520s, Gary Warrick (2003:268) found stable Huron-Petun populations between 1475 and 1633: "There is no evidence of sixteenth-century disease epidemics or depopulation." Even though contact between southeastern tribes and Europeans began in the 1500s, Paul Kelton (2007:36) found no evidence of serious epidemics until the late seventeenth century: "The spread of the Columbian Exchange's human-to-human diseases thus was not an automatic consequence of their introduction to a virgin population." Does the lack of evidence of epidemics mean that no epidemics took place? It is certainly possible that epidemics afflicted populations without leaving a trace in the archaeologic or historic records. Historians, however, should be cautious before concluding—without evidence—that epidemics did take place. In some cases the evidence of absent epidemics is quite good. Steven Hackel's (2012) analysis of mission burial records showed that even though the Spanish arrived in California in the eighteenth century, measles and smallpox did not devastate the California missions until 1806 and 1833. Hämäläinen (2010) has shown that the Comanches, empowered by horses, initially prospered from their encounters with Europeans and did not face significant epidemics until after 1840.

When epidemics did strike, the impact was not always catastrophic—
at least initially. Yavapai mortality, for instance, was much lower than
among the more heavily colonized Pueblo peoples and Quechas; only
after their confinement on the Rio Verde reservation in 1871 did they
bear the full brunt of disease (Braatz 2003:67, 147). Ann Carlos and
Frank Lewis (2012) examined records of the Hudson's Bay Company
and found that smallpox, which struck in 1781–82, actually killed far
fewer Indians (likely less than 20 percent) than previous scholars assumed. The fur trade, for instance, returned to its pre-epidemic levels
within six years of the epidemic. Similarly, the Comanches endured episodic smallpox epidemics in the late eighteenth and into the nineteenth
century without substantial population losses. Only after 1840, and in
the setting of drought and famine, did the Comanches suffer seriously
from smallpox and cholera. They managed to begin to recover in the
mid-1860s, when the flood of immigrants after the Civil War broke
their power once and for all (Hämäläinen 2010:188, 206).

These cases, which range from Florida to California and the Hudson Bay, all show that dire epidemics were not the inevitable outcome
of encounter, spreading ahead of the European advance. Instead, they
often arrived only decades later in the setting of encounter-induced social disruption. This, in turn, demonstrates another key point, one that
has also been carefully documented over the past decade: epidemics
were but one of many factors that combined to generate the substantial mortality that most groups did experience. As Livi-Bacci (2011:164)
observed, "the long-term impact of the new diseases was increasingly
severe the more 'damaged' the demographic system and the more
crippled its ability to rebound after a shock." Specific case studies have
made this case in considerable detail. Livi-Bacci's work on Hispaniola
demonstrates this well. Spaniards confiscated Taino labor, disrupted
subsistence activities, displaced populations, and undermined living
conditions: "Neither the 'black legend,' with its exceptional cruelty, nor
the 'virgin soil' paradigm, with its disease-related mortality, are required
to explain the extinction of the Tainos. The unsettling normality of conquest was sufficient cause" (Livi-Bacci 2003:51).

Spanish Florida has again been studied most closely. Larsen's team
has worked to shift the focus off disease and onto other factors, including "the impact of population relocation and aggregation, changing

patterns of work and physical activity and labor exploitation, and shifts in diet and nutrition" (Larsen et al. 2001:71). Groups that entered only into trade relationships with the Europeans sometimes did fine, whereas colonized groups subjected to changes in diet and lifestyle suffered seriously. Hutchinson (2007:171), for instance, shows that it was not the initial contact that caused problems but the imposition of colonial regimes and the disruptions that stemmed from conflict between French, English, and Spanish settlers: "It was not simply new diseases that affected native populations, but the combined effects of warfare, famine, resettlement, and the demoralizing disintegration of native social, political, and economic structures." In this volume, Larsen (chapter 3) has framed his findings in terms of structural violence: "La Florida is an exemplar of structural violence, as Native populations in this setting were dominated and exploited by a European power, so much so that the entire social fabric of these societies was altered in profound ways and with social and biological consequences." Specifically, "The study of health outcomes in this region reveals a subtle, sometimes invisible record of violence, not in the form of trauma and obvious injury but in the form of illness, morbidity, and increased physical activity and workload owing to labor exploitation" (Larsen, chapter 3, this volume).

Similar stories can be found throughout the Americas. Newson has compiled data about pre- and postcontact population size to calculate depopulation ratios. Her work has revealed ever finer evidence of variable outcomes. Not only did mortality vary between highland and lowland regions, it also varied within those regions, depending on "the intensity of Spanish settlement and the types of activities that were established there" (Newson 2003:136). Imposition of mining, for instance, was more disruptive than agriculture, while cotton mills (which left basic subsistence intact) did the least damage of all. The weight of the colonial regime often determined whether populations recovered when epidemics did strike. Alan Covey and colleagues (2011) analyzed a 1569 survey of eight hundred households in the Inca heartland and found that the double burden of epidemics and Spanish colonization was what eroded populations. Even Ann Ramenofsky, who at times had followed Dobyns quite closely, has come to recognize the complex determinants of outcome. What actually happens when a pathogen meets a population "varies according to a whole set of factors, including population distribution, concomitant infections, diet, individual and group genetics, as well as the strain of the pathogen itself" (Ramenofsky et al. 2003:251). In a 2009 study of San Marcos Pueblo, Ramenofsky and her colleagues found that "social conflict—not disease contact— was the key explanatory variable" (Ramenofsky et al. 2009:525). Barrett (2002:77–78, 115–16) has shown that even though Pueblo Indians were spared early mortality in the sixteenth century, they suffered terribly during the seventeenth, with populations falling by 75 percent between 1600 and 1680, the result of epidemics (possibly in the 1630s and cer- tainly in 1677), disrupted subsistence, forced labor, lost land, Apache raids, disrupted trade, drought, and famine. In his study of California missions, Hackel (2012:89) found that while epidemics did take a toll, more mundane causes of death—violence, workplace accidents, and natural disasters—were also significant: "life in a colonial, pre-modern, pre-industrial, pre-antibiotic society was dangerous for Indians and non-Indians alike."

Scholars of early New England have done similar work. Suggesting leptospirosis as the cause of the 1616 epidemic along the Massachu- setts coast, John Marr and John Cathey (2010:283) emphasized not "no immunity" but the barefoot Wampanoags' chronic exposure to the waterborne pathogen: "'genetic weakness' was not as important as the intimate and repeated exposure to an infectious agent among the Indians not shared by Europeans." When Indians adapted to English settlement and began to raise their own livestock, they were drawn into increasing conflict with the English over control of land. Virginia Anderson (2004) showed how these tensions contributed to King Philip's War and the ensuing decimation of the Indians in southern New England.

The situation in the Southeast is especially revealing. As Kelton has shown, Spanish colonialism had a light touch in this region, introduc- ing trade but little more. This changed in 1692 when slavers based in South Carolina moved into the Indian interior: "Thousands of Natives huddled in fortified, compact, and unsanitary towns, where the fear of being captured kept them from going out to hunt game or harvest crops. It was into this new social landscape—one dramatically altered by nonepidemiological aspects of colonialism—that smallpox did the most damage it would ever do to the region and its people" (Kelton

2007:102). It was not pathogens alone but pathogens in the context of slavery that wreaked havoc: "English-inspired commerce in Native slaves was the element of colonialism most responsible for making indigenous peoples across the region vulnerable to newly introduced diseases" (Kelton 2007:xviii). In this volume, Kelton examines Cherokee experiences during the American Revolution. To punish the Cherokees, who sided with the British, armies from North and South Carolina brought total war to Cherokee towns: "By waging a scorched earth policy, something completely intended, they purposely altered material conditions knowing that severe human suffering and fatalities would result" (Kelton, chapter 8, this volume). Catherine Cameron (also in this volume) looks more broadly to show how captive-taking and warfare both exacerbated Indian mortality.

Studies of Plains tribes, meanwhile, have emphasized the importance of the physical environment. Adam Hodge (2012:366) has shown that while smallpox spread throughout the Great Plains in the early 1780s, its local intensity varied: "Close attention to the interrelationships among climate fluctuations, wildlife population demography, and food shortages can throw new light on the environmental and cultural factors affecting disease epidemics." Northern tribes, for instance, had been weakened by starvation, the consequence of a powerful La Niña climatic episode. Blanca Tovías (2007) argued that Blackfoot mortality should not be traced solely to "lack of immunity." Instead it depended critically on the consequences of their transformation from a nomadic to a sedentary existence. Mary-Ellen Kelm (1998:38) emphasized the inadequate food and appalling sanitary conditions prevalent on reservations: "More than any other factor, environmental conditions probably contributed to the continued prevalence and virulence of infectious diseases in aboriginal communities." Human agency, not microbes, was the key: "Aboriginal ill-health was created not just by faceless pathogens but by the colonial policies and practices of the Canadian government" (Kelm 1998:xix). Raymond Obomsawin (2007:11), reviewing the fates of the First Nations more broadly, supported this analysis: "the first peoples of Canada fell prey to the old world infectious diseases not upon contact, as the germ theory would require, but after their pattern of life and relationships with the natural world were increasingly (oft times precipitously) and drastically altered." Farther north, beyond the "temperate Neo-Europes," outcomes were even more heterogeneous. As Liza Piper and John Sandlos (2007:763) have shown, mortality depended on the synergistic effects of epidemics, malnutrition, and economic imperialism: "the simultaneous progression of colonization and environmental change occurred not as an all-encompassing invasion along a single line of advance, but as a series of sporadic and limited changes on the uneven border of a broken frontier."

Recent scholarship has focused not only on diseases per se but also on how Indian societies responded. Traditional virgin soil narratives described how maladaptive Indian behaviors—the result of having not co-evolved with the pathogens—accelerated the spread of epidemics and how the unstoppable mortality led to the collapse of Indian religious and cultural practices. The counternarratives have taken many forms. Alchon's *A Pest in the Land* worked to demystify Indian reactions to the epidemics. Although the record is full of stories of epidemic-induced disillusionment and horror, similar scenes have occurred throughout human history, as seen in the literary and artistic responses in Europe to the Black Death: "The emotions experienced, the explanations offered, and the treatments adopted by native Americans all demonstrate the universal nature of the human response to epidemic disease" (Alchon 2003:123).

Other recent work has taken this revisioning further. It has documented adaptation, accommodation, agency, and even limited recovery in the face of dire mortality. Kelton's (2004:47) analysis of southeastern Indian experiences with smallpox provides one of the most carefully argued examples: "Native Americans were capable of responding creatively to epidemics and avoiding complete physical and spiritual destruction." Religious leaders, for instance, offered explanations that reinforced tribal beliefs, led ceremonies to regain divine favor, advised their communities about possible responses, and improvised treatments for the new disease. Hull told a similar story in *Pestilence and Persistence*. The archaeological record shows that the Yosemite region had endured repeated episodes of population loss, even before European arrival, and the Yosemite Indians had developed cultural systems to manage these losses (for example, patterns of exchange and even amalgamation with neighboring groups to foster population recovery). This skill set equipped them to manage the turbulence of European arrival:

"The outcome of specific colonial encounters was the result of choices made by those who participated or survived, exercised within the context of both their own personal experience and the experiences of their ancestors that were preserved in oral tradition" (Hull 2009:23). This was not unique. She examined the reactions of ten other Native groups and found widespread evidence of the "the ability of the native people to make decisions, chart their own course, and persist in the midst of colonial upheaval, often drawing on a dynamic long-term history and inherent cultural flexibility in order to do so" (Hull 2009:281–82). Kerri Inglis (2013) documents similar resilience among Native Hawaiians confronted with the challenges of leprosy. They pushed back against a government policy that banished thousands to a remote peninsula on Molokai, challenged the terms of their confinement, demanded better care, and would not let themselves be forgotten.

In this volume, Hull extends this analysis and situates Indian agency in the context of community resilience. Criticizing the simplistic narratives of Diamond and Mann, she calls for more careful work: "the issues of health and survival are much more complex than we are often led to believe. It is a disservice to both descendant communities and our collective heritage and history to ignore the myriad factors that contributed to when and how Native peoples confronted such challenges to survival, and how groups, if not many individuals, often endured" (Hull, chapter 9, this volume).

Time and time again, scholars working to document the complexity and contingency of epidemics have concluded with summary statements that advocate for more-nuanced analyses. Kelton, in this volume (chapter 8), wants "scholars to critically examine and carefully contextualize the evidence that is used when discussing colonial germs and their impact on indigenous peoples." Only then will they be able to purge the "[f]aulty memories and frontier mythology" that "contaminate" so many analyses (Kelton, chapter 8, this volume). Brendan Rensink (2011:15) warns that hemispheric generalizations divert historians away from a meaningful understanding of historical causality: "To presume that the tragic fate of many indigenous peoples was unavoidable precludes carrying out any inquiry into the causal relationships between cultures, empires, and individuals." Hutchinson (2007:172) agrees: "treating disease as a force capable of reducing entire populations to mere remnants of former civilizations also reduces the scholarship we practice to mere 'before and after' pictures of mono-causality rather than to processes of evolving biological and social relationships." Hämäläinen (2010:173, 174) critiques the "grand, large-scale biohistories" that "obscure as much as they reveal. Preoccupied with global patterns, they often distort the realities on the ground, where Europeans did not expand as a monolith and Indians did not die in the aggregate." He wants historians "to envision alternative narratives" that focus "on the interplay among political, economic, cultural, and biological forces" (Hämäläinen 2010:207, 175). Debra Martin, in this volume, calls on historians to see through the superficial epidemics and recognize the underlying structures: "While epidemics were horrifying and caused untold thousands of deaths, the relentless domination and subjugation of the Pueblo people was likely much more of a factor in explaining the impact of contact on biological and cultural adaptation. The Spanish needed labor and resources in their quest to conquer and colonize, and so the forces that produced morbidity and mortality in Pueblo groups were a formulation of many injustices, including coercion and mistreatment" (Martin, chapter 4, this volume). Only by acknowledging the "creeping genocide" will scholars be able to understand what really happened.

Some scholars are optimistic that the tide has turned. Warwick Anderson (2007:144) believes that the old biological histories "are largely out of fashion." Historians, especially those working on contemporary indigenous issues, "now are more likely to address the lasting effects of racial discrimination, dispossession, family disruption, poverty, social marginalisation, and limited access to health care" (Anderson 2007:145). The editors of this volume similarly describe a shift that has taken place since the 1992 quincentenary: "The fate of indigenous populations in regard to health was much more complex, involving, at the least, interactions among the environment, demography, disease ecology, cultural practices, and political-economic forces and power" (Kelton et al., introduction to this volume). However, they go on to warn that "we cannot disregard the seductiveness of a simple, unicausal explanation." The very explanations that historians and others have worked so hard to rebut remain popular. As McMillen (2008:641) reminds us, "Virgin soil theory is not a thing of the past." Scientists continue to search for genes that link race and disease susceptibility, while writers like Diamond and Mann keep claims of "no immunity" in the popular and academic spotlight.

## The Persistence of Simplicity

There is good reason to be concerned. Despite the quality of the careful work that now documents the problems with high counters, the delayed and contingent arrival of epidemics, the multifactorial causes of Indian susceptibility, and the resilience of Indian communities, simplistic biohistories and their claims of "no immunity" circulate widely. The problem is not confined to the popular literature epitomized by the work of Charles Mann. Instead, the traditional narratives circulate widely in academic writing, sometimes even in the writing of those who explicitly critique it.

Some scientists continue to seek evidence of genetic or other immunological liabilities. Magdalena Hurtado and colleagues (2003), for instance, studied the Northern Achés' high susceptibility to tuberculosis and speculated about their low genetic diversity and diminished cell-mediated immunity. James Riley (2010:477), seeking to explain high smallpox mortality rates, concluded that the novelty of the disease caused a particular problem: "Mothers who had not had smallpox could not pass protective antibodies to their developing infants, and they could not care for their young children when they themselves were sick."

Others did not study Indian immunity directly but instead made assumptions about it to explain other findings. In his history of the Yavapais and other southwestern tribes, Braatz (2003:67) described the impact of smallpox and measles: "Southwestern peoples had not yet developed immunities to these germs, had little understanding of how they spread, and died in astounding numbers." Diana Loren (2008:61), writing about the Eastern Woodlands, exhibited a common mix of speculation and confidence: "while the exact numbers will perhaps never be known, it can be said with some certainty that many Eastern Woodlands Indian people were unable to survive introduced diseases such as epidemic syphilis, smallpox, and tuberculosis." Eric Jones and Sharon DeWitte (2012) modeled the spatiotemporal dimensions of

Indian mortality in New England and found that the Western Abenakis along the Connecticut River had the highest mortality. Why them?
Jones and DeWitte speculated about differences in mitochondrial DNA
haplotype diversity and other genetic variants that altered susceptibility
to disease.

A striking example can be found in Sherry Fields's discussion of the
diseases of colonial Mexico. She followed Diamond's basic narrative
quite closely and emphasized stark biological differences between the
Europeans and Americans. Spaniards had evolved at the crossroads of
Europe and Africa, in cities filled with sewage and rodents, and without
regular bathing: "their skin, hair, body fluids, and breath swarmed with
pathogens" (Fields 2008:10). This left them immunologically privileged,
in possession of "one of the most evolved immunological systems in
the world at that time" (Fields 2008:10). Native Americans, in contrast,
"had no previous exposure to the crowd diseases that had forced the
immunological systems of Old World people to erect defenses" (Fields
2008:9). Columbus exposed "the immunologically naive inhabitants of
the New World" to "the 'immunological supermen' of the Old World"
(Fields 2008:10).[6] It was no surprise that "Old World epidemic diseases
found very receptive hosts for their pathogens in the virgin-soil populations of the New World" (Fields 2008:x). With "no immunity," they
suffered a "virulent, and from the point of view of the sufferers, incom-
prehensible onslaught of disease" (Fields 2008:2). As they died, they
could only watch in awe as the Spanish survived: the Spaniards' "immunological systems indeed made them seem superhuman in the eyes
of the natives being destroyed incomprehensibly by pestilence" (Fields
2008:10).[7]

Equally striking is the way in which writers continue to blame Indians for their own mortality. Braatz (2003:67) described how the Yavapais,
initially protected from Spanish smallpox by their isolation, brought the
disease on themselves: "According to Yavapai oral tradition, this contact
first occurred when Yavapai raiders swept down on disease-ridden Pima
villages." Loren showed how Indians in early New England exacerbated
the epidemics in two ways. First, "Native trade networks, so useful for
transporting objects and ideas, also carried lethal pathogens to other
Native peoples" (Loren 2008:61). Second, "Native healing traditions,
such as sweat lodges, tended to exacerbate conditions and caused the

diseases to spread faster" (Loren 2008:61). Warrick (2003:271) described how, among the Iroquois, the "deep spiritual concern for sick relatives, longhouse living conditions, and lack of quarantine" heightened their mortality. Dixon emphasized the Kansas' maladaptive funerary customs. When relatives died, Kansa families sacrificed horses and food, fasted, went on raids, and hunted less, all of which exacerbated mortality, "creating a vicious cycle of increasing starvation, illness, and death that accelerated their population collapse" (Dixon 2007:474). The synergy of disease, famine, and cultural practices was like "a flaming match meeting a powder keg. The powder keg of death customs was fine by itself. Disease and game depletion created a flame that burned plenty of those it touched. When these elements combined (as they did from 1838 to 1840), Kansa losses exploded" (Dixon 2007:499). Even Hämäläinen, normally so impressed with Comanche success, joined this bandwagon. As Comanche power increased, their growing horse and bison herds overgrazed the prairie, leading to famine, while their slave raids increased their exposure to pathogens (Hämäläinen 2010:200).

Charles Mann (2011b) was not an outlier when he described how Indians accelerated their own epidemics: "So somebody would get smallpox, and the whole village would come around and try to comfort that person. They would all get sick, they'd flee in panic, they'd run to the next village. They'd spread it there." Despite decades of work in history, anthropology, and archaeology, Mann can endorse the estimates of high counters, channel Dobyns's and Diamond's faith in no immunity, blame Indian suffering on Indians, and remain in the good company of many scholars who would agree with him.

## The Resilience of Narratives

In a review of recent work on disease in early American studies, Kelly Wisecup (2012) contrasted two visions. Ottawa Andrew Blackbird, writing in 1887 about an epidemic in the 1750s, focused on European deception and trade, highlighting the importance of human agency during the encounter. Diamond, writing in 1997 about hemispheric patterns of mortality, emphasized inevitable forces of genetics and human biology, the product of macro-scale forces of human evolution and global geography. Wisecup placed contemporary writers into one of these camps—the biological approach (for example, Philip Curtin and Alfred Crosby) and the historical-cultural approach (for example, Joyce Chaplin, Cristobal Silva, and me).

This is the phenomenon that interests me. There are two competing narratives. Each has a compelling logical structure, whether of evolutionary biology or of social contingency. Each has well-documented cases, of tribes who collapsed without having ever seen Europeans and of those who escaped disease until worn down by the oppressive forces of European colonial regimes. Given the choice between these two worldviews, readers must decide what makes a historical narrative persuasive.

One initial challenge is that each camp relies on speculation, assumption, and rhetorical gambits. Many of the most deterministic accounts of mortality rely on specific assumptions about what might have happened. Mann, for instance, acknowledged that there is no direct evidence of the hemispheric epidemics described by Dobyns. He acknowledged Henige's critiques of the high counters. He described how archaeologists such as Douglas Ubelaker and Dean Snow have found no evidence of early epidemics and, in fact, found evidence of stable sixteenth-century populations. But none of that cooled his enthusiasm for catastrophe. He simply asserted, "The High Counters seem to be winning the argument, at least for now" (Mann 2005:133). Similarly, he admitted that his discussion of whether Columbus's crew introduced malaria "is highly speculative, to say the least" (Mann 2011a:78). But that did not give him pause: "Yet the impossibility of finding definitive answers does not mean historians should stop seeking them" (Mann 2011a:78). His standard of evidence is not whether a claim is true or even likely to be true but that "it would not be completely wrong" (Mann 2011a:79).[8]

Cavalier assumptions are not limited to popular writers. Dobyns and all of the high counters assumed there was high mortality before Europeans made their first population counts and that, as a result, demographers can multiply those counts to account for 50 percent, 90 percent, or even 99 percent prior mortality. Crosby generalized as well. He based his theories on the "reports of horrendous epidemics and steep population declines, confirmed in many cases by recent quantitative analyses of Spanish tribute records and other sources" (Crosby 1976:290). Did similar epidemics occur outside of New Spain? English and French records were "not as definitively supportive" (Crosby 1976:290). This did not mean that these Europeans introduced fewer epidemics; instead, he asserted, it could simply be that the French and English did not "keep continuous records until the seventeenth century, by which time at least some of the worst epidemics of imported diseases had probably already taken place" (Crosby 1976:290). It is not unreasonable, in Crosby's view, to assume that "many of the most important events of aboriginal history in British America occurred beyond the range of direct observation by literate witnesses" (Crosby 1976:290).

Confronted with a dearth of evidence on early epidemics on Hispaniola, Noble David Cook (2002) proposed a clever hypothesis: an early, unrecorded epidemic of smallpox did take place, granting acquired immunity to the population, something that accounted for the lack of another epidemic until 1518. Like Crosby, he suspected that the colonists, often ill-prepared and struggling to survive, were poor record-keepers. Archaeologists sometimes invoke a similar dodge. Why do many skeletal series show little change in health in the early years of Spanish colonization? As Newson and Ubelaker reminded us, bone keeps imperfect records: "traumatic events, such as epidemics that are noted in the documentary sources, left no mark on the skeleton" (Newson and Ubelaker 2002:343).

The imperfection of the documentary and osteological records empowered scholars to speculate and assume. Although southwestern epidemics are documented only for the seventeenth century, Braatz explained that early epidemics cannot be ruled out. The diseases "could easily have moved on to the Zuni and Hopi villages and their trading partners" (Braatz 2003:66). As Barrett (2002:2) noted, "Although no evidence of such epidemics in the Rio Grande region prior to the 1630s had yet been discovered, elsewhere most such disasters began near the time of contact, and it is likely [that] Puebloans suffered a similar fate." Although the first major epidemic began in 1629, "It is difficult to believe . . . that the Pueblo population had not been previously affected by epidemics of European diseases, particularly smallpox, during the one hundred years that had elapsed since Spaniards first entered the region" (Barrett 2002:79). Like Cook, Barrett speculated about undocumented epidemics that struck, conferred immunity, and then receded until a new generation became susceptible, a cycle that could have run several times before good record keeping began. This is a "just-so" story that would make Rudyard Kipling proud.

Where no evidence exists, writers turn to the realm of the possible. Ramenofsky and Patricia Galloway (2005:261), for instance, wanted to understand the impact of the de Soto expedition even though limitations of the extant sources "preclude definitive conclusions." And so, informed by "the perspective of infectious disease," they speculated about "possible routes or types of infection that could have been transmitted" (Ramenofsky and Galloway 2005:261). Spaniards and their livestock (especially pigs—"the probability that swine-derived infections were transmitted seems inescapable" [Ramenofsky and Galloway 2005:275]) could have transmitted nineteen named pathogens. Ramenofsky and Galloway (2005:268) placed their bets on smallpox, pertussis, typhoid, and venereal syphilis, a quartet that "is more than sufficient to have caused high levels of mortality among the non-immune."[9]

Such assumptions have been widely criticized. Richard Steckel (2005:2) complained that writings about pre-Columbian health and demography are "characterized by an unusually high ratio of debate to factual information." Henige (2008:186) noted that the assumptions of the high counters "need not be accepted by anyone who might choose to reject them on any of a number of grounds." Kelton (chapter 8, this volume) warns scholars not to assume that every possible epidemic was an actual epidemic, a style of speculation that "detracts from the more potent and devastating aspect of colonialism."

While these criticisms are easy to make, it is important to acknowledge that the advocates of contingent mortality also rely on significant assumptions. When I encountered the two competing narratives—one evolutionary and biological, the other contingent and social—I was drawn to the contingent. As an undergraduate, I worked with Stephen Jay Gould, whose tastes in evolutionary theory leaned toward the accidental and contingent, not the deterministic and inevitable (Gould 1989; Gould and Lewontin 1978). This colored my thoughts. A key argument in my "Virgin Soils Revisited" hinged on the interpretation of depopulation ratios, which varied from 3:1 to nearly 60:1. Is this really evidence of contingency? Even the low estimates indicate very high baseline mortality, for instance, 75 percent for 4:1 depopulation. This could be explained in two ways: either "a shared genetic vulnerability, whose final intensity was shaped by social variables" or "a shared social experience, of pre-existing nutritional stress exacerbated by the widespread chaos of encounter and colonization" (Jones 2003:740). Both positions are defensible, and I had—and have—no way of answering this question. I hedged and asserted that while high mortality must have been "a likely consequence of encounter," it was not necessarily "the inevitable result of inherent immunological vulnerability" (Jones 2003:741). I then executed a sleight of hand. Because scholars and readers generally balk at attributing the high prevalence of AIDS in sub-Saharan Africa to the genetic deficiencies of Africans, they should be equally cautious about using "no immunity" to explain the devastation of America. While this argument has rhetorical appeal, it would not convince a logician.

Many scholars have given up hope for a definitive resolution. Henige (2008:198) does not think that data will ever resolve the ambiguity: "But since the debate is based on argument rather than evidence, it is hard to see just what could ever bring it to an end, or even to give one side or another a decided advantage." Ramenofsky and her colleagues (2003:242) agreed: "Given that the same documentary sources are frequently employed to argue all sides of any question, current investigations are inadequate for falsifying any position or for building new knowledge."

Unfortunately, the stakes of the lingering debate are substantial. Debates about contact demography are not technical academic questions but important moral ones. Livi-Bacci (2011:162) argues that the size of precontact populations must be known so that we can understand the real magnitude of—and moral responsibility for—what happened next: "So the assumed dimensions of the population at contact are a relevant aspect of judgment when assessing the impact of the new pathologies—or of confiscation of labor, or of the atrocities perpetrated—on the demographic collapse." This puts a clear burden on current scholars. Because ongoing writing will involve scholars passing judgment on patchy data, it is essential that they understand explicitly the assumptions on which their judgments rest.

Moreover, this problem of assumption, interpretation, and moral consequence is broader than just the literature on demography and depopulation. Daniel Usner (2009:71–72) sees it as but one example of how scholars write about Indians, one that is only slowly starting to change: "Recent attention to medical discourse over American Indian health has been especially informative in demonstrating how much can be learned through this kind of analysis." He sees less to praise in other areas of Indian scholarship. Reading widely in recent work, he "demonstrates how language about American Indian livelihood has operated as an instrument of colonialism. The ideological use of notions such as *backwardness, wastefulness, idleness,* and *timelessness*—through writing, illustrating, painting, or photographing—proved to be as damaging as the material impact of unfair or coercive market forces" (Usner 2009:142).

James Merrell makes a similar point in his 2012 reflection on the current state of Indian history. Even though modern scholars believe that they have moved past the narratives and assumptions of past generations, "The hard truth is that most of us still use much of the same stale rhetoric as 'traditional colonialists'" (Merrell 2012:510). He believes that the "theater still resounds with words drafted ages ago by people with an agenda, words that have been (and still can be) weapons . . . we are all, in more ways than one, 'colonial historians.' In the never-ending struggle to come to terms with early America, as a twentieth-century philosopher put it, 'we have met the enemy and he is us'" (Merrell 2012:512). Swedlund (chapter 6, this volume) agrees: "the discursive practices we employ to talk about the history of Native American health still often carry the echoes of past colonial studies."

How should we move forward? Scholars must continue to do their part to find valuable data that have not yet been found, in hopes (however thin) of proving Usner and Ramenofsky wrong in asserting that empirical data will never settle the debates. Beyond that, they have two choices. They can embrace both narratives, acknowledge that the determinists and the contingents have both produced powerful arguments and detailed case studies, and as a result, give both a seat at the table. Or if they believe that such compromise is not warranted, they need to figure out how to make the case for contingency more persuasively and more publicly so that books like Diamond's and Mann's become more difficult to publish.

## Acknowledgments

This chapter would not have been possible without the intrepid work of my research assistant, Alison Kraemer, and the invaluable feedback from Alan Swedlund, Catherine Cameron, Paul Kelton, and the other participants in this project.

## Notes

1. For other reviews of the biological turn, see Alchon 2003:4–5; Covey et al. 2011:336; Henige 2008:185; Pernick 2012:365.

2. Even though Diamond, in this article (Wolfe et al. 2007:279), described *Guns, Germs, and Steel* as a "tentative, earlier formulation," he continued to market the book aggressively. In a 2013 interview with the *New York Times*, Diamond was asked what book he recommended for parents of children who wanted to learn more about geography. Diamond's (2013:8) answer was decisive: "I believe that I'm being realistic, not egotistical and self-promoting, when I answer: my own book, 'Guns, Germs, and Steel: The Fates of Human Societies.'"

3. This emphasis on the potential susceptibility of all humans and the contingency of disease outcomes appears again in the preface Crosby wrote for the thirtieth anniversary edition of *The Columbian Exchange*. Black Death, for instance, devastated Europe, but the populations recovered slowly over many decades. If, however, "the plague and Mongols had arrived in tandem," he noted, "I think it is unlikely that I would be writing this preface in an Indo-European language" (Crosby 2003:xxii).

4. Alchon (2003:59), however, like so many other authors, sometimes does incorporate the message of virgin soil theory, for instance noting that "Native Americans were not immunologically prepared for the devastation that lay ahead."

5. However, such is the power of the popular narratives that Barrett (2002:11) second-guesses the empirical conclusions: "[I]t is difficult to believe that the Rio Grande Pueblo population escaped the fate of other populations in the western hemisphere when contacted by Europeans who carried diseases to which they had no immunity."

6. This echoes Crosby (1986:34), who, in *Ecological Imperialism*, described how thousands of years of disease exposure in Eurasia had created an Old World "superman" with "an impressive assortment of genetic and acquired adaptations to diseases anciently endemic to Old World civilizations, and an immune system of such experience and sophistication as to make him the template for all the humans who would be tempted or obliged to follow the path he pioneered some 8,000 to 10,000 years ago."

7. Fields (2008:8) does admit that "the harsh treatment and ecological devastation that accompanied Spanish colonization certainly magnified the losses."

8. As Mann (2011a:79) explains, "It would be an exaggeration to say that malaria and yellow fever were responsible for the slave trade, just as it would be an exaggeration to say that they explain why much of Latin America is still poor, or why the antebellum cotton plantations in *Gone with the Wind* sat atop great, sweeping

lawns, or why Scotland joined England to form the United Kingdom, or why the weak, divided thirteen colonies won independence from mighty Great Britain in the Revolutionary War. But it would not be completely wrong, either."

9. But amid this focus on the biological, Ramenofsky and Galloway did leave the door open for contingency. The actual outcomes would have depended on duration of stay, winter camps, the details of the encounters, and the role of swine: this "explains the patchwork pattern of population destruction that occurred in the wake of the Hernando de Soto expedition" (Ramenofsky and Galloway 2005:275).

# References

Alchon, Suzanne A. 2003. A Pest in the Land: New World Epidemics in a Global Perspective. Albuquerque: University of New Mexico Press.

Anderson, Virginia DeJohn. 2004. Creatures of Empire: How Domestic Animals Transformed Early America. New York: Oxford University Press.

Anderson, Warwick. 2007. The colonial medicine of settler states: Comparing histories of indigenous health. Health and History 9:144–54.

Axtell, James. 1985. The Invasion Within: The Contest of Cultures in Colonial North America. New York: Oxford University Press.

Barrett, Elinore. 2002. Conquest and Catastrophe: Changing Rio Grande Pueblo Settlement Patterns in the Sixteenth and Seventeenth Centuries. Albuquerque: University of New Mexico Press.

Bombardieri, Marcella. 2005. Another Summers speech questioned. Boston Globe, April 21:B2.

Braatz, Timothy. 2003. Surviving Conquest: A History of the Yavapai Peoples. Lincoln: University of Nebraska Press.

Bushnell, George E. 1920. A Study in the Epidemiology of Tuberculosis, with Especial Reference to Tuberculosis of the Tropics and of the Negro Race. New York: William Wood.

Calloway, Colin G. 1997. New Worlds for All: Indians, Europeans, and the Remaking of Early America. Baltimore, MD: Johns Hopkins University Press.

Carlos, Ann M., and Frank D. Lewis. 2012. Smallpox and Native American mortality: The 1780s epidemic in the Hudson Bay region. Explorations in Economic History 49(3):277–90.

Clinton, William J. 2000. National Medal of Science, 1999. Presented March 14. Text available at http://www.nsf.gov/od/nms/recip_details.cfm?recip_id=103.

Cockburn, Aidan, ed. 1967. Infectious Diseases: Their Evolution and Eradication. Springfield, IL: Charles C. Thomas.

Cook, Noble David. 2002. Sickness, starvation, and death in early Hispaniola. Journal of Interdisciplinary History 32(3):349–86.

Covey, R. Alan, Geoff Childs, and Rebecca Kippen. 2011. Dynamics of indigenous demographic fluctuations: Lessons from sixteenth-century Cusco, Peru. Current Anthropology 52(3):335–60.

Crosby, Alfred W. 1972. The Columbian Exchange: Biological and Cultural Conse-
    quences of 1492. Westport, CT: Greenwood Publishing.
———. 1976. Virgin soil epidemics as a factor in the aboriginal depopulation in
    America. William and Mary Quarterly 33(2):289–99.
———. 1978. "God . . . would destroy them, and give their country to another
    people." American Heritage 29(6):39–42.
———. 1986. Ecological Imperialism: The Biological Expansion of Europe, 900–
    1900. Cambridge: Cambridge University Press.
———. 2003. The Columbian Exchange: Biological and Cultural Consequences
    of 1492. 30th anniversary edition. Westport, CT: Greenwood Publishing.
d'Anghiera, Peter Martyr. 1885 [1516]. The Decades of the Newe Worlde. Trans.
    Richard Eden, 1555. In The First Three English Books on America, [?1511]–
    1555 A.D., edited by Edward Arber, 45–204. Birmingham, UK: privately
    printed.
Diamond, Jared. 1997. Guns, Germs, and Steel: The Fates of Human Societies.
    New York: W. W. Norton.
———. 2013. Interview for "By the Book." New York Times Book Review, Janu-
    ary 20:8.
Dixon, Benjamin Y. 2007. Furthering their own demise: How Kansa Indian death
    customs accelerated their depopulation. Ethnohistory 54(3):473–508.
Dobyns, Henry F. 1963. An outline of Andean epidemic history to 1720. Bulletin of
    the History of Medicine 37:493–515.
Fields, Sherry. 2008. Pestilence and Headcolds: Encountering Illness in Colonial
    Mexico. New York: Columbia University Press.
Gould, Stephen Jay. 1989. Wonderful Life: The Burgess Shale and the Nature of
    History. New York: W. W. Norton.
Gould, Stephen Jay, and Richard Lewontin. 1978. The spandrels of San Marco
    and the panglossian paradigm: A critique of the adaptationist programme.
    Proceedings of the Royal Society of London 205:581–98.
Hackel, Steven. 2012. From Ahogado to Zorrillo: External causes of mortality in
    the California missions. History of the Family 17(1):77–104.
Hämäläinen, Pekka. 2010. The politics of grass: European expansion, ecological
    change, and indigenous power in the Southwest borderlands. William and
    Mary Quarterly 67(2):173–208.
Henige, David. 1998. Numbers from Nowhere: The American Indian Contact
    Population Debate. Norman: University of Oklahoma Press.
———. 2008. Recent work and prospects in American Indian contact population.
    History Compass 6(January):183–206.
Hodge, Adam. 2012. "In want of nourishment for to keep them alive": Climate
    fluctuations, bison scarcity, and the smallpox epidemic of 1780–82 on the
    northern Great Plains. Environmental History 17(2):365–403.
Holder, A. B. 1892. Papers on diseases among Indians. Medical Record (New York)
    42(August 13):177–82.

Hull, Kathleen L. 2009. Pestilence and Persistence: Yosemite Indian Demography and Culture in Colonial California. Berkeley: University of California Press.

Hurtado, A. M., K. R. Hill, W. Rosenblatt, J. Bender, and T. Scharmen. 2003. Longitudinal study of tuberculosis outcomes among immunologically naive Aché natives of Paraguay. American Journal of Physical Anthropology 121(2):134–50.

Hutchinson, Dale L. 2007. Tatham Mound and the Bioarchaeology of European Contact: Disease and Depopulation in Central Gulf Coast Florida. Gainesville: University Press of Florida.

Hutchinson, Woods. 1907. Varieties of tuberculosis according to race and social condition. National Association for the Study and Prevention of Tuberculosis, Transactions of the Annual Meeting 3:191–216.

Inglis, Kerri A. 2013. Ma'i Lepera: Disease and Displacement in Nineteenth-Century Hawai'i. Honolulu: University of Hawai'i Press.

Jennings, Francis. 1975. The Invasion of America: Indians, Colonialism, and the Cant of Conquest. Chapel Hill: University of North Carolina Press.

Jones, David S. 2003. Virgin soils revisited. William and Mary Quarterly 60(4):703–42.

———. 2004. Rationalizing Epidemics: Meanings and Uses of American Indian Mortality Since 1600. Cambridge, MA: Harvard University Press.

———. 2006. The persistence of American Indian health disparities. American Journal of Public Health 96(12):2122–34.

Jones, Eric E., and Sharon N. DeWitte. 2012. Using spatial analysis to estimate depopulation for Native American populations in northeastern North America, AD 1616–1645. Journal of Anthropological Archaeology 31(1):83–92.

Jones, W. A. 1905. Report of commissioner (17 October 1904), part I. In Annual Reports of the Department of the Interior for the Fiscal Year Ended June 30, 1904. House Documents (58-3) 4978. Washington, DC: Government Printing Office.

Kelm, Mary-Ellen. 1998. Colonizing Bodies: Aboriginal Health and Healing in British Columbia, 1900–50. Vancouver: University of British Columbia Press.

Kelton, Paul. 2004. Avoiding the smallpox spirits: Colonial epidemics and Southeastern Indian survival. Ethnohistory 51(1):45–71.

———. 2007. Epidemics and Enslavement: Biological Catastrophe in the Native Southeast, 1492–1715. Lincoln: University of Nebraska Press.

Kleinman, Arthur, Veena Das, and Margaret Lock. 1996. Introduction to the issue "Social Suffering." Daedalus 125(1):xi–xx.

Kunitz, Stephen J. 1994. Disease and Social Diversity: The European Impact on the Health of Non-Europeans. New York: Oxford University Press.

Larsen, Clark S., M. C. Griffin, D. L. Hutchinson, V. E. Noble, L. Norr, R. F. Pator, C. B. Ruff, et al. 2001. Frontiers of contact: Bioarchaeology of Spanish Florida. Journal of World Prehistory 15:69–123.

Las Casas, Bartolomé de. 1992 [1552]. The Devastation of the Indies: A Brief Account. Translated by Herma Briffault. Baltimore, MD: Johns Hopkins University Press.

Livi-Bacci, Massimo. 2003. Return to Hispaniola: Reassessing a demographic catastrophe. Hispanic American Historical Review 83(1):3–51.

———. 2008. Conquest: The Destruction of the American Indios. Translated by Carl Ipsen. Malden, MA: Polity Press.

———. 2011. The demise of the American Indios. Population and Development Review 37(1):161–65.

Loren, Diana DiPaolo. 2008. In Contact: Bodies and Spaces in the Sixteenth- and Seventeenth-Century Eastern Woodlands. Lanham, MD: AltaMira Press.

Mann, Charles C. 2005. 1491: New Revelations of the Americas Before Columbus. New York: Alfred A. Knopf.

———. 2011a. 1493: Uncovering the New World Columbus Created. New York: Alfred A. Knopf.

———. 2011b. Interview with Terry Gross. Fresh Air, WHYY/NPR, August 8. Available at http://www.npr.org/2011/08/08/138924127/in-1493-columbus-shaped-a-world-to-be.

———. 2012. Interview on RadioBoston. WBUR, October 8. Originally aired August 29, 2011. Available at http://radioboston.wbur.org/2012/10/08/columbus-new-world.

Marr, John S., and John T. Cathey. 2010. New hypothesis for cause of epidemic among Native Americans, New England, 1616–1619. Emerging Infectious Diseases 16(2):281–86.

McMillen, Christian W. 2008. "The red man and the white plague": Rethinking race, tuberculosis, and American Indians, ca. 1890–1950. Bulletin of the History of Medicine 82(3):608–45.

McNeill, William H. 1976. Plagues and Peoples. New York: Doubleday.

Merrell, James H. 2012. Second thoughts on colonial historians and American Indians. William and Mary Quarterly 69(3):451–512.

Newson, Linda A. 1985. Indian population patterns in colonial Spanish America. Latin American Research Review 20:41–74.

———. 2003. Patterns of Indian depopulation in early colonial Ecuador. Revista de Indias 63(227):135–56.

Newson, Linda, and Douglas H. Ubelaker. 2002. Patterns of health and nutrition in prehistoric and historic Ecuador. In The Backbone of History: Health and Nutrition in the Western Hemisphere, edited by Richard H. Steckel and Jerome C. Rose, 343–75. Cambridge: Cambridge University Press.

Obomsawin, Raymond. 2007. Historical and scientific perspectives on the health of Canada's First Peoples. Available at http://www.soilandhealth.org/02/0203cat/020335. obomsawin.pdf.

Packard, Randall M. 1989. White Plague, Black Labor: Tuberculosis and the Political Economy of Health and Disease in South Africa. Berkeley: University of California Press.

Pernick, Martin S. 2012. Diseases in motion. *In* A Companion to World History, edited by Douglas Northrop, 365–74. Malden, MA: Blackwell.

Piper, Liza, and John Sandlos. 2007. A broken frontier—ecological imperialism in the Canadian North. Environmental History 12(4):759–95.

Prescott, William H. 2004 [1843]. History of the Conquest of Mexico. New York: Barnes and Noble Publishing.

———. 2005 [1847]. History of the Conquest of Peru. Mineola, NY: Dover Publications.

Ramenofsky, Ann F., and Patricia Galloway. 2005. Disease and the Soto Entrade. *In* The Hernando de Soto Expedition: History, Historiography and "Discovery" in the Southeast, edited by Patricia Galloway, 259–79. Lincoln: University of Nebraska Press.

Ramenofsky, Ann F., Fraser D. Neiman, and Christopher D. Pierce. 2009. Measuring time, population, and residential mobility from the surface at San Marcos Pueblo, north central New Mexico. American Antiquity 74(3):505–30.

Ramenofsky, Ann F., Alicia K. Wilbur, and Anne C. Stone. 2003. Native American disease history: Past, present, and future directions. World Archaeology 35(2):241–57.

Rensink, Brendan. 2011. Genocide of Native Americans: Historical facts and historiographic debates. *In* Genocide of Indigenous Peoples: A Critical Bibliographic Review, vol. 8, edited by Samuel Totten and Robert K. Hitchcock, 15–36. New Brunswick, NJ: Transaction Publishers.

Riley, James. 2010. Smallpox and American Indians revisited. Journal of the History of Medicine and Allied Sciences 65(4):445–77.

Rosenberg, Charles. 1992. Explaining epidemics. *In* Explaining Epidemics and Other Studies in the History of Medicine, 293–304. Cambridge: Cambridge University Press.

Silva, Cristobal. 2011. Miraculous Plagues: An Epidemiology of Early New England Narrative. New York: Oxford University Press.

Smith, John. 1986 [1631]. Advertisements for the unexperienced plants of New England, or anywhere. *In* The Complete Works of Captain John Smith, vol. 3, edited by Philip L. Barbour. Chapel Hill: University of North Carolina Press.

Steckel, Richard H. 2005. Health and nutrition in pre-Columbian America: The skeletal evidence. Journal of Interdisciplinary History 36(1):1–32.

Tovías, Blanca. 2007. Colonialism and demographic catastrophes in the Americas: Blackfoot tribes of the Northwest. *In* Collisions of Cultures and Identities: Settlers and Indigenous Peoples, edited by Patricia Grimshaw and Russell McGregor, 72–78. Melbourne: RMIT Publishing.

Trigger, Bruce F. 1966. Comments on Henry Dobyns, "Estimating aboriginal American population: An appraisal of techniques with a new hemispheric estimate." Current Anthropology 7(4):439–40.

Usner, Daniel H. 2009. Indian Work: Language and Livelihood in Native American History. Cambridge, MA: Harvard University Press.

Warrick, Gary. 2003. European infectious disease and depopulation of the Wendat-Tionontate (Huron-Petun). World Archaeology 35:258–75.

White, Richard. 1991. The Middle Ground: Indians, Empires, and Republics in the Great Lakes Region, 1650–1815. Cambridge: Cambridge University Press.

Wisecup, Kelly. 2012. Microbes and a "magic box": Medicine and disease in early American Studies. Early American Literature 47(1):199–216.

Wolfe, Nathan D., Claire Panosian Dunavan, and Jared Diamond. 2007. Origins of major human infectious diseases. Nature 447(7142):279–83.

# 2

# Population Decline and Culture Change in the American Midcontinent

## Bridging the Prehistoric and Historic Divide

*George R. Milner*

The early steps of what enabled Old World peoples to push aside the original inhabitants of North America, especially deep in the interior beyond the ken of European observers, are only imperfectly understood. Along the Atlantic and Gulf coasts and in the arid Southwest there is a reasonably continuous, although biased, written account of events from the sixteenth or early seventeenth century onward. Elsewhere, archaeological data must be harnessed to later historical sources to identify what happened. One such place is the American Midwest and Upper South.

It is widely recognized that North America's Native population was greatly reduced over hundreds of years, reaching a low point in the nineteenth century, but there remains considerable uncertainty about the magnitude and timing of that decline and attendant cultural change, as well as what was ultimately responsible for the profound transformations that occurred. New diseases certainly figured prominently in that process. There are, however, two different views of the role of epidemics in population decline and societal change during the early postcontact period, especially the sixteenth century, when written documentation is sparse.

The simpler scenario, forcibly argued by Henry Dobyns (1983), holds that massive population losses took place both early and uniformly across the entire continent as a result of newly introduced infectious diseases that repeatedly swept unimpeded across much or all of North America, with virtually everyone suffering from each outbreak. Significant reduction occurred in the sixteenth century, so acute crowd diseases (notably, the terrible killers smallpox and measles) necessarily played a major role in this version of events. These particular diseases were not geographically limited by indispensable animal reservoirs or vectors.[1] The pathogens were directly transmitted from one person to the next; the time between exposure, sickness, and either death or recovery was short; and survival was accompanied by lifelong immunity. Epidemics struck the peoples of eastern North America repeatedly at intervals of less than one generation, to judge from Dobyns's (1983:291–95) Florida Timucuan example. That implies a heavily populated land with frequent intergroup contact. To facilitate pathogen spread, people had to be continuously distributed across the Eastern Woodlands and elsewhere to the extent possible given environmental constraints. Stated baldly, all equally productive places were equally occupied. Because Europeans had yet to establish much of a presence on the continent, the initial and dramatic decline was not attributed to war, slavery, or the forced appropriation of labor.

Its simplicity—a single causal mechanism uncomplicated by heterogeneous cultural and natural landscapes—holds a certain appeal. That was especially true when Dobyns (1983:324), building on his earlier work (Dobyns 1966), published his influential account of postcontact collapse, arguing that eastern North America was a single "epidemic region." Given the state of archaeological knowledge at that time, this position could be neither supported nor refuted for the critical sixteenth century. Nevertheless, it soon gained traction, partly because eminent scholars such as Alfred Crosby (1976, 1986) and William McNeill (1976) were also calling attention to the devastating impact of new diseases on recently contacted Native peoples.

The alternative scenario was certainly no less horrifying for the people involved, but the initial Eastern Woodlands population was smaller, settled areas were dispersed, and pathogens spread irregularly beyond initial outbreaks. So during any particular disease episode, some groups were hard-hit while others were spared. That produced a mosaic of suddenly weakened and still-strong populations, thereby upsetting long-standing relations among spatially discrete groups. When the irregular spread of high-mortality diseases was first raised as a possibility (Milner 1980), it too lacked strong archaeological support. Yet soon thereafter information consistent with that scenario began to be assembled (Ramenofsky 1987; Snow and Starna 1989). The direct effects of disease were worsened by ineffectual care and the disruption of essential household tasks when numerous people became sick simultaneously, much like what occurred in mid-twentieth-century outbreaks of measles in isolated villages deep in the South American rainforest (Centerwall 1968; Neel et al. 1970). The immediate death toll from epidemics, however, was not the entire story, since excess mortality also led to a loss of cultural knowledge and traditions, disrupted finely balanced alliance networks, and interfered with the acquisition of food by normally self-sufficient communities (Jones 2010; Milner and Chaplin 2010; Milner et al. 2001; Ubelaker 1992). Historians have recently directed attention to the reinforcing debilitative effects of disease and social disorder, including raids for captives, in eastern North America, especially for the seventeenth century onward (Alchon 2003; Kelton 2007).

At this point, there can be little doubt that historic period population declines and localized recoveries, cultural change, and group movement and reconfiguration varied both temporally and spatially. Yet for the sixteenth century, the situation is somewhat simplified, since direct contacts with Europeans in eastern North America were quite limited relative to those that took place later on. So the effects of epidemics that spread well beyond direct encounters between Natives and newcomers are of primary importance. The systematic detection of diseases such as measles and smallpox is impossible with archaeological materials, but the conditions favoring one disease-and-population scenario over the other are identifiable and potentially measurable. They include the size and organization of societies, their distribution, and interactions among them on the eve of contact. As a step in that direction, this chapter focuses on the several hundred years extending up to and including the sixteenth century. Variation in population densities across the Eastern Woodlands, the distribution of settled areas, and the nature of intergroup relations at the close of prehistory set the stage for what happened when Europeans arrived.

## Study Region

The primary area of interest, for convenience referred to as the midcontinent, extends from the Great Lakes southward to the interior plateaus and from the western edge of the Appalachians to somewhat beyond the

Mississippi River. During the late prehistoric and early historic periods, this region was settled by villagers who cultivated crops, notably maize, but also relied heavily on wild plants and animals.

Much of this area—present-day Tennessee and western Kentucky, extending up the Ohio River to southwestern Indiana, and along the Mississippi and its principal tributaries into southern Wisconsin—was dominated by Mississippian chiefdoms during the late prehistoric period (Griffin 1967; Milner 2004). These societies varied in population size, geographical extent, and organizational complexity, and they featured distinctive stylistic traditions, notably in pottery and domestic architecture. In fact, the largest prehistoric settlement in eastern North America, the Mississippian site known as Cahokia, is located in the Mississippi River valley in Illinois (Fowler 1989; Milner 1998; Schroeder 2004). Despite outward appearances, these societies shared similarities in sociopolitical organization, including ranked kin-based groups with prominent people inheriting or otherwise acquiring key political and ritual positions.

Elsewhere in the midcontinent, tribal-scale groups, also a heterogeneous category, lacked well-developed and reasonably fixed social hierarchies and hereditary leadership positions (Milner 2004; Schroeder 2004). None of these groups, including those referred to as Oneota and Fort Ancient, approached the number of people who lived in the society centered on Cahokia (Milner 1998, 2004). Nevertheless, these societies could be as large as, if not bigger than, typical Mississippian chiefdoms (Harn 1994; Muller 1986, 1997a). So regardless of how one might classify these midcontinental societies according to archaeological or societal characteristics, there was considerable overlap in their overall population sizes as well as those of their constituent communities.

## Late Prehistoric Depopulation, Movement, and Warfare

For over thirty years, archaeologists have recognized that by the close of the fifteenth century, locally important large centers, typically marked by earthen mounds, were abandoned throughout the Ohio-Mississippi River confluence area southward to southeastern Missouri. Skepticism greeted Williams's (1980, 1990) initial discussion of this so-called Vacant

Quarter, although it is widely accepted today (Cobb and Butler 2002; Meeks and Anderson 2013; Schroeder 2004). The extent to which widespread depopulation accompanied societal change, as opposed to a dispersal to sites that are hard to detect, was less certain for many years.

It now appears that Williams's (1980, 1990) original Vacant Quarter was much too small, and the number of its inhabitants indeed plummeted. In fact, much of the Midwest and Upper South was depopulated (Milner and Chaplin 2010). Clusters of settlements, none particularly large, were separated by often-vast tracts of unoccupied land (Brown and Sasso 2001; Milner and Chaplin 2010; Milner et al. 2001; Schroeder 2004). Once-settled areas no doubt remain unrecognized by archaeologists because of imperfect survey knowledge and imprecise temporal controls. Nevertheless, the general outline of the sixteenth-century occupation is clear (figure 2.1; Milner and Chaplin 2010: fig. 1).

A sparsely settled midcontinent is remarkable because only a few centuries earlier, several of the biggest and most organizationally complex societies in prehistoric eastern North America were located in this region. In addition to Cahokia, large sites included Kincaid and Angel in the lower Ohio River valley, Aztalan in southeastern Wisconsin, and many other smaller but still locally prominent centers (Butler 1991; Conrad 1991; Emerson 1991; Fowler 1989; Goldstein and Freeman 1997; Goldstein and Richards 1991; Harn 1994; Kelly 2009; Meeks and Anderson 2013; Milner 1998; Muller 1986, 1997a). All such towns were associated with outlying settlements, producing pockets of population surrounded by unoccupied, but not necessarily unused, land.

There is still uncertainty about the timing of population decline and chiefdom collapse. Yet by the end of the thirteenth century, transformations in the sociopolitical landscape were under way from Aztalan southward to the central Illinois River valley and Cahokia (Conrad 1991; Goldstein and Richards 1991; Kelly 2009; Milner 1998). It would take another century or more for population decline and chiefdom dissolution to follow their course, including the disappearance of formerly impressive centers such as Cahokia, Kincaid, and Angel (Butler 1991; Kelly 2009; Milner 1998; Muller 1986).

By circa 1300, if not before, warfare threatened the very survival of some communities, such as the Oneota villagers at Norris Farms in the central Illinois River valley where at least one-third of the adults were

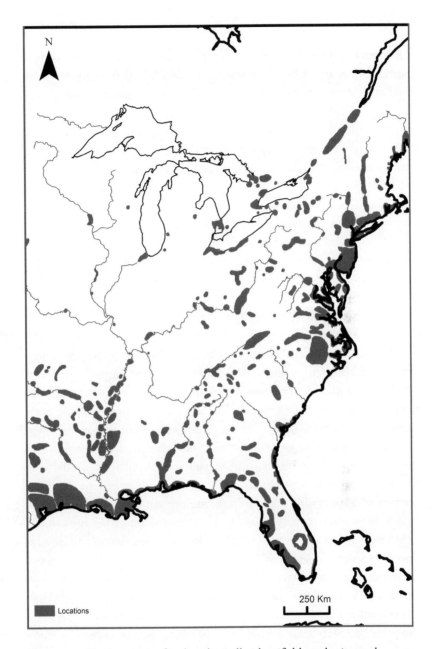

**Figure 2.1.** The locations of archaeologically identifiable early sixteenth-century population aggregates are indicated by dark shading (Milner and Chaplin 2010: fig. 1). Large shaded areas tend to represent places that are poorly known or those occupied by people who moved often. Occupations are surely missed, but the midcontinent was certainly thinly occupied relative to the Deep South and Atlantic Seaboard. (Map by George Chaplin.)

killed in ambushes (Milner et al. 1991; Milner and Ferrell 2011). Other communities also suffered great losses, so conflicts that produced many casualties were not confined to a short time interval (Steadman 2008). In fact, intergroup relations worsened throughout much of the northern Eastern Woodlands during the last centuries of prehistory, to the extent that increasing numbers of settlements protected by palisades reflect troubled times (Milner 1999, 2007).

Population movement accompanied warfare, such as the arrival in the Illinois River valley of the Norris Farms community, as shown by both cranial morphology and artifacts (Esarey and Conrad 1998; Esarey and Santure 1990; Steadman 1998). It was part of a southward expansion of Oneota peoples, the outermost edge of which reached the Cahokia area about two hundred kilometers farther south (Jackson 1992, 1998; Kelly 2009). The geographical distribution of Oneota groups was generally increasing at that time, also extending westward onto the plains beyond the Missouri River (Hollinger 2005; Ritterbush and Logan 2000).

Entire communities moved, but so too did smaller numbers of people, probably down to single individuals. At Norris Farms, about one-half of the mtDNA hypervariable region I sequences examined to date are indicative of separate maternal lineages (Stone and Stoneking 1998, 1999). That could indicate flexible marriage patterns whereby women came from different places, or a community that routinely incorporated captives or the remnants of formerly viable villages. The latter is consistent with hard-pressed historic period Iroquois groups that took in people of diverse backgrounds, including erstwhile enemies (Fenton 1998; Snow 1994, 1995, 1996, 2001). Flexible group membership to meet the exigencies of the moment is also suggested by artifacts and domestic architecture at other midcontinental sites from roughly that point onward, although supporting evidence is not as strong as it is for Norris Farms (Cook 2008; Drooker 1997; Esarey and Conrad 1998; Hollinger 2005; Jackson 1992, 1998). Situationally advantageous coalitions of people from different cultural traditions should not surprise us, especially when the very existence of threatened groups hung in the balance. After all, ways of life were generally similar, despite stylistic distinctions in material culture. Such arrangements, perhaps adopted only during the worst times, allowed groups to maintain or increase their strength, boosting their chances of survival.

Despite fewer people occupying the midcontinent during the sixteenth century, those who remained still had to contend with troublesome intergroup relations. Known population aggregates are situated farther apart than they would be by chance alone (Milner and Chaplin 2010). So these groups—they were few and scattered relative to the situation several centuries earlier—actively distanced themselves from one another.

East and south of the midcontinent there are many sites with remnants of defensive walls or the skeletons of people who died in attacks. Of the sites with temporal spans encompassing part or all of the sixteenth century, those with palisades or casualties ($N$=178) are mostly distributed from southern Ontario and upstate New York to eastern Tennessee, as well as in the lower Mississippi River valley (figure 2.2). Spatial variation in archaeological evidence for warfare can be attributed to occupation density and information quality, as well as the prevalence of conflict. Although not all areas are equally well documented, there is enough information to think the overall picture is unlikely to be wide of the mark. That is, the patterning reflects reasonably well the distribution of people and the places where intergroup conflict frequently broke out. Of particular importance are the sparsely settled midcontinent (hence few sites showing signs of warfare) and a paucity of palisades and casualties in heavily occupied parts of the Deep South and Atlantic Seaboard. The density of pockets of population in the crescent of conflict-prone societies meant that these people were unable to move as far from their enemies as their contemporaries in the thinly occupied midcontinent. Archaeological evidence is consistent with the few written accounts dating to this period, notably from the mid-sixteenth-century de Soto expedition, which encountered large numbers of determined warriors in some parts of the Southeast, including the lower Mississippi River valley, where many settlements feature defensive works (Clayton et al. 1993).

The big question is what set forces in motion that led to chiefdom collapse and depopulation across much of the midcontinent. The principal candidate is climatic deterioration following the Medieval Warm Period when Mississippian societies expanded northward as far as Wisconsin. It tipped the balance for societies perched precariously on a knife-edge between success and failure by raising the specter of famine

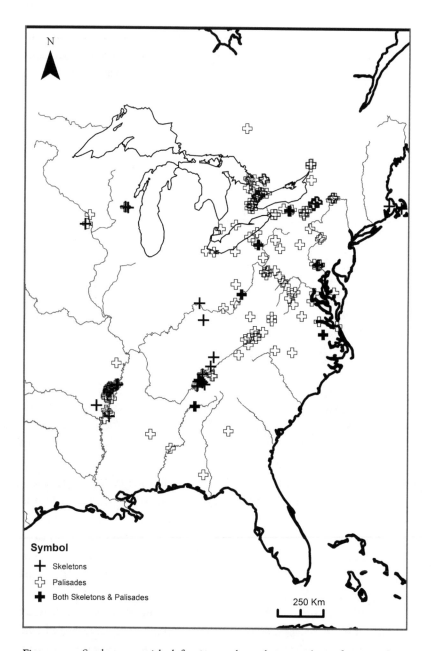

N

Symbol

+ Skeletons

⊹ Palisades

✚ Both Skeletons & Palisades

250 Km

**Figure 2.2.** Settlements with defensive works and sites with warfare casualties (*N*=178) dating to the sixteenth century are unevenly distributed across eastern North America. The midcontinent is bordered on the east and south by many sites with those two markers of conflict. (Map by George Chaplin.)

while eroding the legitimacy of chiefs and souring relations among increasingly desperate groups. Uncertainty stemming from unpredictable crop or wild-food yields presumably aggravated tensions that existed in the midcontinent since the late first millennium AD (Emerson 2007; Milner 1999, 2007). By circa 1300, if not earlier, the depredations of enemies, who perhaps also felt the pinch of hard times, presumably added to the difficulties of acquiring enough to eat. That could have happened when the frequency or length of foraging expeditions were curtailed, crops and stored foods were destroyed, or settlement decisions emphasized safety at the expense of easy access to resources. Taken together, climatic change and intergroup antagonisms increased the risk of severe shortages occurring in back-to-back years, a challenging situation for anyone relying on subsistence systems with modest surplus, storage, and transportation capacities. While the initial push can probably be attributed to climatic change, it is unlikely to have been the sole reason for the difficulties people experienced. Poor intergroup relations contributed to excessive conflict-related mortality, forced movement, and inefficiencies in subsistence practices. These tensions almost certainly had far-reaching and long-lasting effects as they rippled outward to involve groups elsewhere, aggravating any existing resource-related problems people might have experienced.

## Early Epidemics and the Midcontinent

Two aspects of the midcontinental occupation are of primary importance when envisioning what occurred in the sixteenth to early seventeenth centuries: the distance between population aggregates and the nature of interactions among them. The distribution of people is considered first because it is easier to measure than the frequency and nature of contacts along with the numbers of people who participated in them.

During the sixteenth century, the midcontinent was not as heavily occupied and pockets of population were more widely distributed than they were to the east and south (see figure 2.1; Milner et al. 2001; Milner and Chaplin 2010). A physical separation of groups would have impeded the wide dissemination of diseases transmitted through direct human contact, including measles and smallpox.[2] For these diseases to extend across much, or all, of the midcontinent, infected people would have had to travel between clusters of settlements, crossing tens, if not hundreds, of kilometers on foot or by canoe. Distance alone would have interfered with the spread of crowd diseases that are at the heart of the scenario that features frequent and widespread sixteenth-century epidemics.

It might be argued, although not convincingly, that contacts among scattered population aggregates were sufficient for diseases to pass unimpeded from one group to the next, regardless of the distance that separated them. Sixteenth-century midcontinental groups certainly communicated with one another. That is indicated by a thin veneer of nonlocal artifacts and raw materials in site assemblages overwhelmingly composed of locally derived items. Objects from distant places include disk pipes dating to the fifteenth through seventeenth centuries, many fashioned from Minnesota catlinite (Drooker 2004). The long-distance movement of items also included a few European-derived artifacts that reached the middle Ohio River valley by the late sixteenth century and Illinois by the early seventeenth century, if not several decades earlier (Brown and Sasso 2001; Drooker 1996, 1997; Drooker and Cowan 2001; Mazrim and Esarey 2007).

Despite the peaceful communication that took place, intergroup relations were often dominated by quite the opposite tendency: active avoidance of one other (Milner and Chaplin 2010). Widespread hostilities meant that contacts often were infrequent, fleeting, and violent. The disk pipes are instructive because at least some of them might have been used in ceremonies associated with settling differences and forging alliances among groups, much like the historic period Calumet ceremony (Drooker 2004). So while there is evidence for communication among widely separated groups, most face-to-face meetings presumably involved relatively few people who only occasionally met by chance or design during attacks or in various peaceful social interactions.

Eventually midcontinental groups suffered like everyone else. Major historic period losses attributable directly or indirectly to new diseases probably began in earnest during the seventeenth century. They are unlikely to have taken place before the early 1600s, when the first substantial disease-induced declines occurred among the Iroquois and Hurons in upstate New York and southern Ontario, respectively (Jones 2010; Snow 1995, 1996; Snow and Lanphear 1988; Snow and Starna 1989;

Trigger 1976; Warrick 2003, 2008). Yet even among closely allied Iroquoian groups, initial drops in population did not occur simultaneously, most likely because of the nature of contacts among them. There is some archaeological evidence for a reduction in population around that time in one part of the upper Mississippi River valley (Betts 2006). At the southern end of Lake Michigan, there was a strong Oneota presence into the early seventeenth century, and shortly thereafter these people were replaced by newcomers to the area (Brown 1990; Brown and Sasso 2001). Determining what can be attributed to disease as opposed to other societal disruptions—notably, famine and war—is a major challenge since they were not independent events, as shown by the seventeenth-century reduction of the Hurons (Trigger 1976; Warrick 2008). Whatever took place, major changes occurred before the late 1600s, when the French explorers Jacques Marquette and Louis Joliet, followed by others such as René-Robert Cavelier, Sieur de La Salle, encountered relatively few people in their travels through the midcontinent.

A dispersed settlement pattern and uneasy social relations provided a protection of sorts against epidemics, although marked population decline, once initiated, could have taken place rapidly. Dean Snow and Kim Lanphear (1988) have argued convincingly that a sustained European presence consisting of people of all ages, including children, supported by reasonably frequent transoceanic voyages was needed before repeated and widespread epidemics in the interior were likely to occur. Local outbreaks could be devastating, but they were often sharply circumscribed by the irregularity of contacts among neighboring but spatially and socially discrete groups. Yet occasionally outbreaks involved enough separate groups to increase the chance that pathogens might spread far beyond the initial point of introduction, perhaps through multiple routes, striking populations previously isolated by distance and infrequent intergroup contact.

While there was a distinct tendency for midcontinental population aggregates to be widely spaced, there were places where discrete clusters of settlements were situated close to one another (see figure 2.1). Spatial and social proximity is perhaps best illustrated by Fort Ancient groups in the middle Ohio River valley. The risk of an acute crowd disease being transmitted among closely allied groups would have been high once it made its way to one of the affiliated clusters of settlements. At

that point, a pathogen could have been carried by infected but still am-
bulatory people who fled the initial outbreak to seek refuge with close
kin elsewhere.

## Late Prehistoric Legacy

The distributions of sixteenth-century settled areas and conflict-prone
groups provide a context within which early contact period develop-
ments noted in historical documents can be interpreted (see figures 2.1
and 2.2). Several places known for warlike societies, including the lower
Mississippi River valley during the mid-1500s and southern Ontario
and western New York a century later, were not only heavily populated
by the standards of the time but also had long histories of intergroup
conflict quite separate from European influences of any kind. It is not
surprising that antagonisms would last for generations, as small-scale
societies generally find it difficult to escape cycles of violence fueled by
revenge killings.

The midcontinent's turbulent history extended well into the postcontact period. To the extent that Kentucky's "dark and bloody ground"
captures a sense of the dangers people faced, it does not need to be
explained as an isolated or necessarily historic period phenomenon. Instead, what demands attention are the processes of cultural and population change that by the end of prehistory resulted in a largely abandoned
but still bitterly contested land, and how this situation evolved following the arrival of Old World peoples and everything else that followed
in train. Centuries of hostilities, for example, ultimately proved to be an
impediment for those who attempted to forge durable coalitions among
disparate groups to resist the Euro-American onslaught, including Te-
cumseh's failure to do so.

The wide spacing of midcontinental groups and troubled relations
among them were not sufficient to keep these people safe from epidemics forever. After all, they still maintained some contact with one another, as seen most clearly by their possession of nonlocal items. Newly
introduced diseases, when they arrived, accentuated the decline that
was already several centuries in the making. That helped establish conditions necessary for a partial population replacement in the Midwest,
at least by the mid-seventeenth century.

By the mid-1600s, and throughout the subsequent century, large and small groups were moving into and through the Midwest, especially the western Great Lakes area (Bauxar 1978; Brown and Sasso 2001; Mazrim and Esarey 2007; Stone and Chaput 1978; Tanner 1987). Presumably this process started well before such movements were recorded by Europeans. In northern Illinois, for example, replacement is indicated by the sudden appearance of a distinctive pottery style associated with groups that eventually would give the state its name (Brown 1990; Brown and Sasso 2001). A mostly empty land—it was sparsely occupied for centuries and probably emptied still further when epidemics fingered their way into the interior—would have been inviting to those displaced from traditional homelands by incursions of other Native peoples and Euro-Americans.

Historic period groups in general had to replenish their numbers to survive, with the Iroquois and Creeks being highly successful in doing so (Fenton 1998; Knight 1994; Muller 1993; Snow 1994, 1995, 1996, 2001). There was no shortage of remnant groups that urgently sought to join whatever still-powerful society would take them in, including former enemies. The need to maintain a sufficiently large number of people extended down to individual communities, as there is no obvious decline in southeastern settlement sizes from the sixteenth through nineteenth centuries, despite a much-reduced population overall (Muller 1997b). Incorporating people of diverse origins to form viable groups was not a new practice, because several centuries earlier depleted communities such as Norris Farms apparently did the same.

## Pandemics Versus Localized Outbreaks

Thus, when we return to the two scenarios for the early spread of acute crowd diseases, the archaeological evidence for the first century or so following the European landfall in North America decidedly favors one over the other. In fact, it is hard to imagine how the position vociferously championed by Dobyns (1983, 1993)—multiple devastating epidemics spread repeatedly across vast areas, up to the entire continent—could be supported given current archaeological knowledge. That is because the person-to-person spread of the great killers smallpox and measles would have been greatly facilitated if eastern North America had been heavily populated and the members of culturally and spatially distinct groups had maintained frequent contact with one another. Neither is indicated by the evidence at hand.

Archaeological work instead points toward spatially and temporally variable population loss and societal change. To the extent that early postcontact depopulation was attributable to epidemics, it is because high-mortality diseases (notably, smallpox and measles) spread irregularly, fingering their way into the interior through a series of chance occurrences.

Nevertheless, by the late seventeenth century when French explorers first entered the lower Mississippi River valley, this fertile land was only sparsely occupied, despite having been, relatively speaking, rather crowded several centuries earlier. This near abandonment is all the more remarkable because in the mid-sixteenth century these societies were powerful enough to threaten de Soto's men, and the area had a long record of settlement extending deep into prehistory (Brain 1988; Clayton et al. 1993; Morse and Morse 1983; Phillips et al. 1951). The Coosa chiefdom in the southern Appalachians, which was composed of several spatially discrete but politically affiliated pockets of population, likewise figured prominently in de Soto's journey (Clayton et al. 1993; Hudson et al. 1985; Smith 1987, 2000, 2001, 2002). There is evidence to suggest that only several decades later the chiefdom had suffered reverses, including population decline, and its people had begun to move elsewhere (Smith 2000, 2001, 2002), although not all agree with that assessment, citing conflicting Spanish accounts (Kelton 2007).

While the precise timing of the demise of formerly strong southeastern chiefdoms and accompanying depopulation remains to be determined, their experience appears to have been different from that of tribal-scale groups elsewhere. Marked population reductions occurred among the Iroquois and Hurons in the Northeast during the early seventeenth century, and they took place in piedmont North Carolina only later in that century (Jones 2010; Snow 1995, 1996; Snow and Lanphear 1988; Snow and Starna 1989; Ward and Davis 1991, 1993, 2001; Warrick 2003, 2008). So it appears that organizationally complex societies suffered as early as, and quite possibly before, relatively acephalous societies in places that lacked regular contact with Europeans. Tending to hit chiefdoms somewhat earlier is consistent with what is expected of diseases with short incubation and symptomatic states that are transmitted directly from one host to another. There was simply a greater chance that pathogen transmission was interrupted in areas where atomized tribes were common as opposed to those dominated by chiefdoms, especially where the latter were large, tightly knit, and closely allied with their neighbors.

Greater temporal precision, preferably down to the decade level, is required for multiple places to fully understand the pattern of population reduction in the Eastern Woodlands. Available information, however, raises the possibility that sociopolitical organization, and all it might imply, had an influence on which interior groups were most at risk for early disease-induced declines in population.

Rapid, massive, and demoralizing losses of life from various diseases were only the start of the problems people faced when the entire fabric of society was ripped apart (Milner et al. 2001; Thornton 1997). Many simultaneous deaths exposed military vulnerabilities and disrupted essential household and community functions. What followed in the wake of an outbreak could have been as devastating to local groups as the original losses of life. Warfare, in all of its forms, is highlighted here for the simple reason that conflict can be measured with available archaeological data.

Intergroup conflict likely contributed to a more rapid population decline and greater cultural disruption than would have been the case with disease-induced mortality alone. Communities depleted by illness would have been tempting targets to enemies who had scores to settle. They were thereby pushed to extinction as independent entities when obliged to join others to survive.

To avoid attack, people might have abandoned villages, fields, and stored food, adding hunger to their list of ills. People weakened by famine from war-related interruptions in their food supply would have been more susceptible to both long-established diseases and Old World introductions. The Hurons who fled their homes in the mid-seventeenth century were reduced to "dying skeletons eking out a miserable life" (Thwaites 1899:89). These people "totally without means to guard against the famine were attacked by a contagious malady, which carried off a great number of them, especially of the children" (Thwaites 1899:91). Immunologically compromised through malnutrition, their

resistance was lowered to all manner of infectious diseases, with predictably dreadful results. More than 150 years later and far to the west, the
Lewis and Clark expedition encountered Shoshones who avoided their
enemies by retreating to a remote area where they "suffered . . . great
heardships [sic] for the want of food" (Moulton 1988:91). Malnutrition,
no matter how it came about, certainly worsened the outlook by affecting the sufferer's susceptibility and response to infection, with mortality
rates increasing accordingly.

The long-term impact of high-mortality diseases must have differed
from one place to another, depending on the number of deaths and the
timing of the outbreak. Some seasons, such as when people are engaged
in planting and harvesting, require far more intensive labor than others.
Anything that interfered with the acquisition of food and its preparation for long-term storage, particularly during critical seasons, would
have had a lingering effect on already depleted groups that later lacked
what they needed during lean times of the year.

## Disease and Depopulation in Context

In the midcontinent, migration, conflict, and widespread depopulation were deeply rooted in prehistory. There is no doubt that the Euro-
American presence in North America posed significant challenges to
long-established ways of life and in due course profoundly altered Native societies. The processes that ultimately led to population and cultural collapse, however, cannot be neatly separated into what took place
before Europeans arrived as opposed to what happened afterward. The
spread of new diseases and the economic and political agendas of European nations must be viewed in the context of highly dynamic sociopolitical and demographic landscapes that had long and complex histories
extending back many centuries.

By late prehistoric times, much of the midcontinent was sparsely
settled, surviving groups had spaced themselves as far apart as possible,
and organizationally complex chiefdoms had vanished. When new diseases were introduced, isolation by distance likely impeded the spread of
pathogens transmitted through direct person-to-person contact. Looking at eastern North America as a whole, we might reasonably suppose

that newly introduced diseases such as smallpox and measles fanned out across the land in a markedly uneven manner, striking some groups but not others in each outbreak. That is much different than the scenario in which epidemics are said to have been both frequent and far-reaching, affecting virtually everyone from the sixteenth century onward. The use of large depopulation figures, such as by Dobyns (1966, 1983), that are universally applied to all peoples occupying enormous areas ranging up to the entire continent in order to estimate the precontact population size is based, explicitly or not, on the latter, and likely erroneous, assumption.

We are still far from a complete picture of what happened in eastern North America, when those changes occurred, and why they did so. The historical record tells us that depopulation and cultural change during the seventeenth century and beyond were complex processes that are not reducible to a single cause, no matter how much disease resulted in excess mortality. There is no reason to suspect that the preceding sixteenth century, poorly documented in written records, was any different in that regard. High-mortality epidemics must be put in an appropriate cultural context, one that features a discontinuous population distribution and long-standing cooperative and antagonistic relations among socially and physically separate groups.

## Acknowledgments

George Chaplin produced figures 2.1 and 2.2 based on our work together, partly through grant-supported research (NSF BCS-1049464). Emily Zavodny helped collect information on sites with palisades and victims of violence.

## Notes

1. In that regard they are different from diseases such as malaria, also from the Old World, which was restricted to areas where it could be transmitted by mosquitos.

2. The smallpox virus can remain viable for some time outside the human host, which is why people can become ill when handling contaminated items such as blankets. Nevertheless, a means of transmitting these objects between groups would still be required.

# References

Alchon, Suzanne A. 2003. A Pest in the Land: New World Epidemics in a Global Perspective. Albuquerque: University of New Mexico Press.

Bauxar, J. Joseph. 1978. History of the Illinois area. *In* Handbook of North American Indians, vol. 15: Northeast, edited by Bruce G. Trigger, 594–601. Washington, DC: Smithsonian Institution.

Betts, Colin M. 2006. Pots and pox: The identification of protohistoric epidemics in the upper Mississippi valley. American Antiquity 71:233–59.

Brain, Jeffrey P. 1988. Tunica Archaeology. Papers of the Peabody Museum 78. Cambridge, MA: Harvard University Press / Peabody Museum Press.

Brown, James A. 1990. Ethnohistoric connections. *In* At the Edge of Prehistory: Huber Phase Archaeology in the Chicago Area, edited by James A. Brown and Patricia J. O'Brien, 155–60. Kampsville, IL: Center for American Archeology.

Brown, James A., and Robert F. Sasso. 2001. Prelude to history on the eastern prairies. *In* Societies in Eclipse: Archaeology of the Eastern Woodlands Indians, A.D. 1400–1700, edited by David Brose, C. Wesley Cowan, and Robert C. Mainfort, 205–28. Washington, DC: Smithsonian Institution Press.

Butler, Brian M. 1991. Kincaid revisited: The Mississippian sequence in the lower Ohio valley. *In* Cahokia and the Hinterlands, edited by Thomas E. Emerson and R. Barry Lewis, 264–73. Urbana: University of Illinois Press.

Centerwall, Willard R. 1968. A recent experience with measles in a "virgin-soil" population. *In* Biomedical Challenges Presented by the American Indian, 77–80. Scientific Publication 165. Washington, DC: Pan American Health Organization.

Clayton, Lawrence A., Vernon J. Knight Jr., and Edward C. Moore, eds. 1993. The de Soto Chronicles. 2 vols. Tuscaloosa: University of Alabama Press.

Cobb, Charles R., and Brian M. Butler. 2002. The Vacant Quarter revisited: Late Mississippian abandonment of the lower Ohio valley. American Antiquity 67:625–41.

Conrad, Lawrence A. 1991. The Middle Mississippian cultures of the central Illinois valley. *In* Cahokia and the Hinterlands, edited by Thomas E. Emerson and R. Barry Lewis, 119–56. Urbana: University of Illinois Press.

Cook, Robert A. 2008. Sunwatch: Fort Ancient Development in the Mississippian World. Tuscaloosa: University of Alabama Press.

Crosby, Alfred W., Jr. 1976. Virgin soil epidemics as a factor in the aboriginal depopulation in America. William and Mary Quarterly 33:289–99.

———. 1986. Ecological Imperialism. Cambridge: Cambridge University Press.

Dobyns, Henry F. 1966. Estimating aboriginal American population, 1: An appraisal of techniques, with a new hemispheric estimate. Current Anthropology 7:395–449.

————. 1983. Their Number Become Thinned: Native American Population Dynamics in Eastern North America. Knoxville: University of Tennessee Press.

————. 1993. Disease transfer at contact. Annual Review of Anthropology 22:273–391.

Drooker, Penelope B. 1996. Madisonville metal and glass artifacts: Implications for western Fort Ancient chronology and interaction networks. Midcontinental Journal of Archaeology 21:145–190.

————. 1997. The View from Madisonville. Museum of Anthropology Memoirs 31. Ann Arbor: University of Michigan, Ann Arbor.

————. 2004. Pipes, leadership, and interregional interaction in protohistoric midwestern and northeastern North America. In Smoking and Culture, edited by Sean Rafferty and Rob Mann, 73–123. Knoxville: University of Tennessee Press.

Drooker, Penelope B., and C. Wesley Cowan. 2001. Transformation of the Fort Ancient cultures of the central Ohio valley. In Societies in Eclipse: Archaeology of the Eastern Woodlands Indians, A.D. 1400–1700, edited by David Brose, C. Wesley Cowan, and Robert C. Mainfort, 83–106. Washington, DC: Smithsonian Institution Press.

Emerson, Thomas E. 1991. The Apple River Mississippian culture of northwestern Illinois. In Cahokia and the Hinterlands, edited by Thomas E. Emerson and R. Barry Lewis, 164–82. Urbana: University of Illinois Press.

————. 2007. Cahokia and the evidence for late pre-Columbian war in the North American midcontinent. In North American Indigenous Warfare and Ritual Violence, edited by Richard J. Chacon and Rubén G. Mendoza, 129–48. Tucson: University of Arizona Press.

Esarey, Duane, and Lawrence A. Conrad. 1998. The Bold Counselor phase of the central Illinois River valley: Oneota's Middle Mississippian margin. Wisconsin Archeologist 79:38–61.

Esarey, Duane, and Sharron K. Santure. 1990. The Morton Site Oneota component and the Bold Counselor phase. In Archaeological Investigations at the Morton Village and Norris Farms 36 Cemetery, edited by Sharron K. Santure, Alan D. Harn, and Duane Esarey, 162–66. Reports of Investigations 45. Springfield: Illinois State Museum.

Fenton, William N. 1998. The Great Law and the Longhouse. Norman: University of Oklahoma Press.

Fowler, Melvin L. 1989. The Cahokia Atlas: A Historical Atlas of Cahokia Archaeology. Studies in Illinois Archaeology 6. Springfield: Illinois Historic Preservation Agency.

Goldstein, Lynne G., and Joan Freeman. 1997. Aztalan—A Middle Mississippian village. Wisconsin Archeologist 78:223–48.

Goldstein, Lynne G., and John D. Richards. 1991. Ancient Aztalan: The cultural and ecological context of a late prehistoric site in the Midwest. In Cahokia and the Hinterlands, edited by Thomas E. Emerson and R. Barry Lewis, 193–206. Urbana: University of Illinois Press.

Griffin, James B. 1967. Eastern North American archaeology: A summary. Science 156:175–91.

Harn, Alan D. 1994. The Larson Settlement System in the Central Illinois River Valley. Reports of Investigations 50. Springfield: Illinois State Museum.

Hollinger, R. Eric. 2005. Conflict and Culture Change in the Late Prehistoric and Early Historic American Midcontinent. PhD diss., Department of Anthropology, University of Illinois, Urbana.

Hudson, Charles M., Jr., Marvin T. Smith, David J. Hally, Richard Polhemus, and Chester B. DePratter. 1985. Coosa: A chiefdom in the sixteenth-century southeastern United States. American Antiquity 50:723–37.

Jackson, Douglas. 1992. Interpretation. *In* The Sponemann Site, vol. 2: The Mississippian and Oneota Occupations, edited by Douglas K. Jackson, Andrew C. Fortier, and Joyce A. Williams, 511–16. FAI-270 Site Reports 24. Urbana: University of Illinois Press.

———. 1998. Settlement on the southern frontier: Oneota occupations in the American Bottom. Wisconsin Archeologist 79:93–116.

Jones, Eric E. 2010. Population history of the Onondaga and Oneida Iroquois, A.D. 1500–1700. American Antiquity 75:387–407.

Kelly, John E. 2009. Contemplating Cahokia's collapse. *In* Global Perspectives on the Collapse of Complex Systems, edited by Jim A. Railey and Richard M. Reycraft, 147–68. Anthropological Papers 8. Albuquerque: University of New Mexico.

Kelton, Paul. 2007. Epidemics and Enslavement. Lincoln: University of Nebraska Press.

Knight, Vernon J., Jr. 1994. The formation of the Creeks. *In* The Forgotten Centuries: Indians and Europeans in the American South, 1521–1704, edited by Charles Hudson and Carmen C. Tesser, 373–92. Athens: University of Georgia Press.

Mazrim, Robert, and Duane Esarey. 2007. Rethinking the dawn of history: The schedule, signature, and agency of European goods in protohistoric Illinois. Midcontinental Journal of Archaeology 32:145–200.

McNeill, William H. 1976. Plagues and Peoples. Garden City, NY: Anchor Books.

Meeks, Scott C., and David G. Anderson. 2013. Drought, subsistence stress, and population dynamics: Assessing Mississippian abandonment of the Vacant Quarter. *In* Soils, Climate, and Society, edited by John D. Wingard and Sue E. Hayes, 61–83. Boulder: University Press of Colorado.

Milner, George R. 1980. Epidemic disease in the postcontact Southeast: A reappraisal. Midcontinental Journal of Archaeology 5:39–56.

———. 1998. The Cahokia Chiefdom: The Archaeology of a Mississippian Society. Washington, DC: Smithsonian Institution Press.

———. 1999. Warfare in prehistoric and early historic eastern North America. Journal of Archaeological Research 7:105–51.

———. 2004. The Moundbuilders. Thames and Hudson, London.

———. 2007. Warfare, population, and food production in prehistoric eastern North America. *In* North American Indigenous Warfare and Ritual Violence, edited by Richard J. Chacon and Rubén G. Mendoza, 182–201. Tucson: University of Arizona Press.

Milner, George R., David G. Anderson, and Marvin T. Smith. 2001. The distribution of Eastern Woodlands peoples at the prehistoric and historic interface. *In* Societies in Eclipse: Archaeology of the Eastern Woodlands Indians, A.D. 1400–1700, edited by David Brose, C. Wesley Cowan, and Robert C. Mainfort, 9–18. Washington, DC: Smithsonian Institution Press.

Milner, George R., Eve Anderson, and Virginia G. Smith. 1991. Warfare in late prehistoric west-central Illinois. American Antiquity 56:581–603.

Milner, George R., and George Chaplin. 2010. Eastern North American population at A.D. 1500. American Antiquity 75:707–26.

Milner, George R., and Rebecca J. Ferrell. 2011. Conflict and death in a late prehistoric community in the American Midwest. Anthropologischer Anzeiger 68:415–36.

Morse, Dan A., and Phyllis A. Morse. 1983. Archaeology of the Central Mississippi Valley. New York: Academic Press.

Moulton, Gary E., ed. 1988. The Definitive Journals of Lewis and Clark. Vol. 5. Lincoln: University of Nebraska Press.

Muller, Jon. 1986. Archaeology of the Lower Ohio River Valley. Orlando, FL: Academic Press.

———. 1993. Eastern North American population dynamics. Illinois Archaeology 5:84–99.

———. 1997a. Mississippian Political Economy. New York: Plenum Press.

———. 1997b. Native eastern American population continuity and stability. *In* Integrating Archaeological Demography: Multidisciplinary Approaches to Prehistoric Population, edited by Richard R. Paine, 343–64. Center for Archaeological Investigations, Occasional Paper 24. Carbondale: Southern Illinois University.

Neel, James V., Willard R. Centerwall, Napoleon A. Chagnon, and Helen L. Casey. 1970. Notes on the effect of measles and measles vaccine in a virgin-soil population of South American Indians. American Journal of Epidemiology 91:418–29.

Phillips, Philip, James A. Ford, and James B. Griffin. 1951. Archaeological Survey in the Lower Mississippi Alluvial Valley, 1940–1947. Peabody Museum Papers 25. Cambridge, MA: Harvard University.

Ramenofsky, Ann F. 1987. Vectors of Death. Albuquerque: University of New Mexico Press.

Ritterbush, Lauren W., and Brad Logan. 2000. Late prehistoric Oneota population movement into the central plains. Plains Anthropologist 45:257–72.

Schroeder, Sissel. 2004. Current research on late precontact societies of the mid-continental United States. Journal of Archaeological Research 12:311–72.

Smith, Marvin T. 1987. Archaeology of Aboriginal Culture Change in the Interior Southeast: Depopulation During the Early Historic Period. Gainesville: University of Florida Press.

———. 2000. Coosa: The Rise and Fall of a Southeastern Mississippian Chiefdom. Gainesville: University Press of Florida.

———. 2001. The rise and fall of Coosa, A.D. 1350–1700. *In* Societies in Eclipse: Archaeology of the Eastern Woodlands Indians, A.D. 1400–1700, edited by David Brose, C. Wesley Cowan, and Robert C. Mainfort, 143–55. Washington, DC: Smithsonian Institution Press.

———. 2002. Aboriginal population movements in the postcontact Southeast. *In* The Transformation of the Southeastern Indians, 1540–1760, edited by Robbie Ethridge and Charles Hudson, 3–20. Jackson: University Press of Mississippi.

Snow, Dean R. 1994. The Iroquois. Oxford, UK: Blackwell.

———. 1995. Microchronology and demographic evidence relating to the size of pre-Columbian North American Indian populations. Science 268:1601–4.

———. 1996. Mohawk demography and the effects of exogenous epidemics on American Indian populations. Journal of Anthropological Archaeology 15:160–82.

———. 2001. Evolution of the Mohawk Iroquois. *In* Societies in Eclipse: Archaeology of the Eastern Woodlands Indians, A.D. 1400–1700, edited by David Brose, C. Wesley Cowan, and Robert C. Mainfort, 19–25. Washington, DC: Smithsonian Institution Press.

Snow, Dean R., and Kim M. Lanphear. 1988. European contact and Indian depopulation in the Northeast: The timing of the first epidemics. Ethnohistory 35:15–33.

Snow, Dean R., and William A. Starna. 1989. Sixteenth-century depopulation: A view from the Mohawk valley. American Anthropologist 91:142–49.

Steadman, Dawnie W. 1998. The population shuffle in the central Illinois valley: A diachronic model of Mississippian biocultural interactions. World Archaeology 30:306–26.

———. 2008. Warfare related trauma at Orendorf, a Middle Mississippian site in west-central Illinois. American Journal of Physical Anthropology 136:51–64.

Stone, Anne C., and Mark Stoneking. 1998. MtDNA analysis of a prehistoric Oneota population: Implications for the peopling of the New World. American Journal of Human Genetics 62:1153–70.

———. 1999. Analysis of ancient DNA from a prehistoric Amerindian cemetery. Philosophical Transactions of the Royal Society of London B 354:153–59.

Stone, Lyle M., and Donald Chaput. 1978. History of the upper Great Lakes area. *In* Handbook of North American Indians, vol. 15: Northeast, edited by Bruce G. Trigger, 602–9. Washington, DC: Smithsonian Institution.

Tanner, Helen H. 1987. Atlas of Great Lakes Indian History. Norman: University of Oklahoma Press.

Thornton, Russell. 1997. Aboriginal North American population and rates of decline, ca. A.D. 1500–1900. Current Anthropology 38:310–15.

Thwaites, Reuben G. 1899. The Jesuit Relations and Allied Documents. Vol. 35. Cleveland, OH: Burrows Brothers.

Trigger, Bruce G. 1976. The Children of Aataentsic. Kingston, ON: McGill-Queen's University Press.

Ubelaker, Douglas H. 1992. Patterns of demographic change in the Americas. Human Biology 64:361–79.

Ward, H. Trawick, and R. P. Stephen Davis Jr. 1991. The impact of Old World diseases on the Native inhabitants of the North Carolina piedmont. Archaeology of Eastern North America 19:171–81.

———. 1993. Indian Communities on the North Carolina Piedmont, A.D. 1000 to 1700. Research Laboratories of Anthropology, Monograph 2. Chapel Hill: University of North Carolina.

———. 2001. Tribes and traders on the North Carolina piedmont, A.D. 1000–1710. In Societies in Eclipse: Archaeology of the Eastern Woodlands Indians, A.D. 1400–1700, edited by David Brose, C. Wesley Cowan, and Robert C. Mainfort, 125–41. Washington, DC: Smithsonian Institution Press.

Warrick, Gary. 2003. European infectious disease and depopulation of the Wendat-Tiononate (Huron-Petun). World Archaeology 35:258–75.

———. 2008. A Population History of the Huron-Petun, A.D. 500–1550. Cambridge: Cambridge University Press.

Williams, Stephen. 1980. Armorel: A very late phase in the lower Mississippi valley. Southeastern Archaeological Conference Bulletin 22:105–10.

———. 1990. The Vacant Quarter and other late events in the lower valley. In Temples and Towns Along the Mississippi River, edited by David H. Dye and Cheryl A. Cox, 170–80. Tuscaloosa: University of Alabama Press.

# Colonialism and Decline in the American Southeast

## The Remarkable Record of La Florida

*Clark Spencer Larsen*

A fundamental influence on shaping culture and biology in the modern world was the expansion of the European sphere to regions of the globe well beyond continental Europe. This expansion of European peoples, foods, diseases, and social values set into motion irreversible and dramatic changes in health, foodways, living circumstances, and lifestyle for all Native populations. Following his five-year voyage around the world, a young Charles Darwin (1839:321–22) famously noted, "Wherever the European has trod, death seems to pursue the aboriginal." This and other nineteenth-century scholarship would inspire the direction of future study of the impacts of Western colonization, especially creating a focus on Native population size reduction. Book titles in the 1980s and 1990s on the history of population in Native New World settings tell the story: *Their Number Become Thinned* (Dobyns 1983), *American Indian Holocaust and Survival* (Thornton 1987), and *Born to Die* (Cook 1998). This modern body of work addresses the question, Why was there such a remarkable reduction in Native population size across the Western Hemisphere, beginning with early European exploration?

In regard to the dominant body of scholarship, the answer to this question is best summarized by Alfred Crosby (1986:196) in his reference to the impact of Europeans' arrival in the Americas, namely that "[i]t was their germs, not these imperialists themselves, for all their brutality and callousness, that were chiefly responsible for sweeping aside the indigenes and opening the Neo-Europes to demographic takeover." In this vein, Noble David Cook (1998:9) argued that "we need to identify the sicknesses, date their first and subsequent appearances, and ascertain the rates of morbidity and mortality." Numerous historians (and anthropologists) spent the better part of the past several decades doing just that—searching high and low through archives and libraries to identify population numbers, deaths, descriptions of diseases, and catastrophic health outcomes.

In retrospect, though, what did we gain from this singular focus on European-introduced disease and population decimation? It is abundantly clear that in most settings, their number *did* become "thinned." But is that all there is to understanding this dynamic period of human history and the people involved? In a word, no. From my vantage point as a biological anthropologist, there is much more to be gained by developing an understanding of the profound and varied changes in health and population dynamics in the colonial era and the economic, social, and behavioral circumstances leading to these changes. Moreover, decline and collapse at various times in the evolution of humans can rarely be attributed to just one factor, including disease.

This chapter focuses on the human experience viewed from the record of bioarchaeology, the study of human remains from archaeological context. It shows how colonialism's impact on Native health is far more than germs.

Here, I discuss one of the most comprehensively studied colonial-era regions in the Western Hemisphere, La Florida, named by Ponce de León in 1513. It was in that year that he and his crew set foot on North American soil north of Mexico, the first of the major European powers. This remote frontier was one of Spain's first footholds during the early years of exploration, providing the stage for Native exploitation and decline and setting into motion a series of expeditions and later settlements across the southern part of the continent from Florida to California (Thomas 2012; Weber 1992).

Numerous and diverse tribes were encountered by Ponce de León and later explorers in the region of the modern states of Florida and Georgia, but colonization efforts would eventually focus on several key tribal groups: Guales on the Georgia coast and Timucuas and Apalachees in northern Florida (Bushnell 1994; Hann 1988, 1996; Jones 1978; McEwan 1993; Thomas 1987; Worth 1995, 2001) (figure 3.1). Our knowledge of the Native people and the records of bioarchaeology, ethnohistory, and archaeology in this region are among the most comprehensive for any colonial setting, making possible a well-informed perspective on

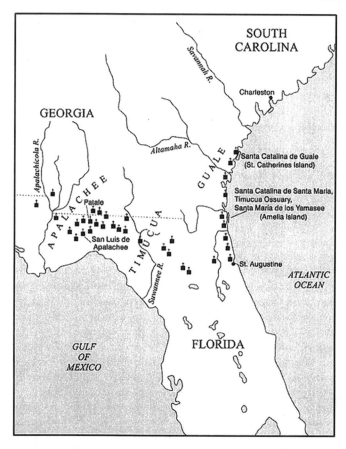

**Figure 3.1.** Map of La Florida showing mission locations and major tribes. Note the presence of two Santa Catalina de Guale missions on the Atlantic coast. Santa Catalina de Guale on St. Catherines Island (ca. 1607–1680) is the original founding mission, and Santa Catalina de Maria (ca. 1680–1702) on Amelia Island is the descendant mission representing the Native population that left St. Catherines Island. (Used with permission, Princeton University Press.)

the impacts and consequences of European colonization, beyond the simple framework of disease and disappearance.

The goals of this chapter are threefold: first, to discuss the region of La Florida, viewing the impacts, changes, and adaptations from the perspective of human biology; second, to place these changes in the regional context of extraction of resources from the tribes exploited by Spain; and third, to examine the social context of health and inequality, revealing a record of structural violence at both a regional and a local level. This chapter focuses primarily on what we have learned from the bioarchaeological record for the region of La Florida, encompassing the period from 1565, the year of the founding of the capital and administrative center at St. Augustine and early attempts at missionization, to 1706, when the last of the mission centers was abandoned. It makes the case that domination and exploitation of a subordinate Native society by an intrusive dominant society had profound, and largely negative, implications for the viability and survival of indigenous populations.

## The Case of La Florida: More Than Disease, Death, and Decline

Spain took a serious interest in La Florida, especially after setting eyes on the landscape and the people occupying it and realizing the economic potential in agricultural production, especially via exploitation through various means, including a mixed strategy of proselytization and resettlement of Native people. Here and throughout the New World, missionaries were at the forefront of establishing relationships with Native groups and founding strategic outposts, an important step in establishing Spain's dominance across a highly varied and complex social, cultural, and economic landscape. At the time of initial contact, indigenous communities coming under the control of Spain pursued various modes of food production reflecting their habitats and cultural histories. Some were hunter-gatherer-fishers exclusively, such as in the Florida peninsula, whereas others were at least in part dependent on farming, especially maize, such as along the Georgia coast and in the Florida panhandle.

From the start, the process of missionization entailed a goal of regional homogenization of Native lifestyles and foodways, emphasizing agricultural production for supplying food to Natives, to Europeans, and in some instances, for export. This homogenization process was also extended to transforming the Native belief systems to Christianity. The material successes of this transformation are illustrated by the presence of religious structures (such as churches) and the near-universal

mode of European-style burial interment, placing the deceased (with
bodies supine and extended, arms flexed on the chest) in shallow pits,
which were located in the church floor or sometimes in the region immediately outside the church in consecrated ground (Larsen 1990, 1993;
Stojanowski 2013).

Most of the settings coming under the auspices of the Spanish
colonial system were agricultural and had a chiefdom form of social
organization, built around maize production (Worth 2001). These "agricultural chiefdoms" and their social hierarchies were instrumental in
facilitating the assimilation of Native societies into the La Florida colonial system. Most of the chiefdoms became subordinate elements of
a Spanish colonial hierarchy centered on labor tribute and the food
produced by this labor. This system of labor tribute had been in place
long before Ponce de León set foot in Florida (Jones 1978; Worth 2001,
2002). The Spanish successfully tapped into the Native social structure
whereby chiefs, who were on top of the Native hierarchy, served as the
direct subordinates to and interfaced with the Spanish colonial authority centered at St. Augustine (Worth 2002). With this system serving as
the conduit to labor tribute, labor exploitation, and food production
via chiefly authorities, the missions provided a combination of spiritual center, labor source, and breadbasket (Bushnell 1994; Jones 1978;
Thomas 1990, 2008, 2012; Worth 1995, 1998, 2001). Importantly, the
chiefdoms retained some autonomy from the Spanish newcomers, especially pertaining to the preservation of a social hierarchy of elites and
subordinates (Thomas 2012).

Although the system described here worked well in various places
and at various times, in the end, it did not survive. The accumulated
pressures of piracy, slave raiding, and encroachment by British interests to the north in the later seventeenth century and conflicts between
chiefdoms led to the abandonment of the region by the much-reduced
population from the Georgia coast and Florida panhandle. Many refugee groups retreated to St. Augustine, whereas others fled westward to
Alabama, and some became assimilated into the Seminoles, a new tribal
identity in peninsular Florida. In this respect, there were profound implications for the viability of these groups here and elsewhere in the
Southeast, including increased mortality rates, declining ability to reproduce, and the inability to recover from colonial traumas, such as

from introduced disease and enslavement (see also Kelton 2007; Worth 1995, 2007).

Complementing the extraordinary ethnohistoric record is an equally extraordinary archaeological record of La Florida. In no other region in the Americas is the archaeology of the contact between Spaniards and the Natives they encountered so well documented. Archaeological excavations at numerous missions and other historic-era localities have produced a remarkably complete picture of what life was like during the late sixteenth, all of the seventeenth, and the early eighteenth centuries, including settlement and habitations, architecture, material culture, and inferences drawn about Native societies (Blair et al. 2009; McEwan 1993; Thomas 2012).

## A Regional Bioarchaeology of La Florida

There are areas of the Americas where there exists a large and comprehensive record of ethnohistory, archaeology, and bioarchaeology dating to the colonial period (e.g., Klaus 2012; and see below). However, for various reasons, often the study of the biological component of the record is either nonexistent or superficial. Owing to the collaborations between bioarchaeologists, ethnohistorians, and archaeologists in the context of organized research programs throughout Spanish Florida over the past four decades, there is a comprehensive understanding of key biological changes reflecting the colonial strategies of Spain in regard to foodways, food production, and labor, as well as a picture of changing social relations.

Viewed broadly under the arena of ethnogenesis, or the development of new ethnic and cultural identities and social relationships, the hegemonic Spanish system involving the domination by a colonial authority over Native societies resulted in profound changes in Native peoples socially, culturally, and biologically. Moreover, the *reducción* system involved the concentration or reduction of once relatively dispersed populations clustered in small villages into larger, more densely crowded mission centers and their associated villages. This planned redistribution of population served to manage Native populations more effectively, as well as to increase the efficiency of agricultural production and labor in general.

## Foodways and Nutritional Transitions

The success of the Spanish colonial system was dependent on a significant increase in maize production, in considerable excess of what was
being produced at the time of first European contact (Worth 2001).
Presumably, an increase in maize production would also translate into
greater relative consumption of maize by Native populations. Therefore,
it is critical to understand whether this major economic shift brought
about by increased maize production did in fact lead to substantial
changes in Native diets. While the study of preserved plant and animal
remains from archaeological contexts is informative regarding various
aspects of precontact and colonial-era food consumption in this region
(e.g., Reitz et al. 2010; Ruhl 1990; Scarry and Reitz 1990; Thompson
and Turck 2010; Thompson and Worth 2011), far more informative is
the documentation and interpretation of carbon and nitrogen stable
isotope ratios by the Native consumers. Analysis of a large record of isotope variation from human remains from La Florida reveals a significant
change in diet reflecting a concomitant reduction in the use of animal
sources of protein, including seafood for coastal populations (that is, a
decrease in stable isotope ratios of nitrogen, or $\delta^{15}N$ values), and an increase in the use of domesticated plants, especially maize (that is, an increase in stable isotope ratios of carbon, or $\delta^{13}C$ values) (Hutchinson et
al. 1998; Larsen et al. 1992, 2007; Larsen, Hutchinson, et al. 2001). The
isotopic record shows that the adoption of and increased dependence
on maize began several centuries prior to the arrival of Europeans, circa
AD 1000–1200 on the Georgia coast and Florida panhandle and following European contact in peninsular Florida. In general, and predictably,
the diet became more homogeneous across Spanish Florida, replacing
what had once been a highly localized and diverse dietary landscape
(Hutchinson et al. 1998; Larsen, Hutchinson, et al. 2001).

Other evidence, based on microscopically visible damage on occlusal
surfaces of teeth (microwear), reveals trends that show the shift from
consumption of relatively hard-textured, abrasive foods (such as meat)
to relatively soft-textured, less-abrasive foods (such as maize-based por-
ridge) (figure 3.2). In some settings, such as among the Guales and
Timucuas, there is a trend toward a reduced number of microwear features (for example, large pits and large scratches), indicating decreased

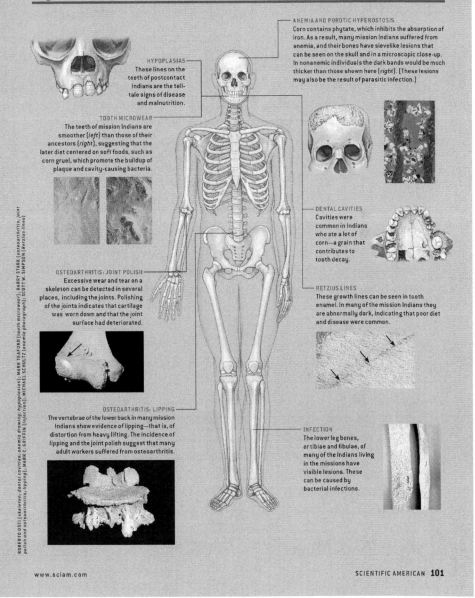

# Signs of Stress in a Skeleton

**ANEMIA AND POROTIC HYPEROSTOSIS**
Corn contains phytate, which inhibits the absorption of iron. As a result, many mission Indians suffered from anemia, and their bones have sievelike lesions that can be seen on the skull and in a microscopic close-up. In nonanemic individuals the dark bands would be much thicker than those shown here (*right*). (These lesions may also be the result of parasitic infection.)

**HYPOPLASIAS**
These lines on the teeth of postcontact Indians are the tell-tale signs of disease and malnutrition.

**TOOTH MICROWEAR**
The teeth of mission Indians are smoother (*left*) than those of their ancestors (*right*), suggesting that the later diet centered on soft foods, such as corn gruel, which promote the buildup of plaque and cavity-causing bacteria.

**DENTAL CAVITIES**
Cavities were common in Indians who ate a lot of corn—a grain that contributes to tooth decay.

**OSTEOARTHRITIS: JOINT POLISH**
Excessive wear and tear on a skeleton can be detected in several places, including the joints. Polishing of the joints indicates that cartilage was worn down and that the joint surface had deteriorated.

**RETZIUS LINES**
These growth lines can be seen in tooth enamel. In many of the mission Indians they are abnormally dark, indicating that poor diet and disease were common.

**OSTEOARTHRITIS: LIPPING**
The vertebrae of the lower back in many mission Indians show evidence of lipping—that is, of distortion from heavy lifting. The incidence of lipping and the joint polish suggest that many adult workers suffered from osteoarthritis.

**INFECTION**
The lower leg bones, or tibiae and fibulae, of many of the Indians living in the missions have visible lesions. These can be caused by bacterial infections.

**Figure 3.2.** Human skeleton rendered with key areas of pathology discussed in text. (Used with permission of Roberto Osti.)

consumption of abrasive foods (e.g., Teaford 1991; Teaford et al. 2001; and see Stojanowski 2013). In addition, there is evidence for regional variation in microwear, including an increased abrasiveness of diet in some settings, such as at San Luis de Apalachee at the far western end of the mission system in the Florida panhandle. We have interpreted the San Luis microwear record as showing relatively low levels of maize consumption and greater access to livestock in this setting than elsewhere in Spanish Florida (Organ et al. 2005), which is consistent with ethnohistoric (Hann 1988), ethnobotanical (Ruhl 1990), zooarchaeological (Reitz 1993), and isotopic (Larsen, Hutchinson, et al. 2001) evidence.

It is clear, then, that the dietary changes occurring across most settings were driven by the aforementioned economic interest in and exploitative strategies put into place by the Spanish colonial authorities. That is, diet changed simultaneously with the introduction of the food tribute system described above. Our analysis reveals that this dietary shift had important implications for the oral and general health of Native populations. In regard to oral health, maize is a carbohydrate (starch), which is a central dietary factor in promoting dental caries. Dental caries is a disease process resulting from the by-products of the bacterial fermentation process taking place in the mouth as bacteria metabolize the carbohydrate-rich diets. These by-products—especially lactic acid—dissolve the tooth enamel, creating the cavities so prevalent in populations that are heavily dependent on carbohydrates. Predictably, the elevated consumption of maize by mission Indians resulted in an increase in dental caries, especially in the later Guale descendant group on Amelia Island (Santa Catalina de Santa Maria) following the abandonment of St. Catherines Island (Santa Catalina de Guale) (Larsen et al. 1991, 2007). While certainly not life threatening, dental caries promotes gingivitis and periodontal disease, which in turn contributes to poor general health, especially in later adulthood.

## Health and Well-Being in a Dynamic Landscape

In addition to its cariogenic properties, maize is deficient in several amino acids (such as lysine and isoleucine), rendering it an incomplete protein. These nutritional deficits can result in the disruption of the cells that are responsible for enamel development, resulting in growth arrest markers called hypoplasias. In the mission settings of northern Florida, the great majority of individuals display these defects. Moreover, there is a tendency for the defects to be wider in the mission settings, suggesting a longer duration of stress (Hutchinson and Larsen 1988; Larsen, Griffin, et al. 2001; Simpson 2001). In addition, our analysis of microscopic growth-related defects in tooth enamel called Wilson bands shows that these defects, like enamel hypoplasias, are much more prevalent in the mission Indians than in their prehistoric ancestors (Simpson 2001).

Several other indicators of health status are consistent with a profile of increased stress and declining health, especially in the contact era. In this regard, comparison of precontact and mission-era communities reveals an increase in cribra orbitalia and porotic hyperostosis, cranial pathological conditions that have been related to chronic iron deficiency anemia. As a result, the body attempts to compensate for iron deficiency by increasing red blood cell production, a process taking place in bone marrow regions of the skeleton (such as the cranium). In particular, marrow expansion in these instances is a response to deficiencies in red blood cells and/or hemoglobin (Moseley 1974; Ortner 2003; Schultz 2001). Both the severity and the prevalence of cribra orbitalia/porotic hyperostosis increase dramatically in the colonial era and reflect a major nutritional decline relating to iron metabolism (Larsen, Griffin, et al. 2001; Larsen et al. 2007).

The practice of relocation of Native groups to mission centers also had the predictable health outcomes involving a record of increasing infectious disease. Comparisons of pathology representing specific diseases are now well documented in the region in the late prehistoric and contact era, especially lesions consistent with a diagnosis of tuberculosis and treponematosis (endemic nonvenereal syphilis) (Hutchinson et al. 2005; Powell 1990). The overall deteriorating circumstances of missionization for Native peoples, especially population aggregation and poor living conditions, suggest that the cause in this setting is largely infection and the associated inflammatory response.

## Lifestyle Changes and Behavioral Adaptations

In addition to fundamental changes in foodways and nutritional outcomes, the most profound change to occur in the lives of Native peoples in the postcontact era was the labor demand placed on them in this highly exploitive system. The labor pool needed to support Spain's imposed economic model was already in place at the time of initial contact by Europeans—that is, the men, women, and children living in the communities that later came to be associated with the mission centers. Bioarchaeology provides an important avenue for reconstructing and interpreting physical activity, workload, and lifestyle. The human skeleton presents a record of lifestyle and activity by reflecting the accumulated bony responses to lifestyle and workload, especially in two key ways. First, bone as a living tissue responds to activity in highly predictable ways, reflecting levels of mechanical demand associated with habitual activity, such as long-distance travel in some settings. Second, heavy mechanical demand on the joints of the skeleton, if sufficiently prolonged and severe, will result in articular damage and other pathological alterations collectively called osteoarthritis. Osteoarthritis, a disorder caused largely by wear and tear on joints of the skeleton, provides a record of the degree to which the Spanish labor system impacted its Native participants.

For this setting, application of biomechanical engineering principles to bone size and shape has provided an avenue for reconstructing behavior and lifestyle. In particular, this approach is based on the phenomenon that the bone tissue in a living person alters itself in response to activity-related demands. Simply, greater demand or stress on bone, such as use of the arms in lifting or the legs in walking and running, will result in increased bone development over the course of a person's years of growth and development and adulthood. For example, a person who is engaged in heavy physical labor throughout his or her lifetime will have larger bones when viewed in cross section than someone who leads a relatively sedentary lifestyle. In fact, comparison of human populations around the world and in specific regions shows predictable variation reflecting the level and type of mechanical loading (Larsen 1997; Ruff 2008).

In such biomechanical analyses, anthropologists apply principles used by civil and mechanical engineers when designing materials for the construction of various kinds of structures, such as buildings and bridges. In particular, these materials are designed so that they are best suited to hold up under very heavy weights. For example, the iconic I beams universally used in the infrastructure of buildings and bridges are used based on one key theory discovered by engineers many years ago. That is, the farther the material is distributed from a central longitudinal axis, the better it is able to resist deforming or breaking (Larsen 1997; Ruff 2008). Specifically, engineers and anthropologists use cross-sectional geometric properties called second moments of area to analyze the "rigidity" or ability of bones (for example, the humerus and femur) to resist bending and torsion (twisting) during activities, such as walking and running or lifting and carrying. Our findings show that compared to the late prehistoric Native populations, the second moments of area are considerably greater in cross sections of arm and leg bones among the mission Indians (Ruff and Larsen 2001). These findings can be interpreted in only one way, namely, that the mission Indians had a lifestyle involving very heavy physical labor, especially in the late mission populations in Guale.

Importantly, the record of biomechanical adaptation shows some interesting differences in comparison of adult males versus females. Comparisons of archaeological populations from a range of prehistoric and historic settings in North America show a decline in differences between men and women over time. That is, sexual dimorphism declines among agriculturalists compared to hunter-gatherers, with very few exceptions (Ruff and Larsen 2001): males and females become increasingly similar in the structural properties of their limb bones. Interestingly, the two mission settings from Guale—first Santa Catalina on St. Catherines Island and later on Amelia Island—show marked differences in the ratio of $I_x/I_y$ in the femur midshaft in comparing males and females. This ratio reflects front-to-back bending of the femur relative to side-to-side bending, providing an indication of degree of mobility. In both missions, numerous males have considerably higher $I_x/I_y$ ratios, indicating much greater levels of mobility than their female counterparts. Almost certainly, and at least for some communities, these differences indicate the use of male draft laborers who traveled long distances for various labor projects (Ruff and Larsen 2001).

The temporal trends in osteoarthritis prevalence for the Guale series are consistent with the observation of increased biomechanical loading and increased work demand in the mission period (Larsen 1994). That is, there are dramatic increases in osteoarthritis, especially in the vertebrae. In addition, five of the fifty-six individuals studied from Santa Catalina de Guale on Amelia Island display spondylolysis, a fatigue fracture involving the lower back caused by heavy mechanical loading.

It is not possible to tell exactly which specific activities were involved in explaining the changes in workload and lifestyle that have been documented in parts of La Florida. However, the ethnohistoric record and especially written accounts about life in colonial communities make clear that Indians were subjected to very heavy labor relating to the economic structure of the Spanish colonial system, namely, focused on the production and distribution of crops, especially maize (Worth 2001). In addition, this repartimiento draft labor system involved the use of hundreds of Indian laborers who traveled by foot for the distribution of food across La Florida, as well as draft labor at St. Augustine to produce the necessary food for the city. By some estimates, 1 million pounds of maize was produced each year in the mid-seventeenth century, much of it in the Guale and Apalachee provinces (Worth 1998). In a nutshell, Native labor was the driving force behind this extractive system put in place by Spanish authorities. In a very real sense, the biological changes documented in the remains of colonial-era Native populations show that these groups underwent excessive labor demand, almost certainly caused by a dominant authority exploiting a subordinate group. Moreover, in addition to the circumstances leading to poorer health owing to nutritional decline, exposure to infectious disease, and the impact of newly introduced pathogens, the Native population declined at a time when the Spanish authorities were most in need of them as a labor source. In fact, outside of St. Augustine, the authorities were entirely dependent on the Native labor pool for maintenance of this extractive repartimiento system.

The labor system could possibly have sustained itself well beyond the seventeenth century. However, the influence of external forces would ultimately exceed any balance provided by a Native population struggling to adapt. In 1659, Native groups from north of La Florida moved into the region armed with English-supplied firearms, affecting this and other areas of the Southeast (Worth 2001). For the province of Guale, this action forced the abandonment of all mainland mission Indians to the coast. In addition, the Yamasees, another tribal group relocated to the coastal region during the later colonial period, were incorporated into the sphere of Spanish authority. It has long been assumed that a mission cemetery and church located near the Santa Catalina de Guale cemetery on Amelia Island, Florida, was the mission Santa María de los Yamasee, representing a later mission-era population (Larsen 1993:328–30). I speculated, however, that the cemetery was likely earlier than the Santa Catalina cemetery and may, therefore, be from the original pre-Guale, Timucua population. Analysis of the $I_x/I_y$ ratio in the femur midshaft shows a level of sexual dimorphism very much like prehistoric agriculturalists (Ruff and Larsen 2001), and the series displays relatively low levels of nonspecific infections, just 6 percent of individuals (five of eighty-three with at least one long bone) (Larsen, unpublished data). Moreover, the stable carbon and nitrogen isotope values are also more like those of prehistoric agriculturalists less focused on maize than the Guale mission populations on St. Catherines Island or the later population on Amelia Island, further supporting the notion that the so-called Santa María de los Yamasee mission and cemetery were associated with the Timucuas and not the Yamasees. Indeed, new biodistance and mortuary analyses of the Santa María cemetery remains from Amelia Island are more consistent with Timucua and not Yamasee people (Stojanowski 2013). Therefore, the pattern described here shows that the workload and behavioral adaptation of the Native people in the early mission period were similar to those of their prehistoric ancestors and preceded the influences of labor tribute developed to its fullest in the late mission period (Larsen et al. 2007; Ruff and Larsen 2001).

## Structural Violence: More Than Just Broken Bones

The historical and archaeological records suggest that for many of the tribes of La Florida, elites exacted labor and other tribute from nonelites. By linking into this system, the Spanish authorities recognized an opportunity to establish an economic foothold and sustainable production. As described in this chapter, there is a comprehensive record of health outcomes and behavioral adaptations demonstrating the profound alterations in quality of life for the Native communities across La Florida. Haagen Klaus (2012) has made the compelling case that health outcomes derived from bioarchaeological contexts provide an important record of violence, not in the form of fractures, decapitations, and dislocations but, rather, in forms that are "more harmful, widespread, and enduring than those that produce broken bones and weapons injuries" (Klaus 2012: 31). Violence viewed from this perspective is but one element of a continuum of social behaviors, interpersonal and inter-group, described by Johan Galtung (1969) as "structural violence." That is, the behaviors are "structural" because they are defined within the context of existing political, economic, and social structures, and they are a record of "violence" because the outcomes cause death and debili-tation (Farmer et al. 2006). In other words, we are seeing a collective of social structures, institutions, and policies that suppress the ability of members of Native societies to reach their full potential. I believe that the record of structural violence revealed by the comparisons of health and behavioral outcomes in contact-era skeletons from La Florida un-derscores this important point and is certainly revealed in this setting via bioarchaeological study.

La Florida is an exemplar of structural violence, as Native popu-lations in this setting were dominated and exploited by a European power, so much so that the entire social fabric of these societies was altered in profound ways and with social and biological consequences. The most obvious cultural consequence was the replacement of tradi-tional religious institutions with European Christianity. This is obvi-ous in the sense that Native mortuary ritual changed from traditional mound burial to placement in European-style cemeteries, often within the church. This replacement of traditional social and cultural behaviors was accompanied by a dramatic shift in expectations involving labor tribute and the movement of entire communities to settings that were more readily exploited by church and civil authorities. The study of health outcomes in this region reveals a subtle, sometimes invisible re-cord of violence, not in the form of trauma and obvious injury but in the form of illness, morbidity, and increased physical activity and work-load owing to labor exploitation. Most importantly, structural violence is tied to population outcomes: namely, the reduction in health and well-being led to an inability to reproduce and recover from the colonial traumas of disease, poor diet, and labor demands.

The record of structural violence described here is not to say that overt violence was not present in this setting. Indeed, historical re-cords on the early years of exploration talk about conquest and the violence that Spaniards directed toward Native people (Hutchinson 1996, 2006). Moreover, there is a bioarchaeological record of violent injury resulting from malicious intent, but it is rare. At the Tatham

Mound in west-central Florida, dating well prior to the mission era, circa AD 1525–50, Hutchinson (1996, 2006) has documented the only record of violence involving the use of metal-edged weapons. In this setting, some eighteen skeletal elements—mostly limb bones—display damage caused by metal-bladed instruments. The site is likely one of many villages visited by Hernando de Soto's exploration through the region in 1539. At San Luis de Apalachee, an adult male from an elite grave interred near the altar likely died from a gunshot wound (Larsen et al. 1996).

Far more profound than these few instances of interpersonal violence, however, is the record of structural violence in La Florida, and it is striking in its similarity to other settings of the Americas colonized by Spain. Like La Florida, in the Lambayeque River valley of north coastal Peru, the Spanish authorities recognized the economic potential of the region, including especially the exploitation of local Native populations for labor (Klaus 2012). Unlike La Florida, where labor was exploited for primarily agricultural production, the Muchik people of Peru were viewed as an important labor source in mining operations, especially the mining of gypsum. Within a half century of initial contact, the conquest of the region resulted in fundamental changes in the political and economic landscapes, accompanied by forced resettlement, a labor tax, and the general deconstruction of traditional Native social structures.

Analysis of a large series of late precontact skeletons and postcontact remains from San Pedro de Morropé revealed a pattern of change in morbidity remarkably similar to that of La Florida. In a comparison of the pre- and postcontact Lambayeque Valley Muchiks, an extraordinarily high increase in the prevalence of dental caries, porotic hyperostosis, and osteoperiostitis has been documented (Klaus 2012). Like the record of structural violence in La Florida, labor exploitation by the dominant Spanish authority in Peru is well displayed in an elevated prevalence of degenerative joint disease (Klaus 2012; Klaus et al. 2009). However, reflecting the different kind of labor in comparison with La Florida, the prevalence of degenerative joint disease among the Muchiks is most pronounced in the shoulder, elbow, wrist, hand, and knee joints. While these specific differences between La Florida and the Lambayeque Valley reflect differences in labor, the overall record of elements of structural violence is similar: the manipulation of Native labor toward privileging the economic gains of the superordinate Spanish society at the expense of the subordinate Native society.

## Equal Before God? Santa Catalina de Guale and Health Outcomes

Different health outcomes in comparison of social classes within chiefdoms like those associated with La Florida do not appear to represent structural violence. Structural violence is a concept applied to settings involving the planned application by a major dominant authority exerting social, political, and economic control over a subjugated nondominant society, such as in the case of the many settings of colonization across the globe by major European powers, including, as in this setting, Spain (see Klaus 2012, for discussion and application to bioarchaeology). This is not to say that chiefdoms and their unequal components do not produce different health outcomes. Indeed, there are numerous instances in prehistoric North America where elites and nonelites display different outcomes in health (Larsen 1997).

Social hierarchy and variability in access to resources may have been in place in the region prior to the arrival of Spaniards. The Spanish recognized the different classes in the chiefdoms they encountered and tapped into the established social hierarchy for extracting labor tribute. On the Georgia coast, in particular, the Guales had social ranking, with a smaller elite class likely controlling food and other resources. Analysis of the distribution of types and quantities of burial-related material culture provides one important avenue for estimating the general degree of social differentiation within this society. Contrary to the expectation of church doctrine (wherein, in Christian belief, everyone is equal before God), interments in some Native cemeteries during the mission era have been found in association with material culture, some including elaborate grave goods. The most spectacular in this regard is the church cemetery at Santa Catalina de Guale on St. Catherines Island. This cemetery contained an extraordinary record of material culture, including some 70,000 glass beads, largely from rosaries, ceramic plates and other vessels, crucifixes, religious medallions, and a mirror (Blair et al. 2009). In addition, at the altar end of the church (the nave), the remains of one individual were found in association with a coffin. The distribution of this material culture was not random: the more elaborate grave

inclusions and greater density of these inclusions tended to be associated with the altar end of the church. These grave inclusions were likely
the personal possessions of the deceased or those of close relatives. This
assumed pattern of ownership suggests that individuals interred closest
to the altar were of higher ranks than individuals interred farthest from
the altar (Larsen 1990; Winkler et al. 2012).

To document a potential relationship between health and rank, we
analyzed indicators of physiological stress (hypoplasia) and diet (dental
caries) with reference to the association with three distinctive clusters of
burials, namely, the front, middle, and back thirds of the church, here
called the altar, midnave, and back nave. Comparison of individuals
from the three clusters revealed a near statistically significant (ANOVA;
$p < .06$) association between location and hypoplasia: higher-ranked
individuals (closer to the front) tended to have no hypoplasias, whereas
lower-ranked individuals (farther from the altar) tended to have hypoplasias. We interpret this record to suggest that the higher-ranked elites
had lower levels of physiological stress than the lower-ranked subelites
in Guale society.

Analysis of the distribution of dental caries provides an even more
compelling case for the relationship between health and status. In this
regard, the lowest frequency of individuals having dental caries was in
the altar area (24.8 percent of 113 individuals) versus the midnave (37.8
percent of 82 individuals) or the back nave (39.2 percent of 97 individuals). The difference between altar and other areas is statistically significant (chi square; $p < .05$). The differences between the midnave and
back nave are not statistically significant (chi square; $p > .05$).

This record suggests that elite individuals had a different experience
in diet and oral health than nonelite individuals. That is, higher-status
individuals consumed a lower amount of cariogenic foods (especially
maize) than did lower-status individuals. Overall, then, diets of nonelites were more dominated by protein-poor maize than were those
of elites. These findings suggest that (1) social inequality is expressed
in health and access to resources; (2) individuals nearest the altar had
greater access to meat and resources to mitigate stress during growth
and development and adulthood; (3) Guale social positions (such as
high-status chiefs and other elites) were not preserved in name only,
for their positions represented tangible differences in stress and access
to quality dietary resources; (4) stress and diet among the Guales were

factors of socially constructed statuses, as well as later ways in which individuals mediated the colonial landscape through individual action; and (5) the Guale setting at Santa Catalina was likely part of the larger fabric of structural violence representing a record of social inequality. We do not know whether colonialism created or exacerbated inequality and health disparities in La Florida, where the brunt of structural violence was greater for the lesser elites than the higher elites. What the record does show is social differentiation in health in the contact era and that elite individuals were more buffered from structural violence than were nonelite individuals.

Other intracommunity comparisons of morbidity reveal similarities and differences across La Florida. For example, at San Pedro y San Pablo de Patale in Apalachee province, like Santa Catalina de Guale in Guale province, there was a higher prevalence of hypoplasia in the altar end of the church (Stojanowski 2013). Similarly, the diachronic comparison of earlier and later series at San Martín revealed an increase in dental caries, a pattern also shown in ancestral-descendant comparisons in Guale. In contrast, in Patale and San Martín cemeteries in Timucua province there is a random distribution of dental caries, suggesting little or no variation in diet by social class (Stojanowski 2013).

For all bioarchaeological research in mission cemeteries, the focus of study has been on each skeletal assemblage as representing a single temporal unit. Future research will explore the possibility that health variation may be at least in part temporal. Perhaps, then, earlier deaths at Santa Catalina de Guale were interred closer to the altar than later deaths. If that is the case, then caries variation may simply reflect an increasing emphasis on carbohydrates (maize) over the eighty or so years of the history of the church and cemetery. However, at this point of study, the health record described in this chapter is far more consistent with expectation for a socially stratified society, whereby there are clear differences in access to quality nutrition in subordinates versus elites.

## The Cumulative Process of Structural Violence

An important theme for colonial-era La Florida is the presence of structural violence, subjugation, and exploitation of subordinate Native societies by a dominant Spanish authority. Viewed from this perspective,

Native groups were weakened by a host of factors affecting health and well-being, including labor exploitation, an increasing reliance on poor-quality protein, and the impact of European-introduced diseases. The key lesson to be learned is that the singular focus on germs is only a part of the complex story of why these and other societies in the Americas saw decline and disappearance. These declines did not happen in weeks or months. Rather, it was the cumulative insult of increasingly poor circumstances that promoted population loss, perhaps the most important of which was structural violence and its contribution to the inability to rebound in the face of declining living conditions.

## Acknowledgments

The research presented in this chapter represents conclusions drawn from the La Florida Bioarchaeology Project, directed by me since 1982. The research was possible only through my collaborations with several mission-era archaeology research programs directed by David Hurst Thomas on St. Catherines Island, Georgia; Jerald T. Milanich and Rebecca Saunders on Amelia Island, Florida; and Bonnie G. McEwan at Mission San Luis in Tallahassee, Florida. The bioarchaeology program was funded by the National Science Foundation, St. Catherines Island Foundation, and the National Endowment for the Humanities. I am indebted to the many collaborators, including especially Hong Huynh, Katherine Ford Russell, Leslie Sering, Elizabeth Miller, Christopher Schmidt, Dale Hutchinson, Christopher Stojanowski, Matthew Williamson, Mark Griffin, Scott Simpson, Christopher Ruff, Margaret Schoeninger, Lynette Norr, Mark Teaford, Jason Organ, Elizabeth Monahan Driscoll, Tiffiny Tung, Susan Simmons, Lauren Winkler, Nikolaas van der Merwe, Julia Lee-Thorp, Victor Thompson, and Paul Sciulli. I also acknowledge the research programs directed by Dale Hutchinson and Christopher Stojanowski in La Florida, as well as the tremendous value of my collaborations with them. I thank the Amerind Foundation Seminar organizers—Alan Swedlund, Catherine Cameron, and Paul Kelton—for inviting me to participate and for their guidance in the preparation of this contribution to the book. Haagen Klaus and Joshua Sadvari provided many helpful suggestions on an earlier draft.

# References

Blair, Elliot H., Lorann S. A. Pendleton, and Peter Francis Jr. 2009. The Beads of St. Catherines Island. Anthropological Papers 89. New York: American Museum of Natural History.

Bushnell, A. Turner. 1994. Situado and Sabana: Spain's Support System for the Presidio and Mission Provinces of Florida. Anthropological Papers 74. New York: American Museum of Natural History.

Cook, Noble David. 1998. Born to Die: Disease and New World Conquest, 1492–1650. Cambridge: Cambridge University Press.

Crosby, Alfred W. 1986. Ecological Imperialism: The Biological Expansion of Europe, 900–1900. Cambridge: Cambridge University Press.

Darwin, Charles R., ed. 1839. Mammalia. Part 2 of The Zoology of the Voyage of HMS *Beagle*. London: Smith Elder.

Dobyns, Henry F. 1983. Their Number Become Thinned: Native American Population Dynamics in Eastern North America. Knoxville: University of Tennessee Press.

Farmer, Paul E., Bruce Nizeye, Sara Stulac, and Salmaan Keshavjee. 2006. Structural violence and clinical medicine. PLoS Medicine 3:1686–1791.

Galtung, Johan. 1969. Violence, peace and peace research. Journal of Peace Research 6:167–91.

Hann, John H. 1988. Apalachee: The Land Between the Rivers. Gainesville: University Press of Florida.

———. 1996. A History of the Timucua Indians and Missions. Gainesville: University Press of Florida.

Hutchinson, Dale L. 1996. Brief encounters: Tatham Mound and the evidence for Spanish and Native American confrontation. International Journal of Osteoarchaeology 6:51–65.

———. 2006. Tatham Mound and the Bioarchaeology of European Contact: Disease and Depopulation in Central Gulf Coast Florida. Gainesville: University Press of Florida.

Hutchinson, Dale L., and Clark Spencer Larsen. 1988. Determination of stress episode duration from linear enamel hypoplasias: A case study from St. Catherines Island, Georgia. Human Biology 60:93–110.

Hutchinson, Dale L., Clark Spencer Larsen, Margaret J. Schoeninger, and Lynette Norr. 1998. Regional variation in the pattern of maize adoption and use in Florida and Georgia. American Antiquity 63:397–416.

Hutchinson, Dale L., Clark Spencer Larsen, Matthew A. Williamson, Virginia D. Green Clow, and Mary Lucas Powell. 2005. Temporal and spatial variation in the patterns of treponematosis in Georgia and Florida. *In* The Myth of Syphilis: The Natural History of Treponematosis in North America, edited by Mary Lucas Powell and Della Collins Cook, 92–116. Gainesville: University Press of Florida.

Jones, Grant D. 1978. The ethnohistory of the Guale coast through 1684. *In* The Anthropology of St. Catherines Island, vol. 1: Natural and Cultural History, edited by David Hurst Thomas, Grant D. Jones, Roger S. Durham, and Clark Spencer Larsen, 178–210. Anthropological Papers 55 (part 2). New York: American Museum of Natural History.

Kelton, Paul. 2007. Epidemics and Enslavement: Biological Catastrophe in the Native Southeast, 1492–1715. Lincoln: University of Nebraska Press.

Klaus, Haagen D. 2012. Bioarchaeology of structural violence: Theoretical model and case study. *In* Bioarchaeology of Violence: Small-Scale Conflict, Warfare, and Ritualized Violence in the Past, edited by Debra L. Martin, Ryan P. Harrod, and Ventura R. Pérez, 29–62. Gainesville: University Press of Florida.

Klaus, Haagen D., Clark Spencer Larsen, and Manuel E. Tam. 2009. Economic intensification and degenerative joint disease: Life and labor on the post-contact north coast of Peru. American Journal of Physical Anthropology 139:204–21.

Larsen, Clark Spencer. 1990. The Archaeology of Mission Santa Catalina de Guale. Vol. 2: Biocultural Interpretations of a Population in Transition. Anthropological Papers 68. New York: American Museum of Natural History.

———. 1993. On the frontier of contact: Mission bioarchaeology in La Florida. *In* The Spanish Missions of La Florida, edited by Bonnie G. McEwan, 322–56. Gainesville: University Press of Florida.

———. 1994. In the wake of Columbus: Native population biology in the post-contact Americas. Yearbook of Physical Anthropology 37:109–154.

———. 1997. Bioarchaeology: Interpreting Behavior from the Human Skeleton. Cambridge: Cambridge University Press.

———. 2001. Bioarchaeology of Spanish Florida. *In* Bioarchaeology of Spanish Florida: The Impact of Colonialism, edited by Clark Spencer Larsen, 22–51. Gainesville: University Press of Florida.

Larsen, Clark Spencer, Mark C. Griffin, Dale L. Hutchinson, Vivian E. Noble, Lynette Norr, Robert F. Pastor, Christopher B. Ruff, et al. 2001. Frontiers of contact: Bioarchaeology of Spanish Florida. Journal of World Prehistory 15:69–123.

Larsen, Clark Spencer, Dale L. Hutchinson, Margaret J. Schoeninger, and Lynette Norr. 2001. Food and stable isotopes in La Florida: Diet and nutrition before and after contact. *In* Bioarchaeology of Spanish Florida: The Impact of Colonialism, edited by Clark Spencer Larsen, 52–81. Gainesville: University Press of Florida.

Larsen, Clark Spencer, Dale L. Hutchinson, Christopher M. Stojanowski, Matthew A. Williamson, Mark C. Griffin, Scott W. Simpson, Christopher B. Ruff, et al. 2007. Health and lifestyle in Georgia and Florida: Agricultural origins and intensification in regional perspective. *In* Ancient Health: Skeletal Indicators of Agricultural and Economic Intensification, edited by

Mark Nathan Cohen and Gillian M. M. Crane-Kramer, 20–34. Gainesville: University Press of Florida.

Larsen, Clark Spencer, Hong P. Huynh, and Bonnie G. McEwan. 1996. Death by
gunshot: Biocultural implications of trauma at Mission San Luis. International Journal of Osteoarchaeology 6:42–50.

Larsen, Clark Spencer, Margaret J. Schoeninger, Nikolaas J. van der Merwe, Katherine M. Moore, and Julia A. Lee-Thorp. 1992. Carbon and nitrogen stable
isotopic signatures of human dietary change in the Georgia Bight. American Journal of Physical Anthropology 89:197–214.

Larsen, Clark Spencer, Rebecca Shavit, and Mark C. Griffin. 1991. Dental caries
evidence for dietary change: An archaeological context. In Advances in
Dental Anthropology, edited by Marc A. Kelley and Clark Spencer Larsen,
179–202. New York: Wiley-Liss.

McEwan, Bonnie G., ed. 1993. The Spanish Missions of La Florida. Gainesville:
University Press of Florida.

Moseley, J. E. 1974. Skeletal changes in the anemias. Seminars in Roentgenology
9:169–184.

Organ, Jason M., Mark F. Teaford, and Clark Spencer Larsen. 2005. Dietary inferences from dental occlusal microwear at Mission San Luis de Apalachee.
American Journal of Physical Anthropology 128:801–11.

Ortner, Donald J. 2003. Identification of Pathological Conditions in Human Skeletal Remains. 2nd ed. San Diego, CA: Academic Press.

Powell, Mary Lucas. 1990. On the eve of conquest: Life and death at Irene Mound,
Georgia. In The Archaeology of Mission Santa Catalina de Guale, vol. 2:
Biocultural Interpretations of a Population in Transition, edited by Clark
Spencer Larsen, 26–35. Anthropological Papers 68. New York: American
Museum of Natural History.

Reitz, Elizabeth J. 1993. Evidence for animal use at the missions of Spanish Florida.
In The Spanish Missions of La Florida, edited by Bonnie G. McEwan,
376–98. Gainesville: University Press of Florida.

Reitz, Elizabeth J., Barnet Pavao-Zuckerman, Daniel C. Weinand, and Gwyneth A.
Duncan. 2010. Mission and Pueblo of Santa Catalina de Guale, St. Catherines Island, Georgia: A Comparative Zooarchaeological Analysis. Anthropological Papers 91. New York: American Museum of Natural History.

Ruff, Christopher B. 2008. Biomechanical analyses of archaeological human skel-
etons. In Biological Anthropology of the Human Skeleton, edited by
M. Anne Katzenberg and Shelley R. Saunders, 183–206. 2nd ed. Hoboken,
NJ: Wiley-Liss.

Ruff, Christopher B., and Clark Spencer Larsen. 2001. Reconstructing behavior in
Spanish Florida: The biomechanical evidence. In Bioarchaeology of Spanish Florida: The Impact of Colonialism, edited by Clark Spencer Larsen,
113–45. Gainesville: University Press of Florida.

Ruhl, Donna L. 1990. Spanish mission paleoethnobotany and culture change: A survey of the archaeobotanical data and some speculations on aboriginal and Spanish agrarian interactions in La Florida. *In* Columbian Consequences, vol. 2: Archaeological and Historical Perspectives on the Spanish Borderlands East, edited by David Hurst Thomas, 555–80. Washington, DC: Smithsonian Institution Press.

Scarry, C. Margaret, and Elizabeth J. Reitz. 1990. Herbs, fish, scum, and vermin: Subsistence strategies in sixteenth-century Spanish Florida. *In* Columbian Consequences, vol. 2: Archaeological and Historical Perspectives on the Spanish Borderlands East, edited by David Hurst Thomas, 343–54. Washington, DC: Smithsonian Institution Press.

Schultz, Michael 2001. Paleohistology of bone: A new approach to the study of ancient diseases. Yearbook of Physical Anthropology 44:106–47.

Simpson, Scott W. 2001. Patterns of growth disruption in La Florida: Evidence from enamel microstructure. *In* Bioarchaeology of Spanish Florida: The Impact of Colonialism, edited by Clark Spencer Larsen, 146–80. Gainesville: University Press of Florida.

Stojanowski, Christopher M. 2013. Mission Cemeteries, Mission Peoples: Historical and Evolutionary Dimensions of Intracemetery Bioarchaeology in Spanish Florida. Gainesville: University Press of Florida.

Teaford, Mark F. 1991. Dental microwear: What can it tell us about diet and dental function? *In* Advances in Dental Anthropology, edited by Marc A. Kelley and Clark Spencer Larsen, 341–56. New York: Wiley-Liss.

Teaford, Mark F., Clark Spencer Larsen, Robert F. Pastor, and Vivian E. Noble. 2001. Pits and scratches: Microscopic evidence of tooth use and masticatory behavior in La Florida. *In* Bioarchaeology of Spanish Florida: The Impact of Colonialism, edited by Clark Spencer Larsen, 82–112. Gainesville: University Press of Florida.

Thomas, David Hurst. 1987. The Archaeology of Mission Santa Catalina de Guale. Vol. 1: Search and Discovery. Anthropological Papers 63 (part 2). New York: American Museum of Natural History.

———. 1990. The Spanish missions of La Florida: An overview. *In* Columbian Consequences, vol. 2: Archaeological and Historical Perspectives on the Spanish Borderlands East, edited by David Hurst Thomas, 357–97. Washington, DC: Smithsonian Institution Press.

———. 2008. Native American Landscapes of St. Catherines Island, Georgia. Vol. 1: The Theoretical Framework. Anthropological Papers 88. New York: American Museum of Natural History.

———. 2012. War and peace on the Franciscan frontier. *In* From La Florida to La California: Franciscan Evangelization in the Spanish Borderlands, edited by Timothy J. Johnson and Gert Melville, 105–30. Berkeley, CA: Academy of Franciscan History.

Thompson, Victor D., and John A. Turck. 2010. Island archaeology and Native American economies (2500 B.C. to A.D. 1700) of the Georgia coast, USA. Journal of Field Archaeology 35:283–97.

Thompson, Victor D., and John E. Worth. 2011. Dwellers by the sea: Native American coastal adaptations along the southern coasts of eastern North America. Journal of Anthropological Research 19:51–101.

Thornton, Russell. 1987. American Indian Holocaust and Survival: A Population History Since 1492. Norman: University of Oklahoma Press.

Walker, Phillip L., Rhonda R. Bathurst, Rebecca Richman, Thor Gjerdrum, and Valerie A. Andrushko. 2009. The causes of porotic hyperostosis and cribra orbitalia: A reappraisal of the iron-deficiency-anemia hypothesis. American Journal of Physical Anthropology 139:109–25.

Weber, David J. 1992. The Spanish Frontier in North America. New Haven, CT: Yale University Press.

Winkler, Lauren A., Clark Spencer Larsen, Victor D. Thompson, Paul W. Sciulli, and Dale L. Hutchinson. 2012. The social structuring of stress in contact-era Spanish Florida: A bioarchaeological case study from Santa Catalina de Guale, St. Catherines Island, Georgia. American Journal of Physical Anthropology Supplement 54:305.

Worth, John E. 1995. The Struggle for the Georgia Coast: An Eighteenth-Century Spanish Retrospective on Guale and Mocama. Anthropological Papers 75. New York: American Museum of Natural History.

———. 1998. The Timucuan Chiefdoms of Spanish Florida. Gainesville: University Press of Florida.

———. 2001. The ethnohistorical context of bioarchaeology in Spanish Florida. In Bioarchaeology of Spanish Florida: The Impact of Colonialism, edited by Clark Spencer Larsen, 1–21. Gainesville: University Press of Florida.

———. 2002. Spanish missions and the persistence of chiefly power. In The Transformation of Southeastern Indians, 1540–1760, edited by Robbie Ethridge and Charles Hudson, 39–64. Jackson: University Press of Mississippi.

———. 2007. The Struggle for the Georgia Coast. Tuscaloosa: University of Alabama Press.

# 4

# Beyond Epidemics

## A Bioarchaeological Perspective on Pueblo-Spanish Encounters in the American Southwest

*Debra L. Martin*

Tourists flock to the American Southwest in part because it is home to many groups of Native Americans whose tribal names (such as Hopi and Zuni) are familiar and iconic in the collective national imagination. The Southwest is one of a small number of places in the United States where Native groups were not completely decimated by the colonial encounter or relocated to reservations far from their homelands. The reservations that they live on today are the same spaces (although much smaller in size) that their ancestors lived for hundreds of years. Patricia Limerick (1987:25) argues that all of the American Southwest has essentially been "museumized," beginning in the early 1800s when tourists discovered that these ancient/modern pueblos could be visited. Tourists (historically and even today) hope to see ancient customs and traditions enacted for them in ways that let them imagine what life was like for Native people prior to contact. Simultaneously and at odds with this romanticized version of the past, the most popular narrative of colonial contact has been written about as "the history of interactions among disparate peoples . . . [that] shaped the modern world through conquest, epidemics and genocide" (Diamond 1997:16).

Part of the lure and charm of visiting these areas is the wonder that Native people still exist at all, given the popularized notions about the epidemics that occurred during the contact period. Tourists are at once lulled into imagining a disease-free and violence-free world prior to colonial contact and are then told to imagine an explosion of epidemics and violent encounters that led to a pacified and diminished people that can be seen today. Emphasizing epidemics (as addressed in the chapters by Swedlund, Kelton, and others in this volume) is as problematic as emphasizing the idealized disease-free paradise that indigenous people must have lived in prior to 1492. Bioarchaeological and other scientific data reveal that life on the ground as farmers in the desert Southwest was not a paradise. In the Southwest, life prior to contact was challenged by dietary and health issues compounded by sporadic small-scale warfare and interpersonal violence (Cordell and McBrinn 2012; Martin 1994, 1997). And at contact, epidemics were only one of many challenges faced by Native people (Stodder 1996, 2012; Stodder et al. 2002).

## Spanish Colonization Tactics and Pueblo Resistance

The indigenous Pueblo people of the Southwest have not become extinct, nor have they been assimilated into the dominant culture. An understanding of their long in situ histories, particularly with respect to health, presents a unique opportunity to understand biological stress and its interplay with environmental and cultural variables over long periods of time. Beginning with the Columbian quincentennial in 1992, there was an explosion of bioarchaeological studies, meaning studies focused on what the human skeletal remains revealed about age at death and pathology before, during, and after contact. These studies provided biological data that helped to make an assessment of the impact of colonial expansion on indigenous populations (see, for examples, Baker and Kealhofer 1996; Larsen 2001; Larsen and Milner 1994; Verano and Ubelaker 1992). Because of the focus on biological human remains, these studies provided important insights into what life was really like prior to and during the contact period. This was especially true when there were chronological series that spanned the precontact and contact periods.

Bioarchaeological studies provided important correctives to the narratives about life before, during, and after colonial expansion in that they helped establish baseline data regarding patterns of morbidity and mortality. This information is crucial because it permits an analysis of what transpired with contact within a much more dynamic, complex, and nuanced context. Both Clark Spencer Larsen and George Milner (chapters 3 and 2, respectively, in this volume) demonstrate with regional case studies that while epidemics were part of the story of what transpired at contact, epidemics by no means were the only important factor to consider.

Via a complex interrelated set of goals that included missionization, labor exploitation, and the necessity for females by the all-male armies, epidemics were not the only or primary source of sickness and death at contact (Voss 2008). Massacres and other fear-invoking and terrorist activities were palpable forces in the colonial experience for Native men, women, and children in highly variable ways in the Southwest. For the Pueblo Indians in the 1500s, historian Ramón Gutiérrez (1991) suggests for one group living at the pueblo of Acoma that the Spanish not only controlled all labor and hence political-economic aspects of power but also controlled sexual intercourse, marriage, and reproduction. Yet these narratives demonstrate agency and nuance as well. Gutiérrez theorizes that in Pueblo traditional (precontact) societies, females had power to control factors having to do with households and with their sexuality and reproductive capabilities.

Historian James Brooks (2002) adds many additional dimensions to understanding the motivations of the Spanish colonists in the Pueblo Southwest with his unpacking of the role of captivity and slavery within and between various indigenous groups as well as the imposition of particular kinds of marriage rules and the incorporation of captivity and slavery into new definitions of family. Catherine Cameron (chapter 7, this volume) provides examples of the complex ways that indigenous systems of captivity and slavery were exploited by various other groups. Marc Simmons (1979) documents the role of massacres and intimidation in the colonial process. In retaliation for Native resistance, the Spanish would often burn at the stake whole villages (Cajete 2010:24). Katherine Spielmann and colleagues (2009) have provided archaeological and bioarchaeological evidence supporting these claims using data collected from precontact and contact human remains and detailed excavation data on diet, subsistence strategies, and gendered labor patterns. What these kinds of studies reveal are Pueblo groups who increasingly were forced to hunt more, farm more intensively, and succumb to harsh assimilation tactics to meet the Spanish tribute levies that increasingly defined their lives.

Thus, focusing solely on the effects of germs and epidemics and not on the everyday practices and experiences of Native people misses the point about the ways that Pueblo people adapted to, resisted, were transformed by, and succumbed to colonial rule. This is an important part of the historical narrative that is not represented in popular writing. What historians, ethnographers, and archaeologists reveal in this volume is that while epidemics were important, there were many other factors that contributed to subordinating and remaking the indigenous presence into a controllable part of the political-economic Spanish superstructure.

## Applying the Concept of Creeping Genocide to the Southwest

In the Pueblo Southwest, it is clear that while indigenous people did suffer from sporadic and variable waves of epidemics that have been well documented (Reff 1991; Stodder and Martin 1992), small-scale warfare, burning at the stake, taking of lands, fragmentation of communities, extraction of labor and taxes, use of captives and slaves for labor, and extreme forms of missionization and assimilation are important forces to consider in the ultimate transformation, subordination, and depopulation of groups in the Southwest (Brown 2013; Wilcox 2009:75–94). This constant wearing down of Pueblo people resulted in one of the few successful rebellions by Native people against their colonizers, the Pueblo Revolt of 1680 (Liebmann and Preucel 2007; Spielmann et al. 2009).

It is a useful heuristic to frame these other factors as a form of genocide. However, *genocide* as a label is fraught with legal and modern definitions that may or may not capture the collective activities of the European colonists. For the colonial invaders and the ways that Native people experienced this invasion, Norbert Finzsch (2008:220) used the work of Mark Levene (1999), who coined the phrase *creeping genocide* to capture the complexities of colonization. This distinguishes genocide from the more straightforward colonial encounters that were accomplished through outright slaughter of all people encountered. In a survey of colonial encounters from historic to contemporary cases, Levene (1999:342) notes that "most genocides do not follow an absolute trajectory but are usually aborted at some point or, possibly, succeeded by a return to other carrot and stick strategies of forcible integration or exclusion, even in some instances, running parallel to, genocide itself." This is more in line with what has been documented for the Pueblo people. While sometimes whole villages (such as the Tiwa pueblo referred to as Tiguex) were massacred, the colonial violence visited upon the Pueblo people was more sporadic, with the intent to communicate fear and to force particular kinds of behaviors rather than to exterminate all of the Native inhabitants (Bellesiles 2004:163; Rabasa 1993:47).

In thinking, then, about the different events, practices, and activities related to colonization that constitute creeping genocide, we can see epidemics in the Pueblo Southwest as one part of an intertwined and systematic set of culturally and politically motivated practices that colonists implemented. Creeping genocide is a useful framework to use because it permits individual events to be seen within a much larger, enmeshed, and dynamic set of processes (Levene 1999:365). When massacres, enslavement, harsh taxation, and assimilation failed to work, stronger tactics were operationalized that led to things such as broken treaties, more massacres, separation of children from families, forced assimilation, and the creation of reservations as marginalized welfare states (Thornton 1987). Elinor Barrett (2004) suggests further the ways that the introduction of encomiendas (a legal system imposed on indigenous people to control them) also contributed to hardships and depopulation. The importance of identifying these collective tactics as creeping genocide is that it brings into sharper focus important analytical binaries such as resistance and compliance, adaptation and death, agency and pacifism, and identity and assimilation.

There are likely more factors at work than can ever be reconstructed historically or archaeologically for Native groups, but it is important to try to look for connections among different underlying political-economic processes. In this light, creeping genocide can be seen as a continuum of everyday practices. Captivity, enslavement, losing lands, forced missionization, forced detentions, forced exoduses, forcing religious conversion, expulsion, confinement, rape of women, and torture or public brutalization of resistors, warriors, and elders—all of these are part of the everyday experiences that deserve attention (Finzsch 2008). These processes accumulate so broadly and often invisibly that one literally has to excavate a wide variety of sources to unearth them. To pave over this complexity with a single narrative about the impact of epidemics is a flawed scientific approach to explaining the impact and legacy of colonial encounters in the Southwest.

Creeping genocide abounds in the world today, making the studies in the current volume all the more relevant. Levene (1999:339) argues that "not only is the destruction or attempted destruction of fourth world peoples central to the pattern of contemporary genocide but [also], by examining such specific examples, we can more clearly delineate the phenomenon's more general wellsprings and processes." In fleshing out what really happened and what was really experienced by people under colonial attack, new models for prevention and intervention in today's secular and religious wars may emerge.

## A Confluence of Factors on the Eve of Contact

Study of the ancestral Pueblo groups during the period preceding the colonial presence (approximately AD 1250 to 1450) offers important insights into mechanisms underlying cultural processes, adaptability, and behavioral flexibility in a fluctuating, unpredictable, and marginal environment. Without information derived from archaeological and bioarchaeological sources of this precontact period, it would be nearly impossible to estimate the full impact of the changes and transformations wrought by colonial encounters. While there were many interrelated factors at play, climate change, endemic disease, and small-scale warfare are three interrelated challenges for which there is an increasingly rich set of supporting data (from bioarchaeological, archaeological, paleoclimate, and ethnohistoric studies). Determining how the Pueblo people coped with and reacted to outside and inside forces impinging on their communities and being able to measure levels of short- and long-term adaptability under multiple stressors are fundamental to addressing the impact of colonization. The two hundred or so years preceding the arrival of the Spanish were extremely difficult for Pueblo farmers, yet there is strong evidence for resilience and survival during the confluence of these factors that included environmental uncertainties, chronic and persistent disease loads, and sporadic warfare and violence. Knowing this context makes even more remarkable the ways that various Pueblo groups persisted and survived given the additional stressors of the colonial encounters.

### Environmental Marginality and Climate Change

An impressive wealth of archaeological data for the Southwest exists because of intensive excavation and study since the 1890s. The reconstruction of environment, climate, trade networks, population movements, settlement patterns, ceramic and lithic technology, architecture, diet, subsistence activities, and other facets of ancient Pueblo life has provided a great deal of data, recently summarized by Linda Cordell and Maxine McBrinn (2012) and John Kantner (2004). The many archaeological reconstructions of Pueblo people's environment and subsistence strategies suggest that they were constantly challenged by the vicissitudes of farming in an arid and marginal environment with periodic and long-lasting droughts (Spielmann et al. 2009). Constant movement and migration involved small-scale and larger region-wide patterns of leaving older communities and establishing new communities. This was part of an adaptive strategy to marginal and water-poor microenvironments, but it was also a deeply embedded part of Pueblo ideology.

According to Cordell and McBrinn (2012:223), the eve of contact was a turbulent time that produced large-scale depopulations through a process of residential mobility. Particularly, between AD 1250 and 1450, there is evidence of severe and long-lasting droughts, arroyo entrenchment, falling water tables, and major changes in rainfall periodicity (Kohler 2010).

Yet throughout this period, overall population size continued to grow and Pueblo groups formed complex regional and interregional alliances, practiced risk-avoidance strategies, shared resources, exchanged goods between regions, moved around the landscape to maximize resource acquisitions, and traded for nonindigenous items with people outside of the boundaries of the Pueblo Southwest (Cordell and McBrinn 2012:238). In the broadest picture, institutionalization of cooperative ventures and formation of local and distant alliances were likely dominant political-economic activities solidified through complex sodality, kin, clan, locality, marriage, and trade relationships. As resources dwindled and the ability to maintain large and dense population centers decreased, massive migrations and population movements have been documented. Crop failure, empty storage bins, and food shortage may have caused "lean years" and even starvation (White 1992:363).

This brief overview of the environmental challenges posed in the two-hundred-year period prior to the arrival of the Spanish is important because it shows that Pueblo people were already under quite a bit of strain without interjecting contact into the picture. Furthermore, the

1500s continued to have problematic climatic shifts with the onset of the Little Ice Age, during which colder weather patterns made farming even more challenging.

### Endemic Diseases

The Southwest in the late precontact period (1400–1500s) was a highly interactive and dynamic region with networks that were far-reaching. Trade goods found at sites revealed connections to the California coast, Mexico, the Great Plains to the east, and the Great Basin to the north (Cordell and McBrinn 2012). Bioarchaeological research conducted on human remains from this period from the archaeological sites of Hawikku, San Cristobal, and Pecos dismiss any notions about a disease-free paradise on the eve of contact (Morgan 2010; Stodder 1994, 1996). Techniques for the identification of pathologies related to communicable diseases such as *Staphylococcus* and *Streptococcus* infections, malnutrition, iron deficiency anemia, and traumatic injuries show frequencies within the burial populations by age and sex that are equal to or worse than frequencies discussed for other New World precontact populations (see, for examples, the chapters by Larsen and Milner in this volume).

These occurrences of pathologies and underlying disease stressors were also present in the time periods leading up to the 1200s. Studies have noted the ubiquity of health problems throughout the Southwest and for all precontact time periods (Martin et al. 1991; Nelson et al. 1994; Stodder 1994; Stodder and Martin 1992). In part because of the climate changes and unpredictable weather patterns that started in the 1200s, cultivation of crops and availability of local resources made these health problems all the more problematic, and increases in almost all categories of disease are higher when compared to earlier groups.

While the frequencies of pathologies such as nutritional anemia and infectious diseases suggest that they were ubiquitous across the Southwest, demographic trends in age-at-dying reveal patterns of differential survival. For example, developmental and endemic health problems such as nutritional anemia and infectious disease were less of a problem in the small dispersed farming hamlets that existed prior to the 1400s versus the aggregated villages found along the Rio Grande River at the time of contact.

High rates of dental disease (Stodder and Martin 1992:57) across fifteen communities ranging from AD 900 to contact had a mean of approximately 50 percent of the dentition from individuals showing caries and about 30 percent showing abscesses. Cranial lesions indicative of some kind of nutritional problems (such as B-12, iron, or other deficiencies) are consistently represented across all sites and most age categories, with the highest rates in children (from 15 percent to 88 percent) from some of the larger and later communities (Stodder and Martin 1992:58).

## Small-Scale Warfare, Raiding, and Interpersonal Violence

In the two hundred years or so prior to contact, the skeletal remains reveal evidence for sustained but highly variable behaviors that led to interpersonal conflict, various forms of violence, raiding, ambushes, possible cannibalism, massacres, enslavement of some captives, small-scale warfare, unequal distribution of high-quality food resources (leading to disease and morbidity), and shifts in sexual division of labor (for detailed regional case studies, see Baustian et al. 2012; Harrod 2012; LeBlanc 1999; Lekson 2002; Pérez 2012).

Around AD 1150 and onward, researchers suggest that there was a collapse of the Chaco Canyon populations, which represented a powerful sphere of influence. This collapse caused population movement and growth of population sizes in other regions (Harrod 2012; LeBlanc 1999; Lekson 1999, 2012). While the period of AD 900–1150 has been thought to be relatively peaceful, there is compelling data to suggest that warfare became more pronounced. The osteological record indicates the probability of large-scale village massacres in places such as Castle Rock (Kuckelman et al. 2002) and Cowboy Wash (Billman et al. 2000). However, the assemblages and burials found at these sites are not composed simply of dead bodies struck down while fighting. There is a remarkable range of variability in the kinds of corpse treatment (by both the perpetrators of the attack and possibly returning survivors), rituals for burial of the dead that are unique to this time period, and cases of violent deaths. In addition, there is skeletal evidence documenting victims of violent interactions who escaped death. Healed (nonlethal) traumatic injuries and head wounds are present at many Pueblo sites but seem to have increased during the twelfth and thirteenth centuries (Martin 1997).

The underlying causal relationships between violence and food shortage (Haas and Creamer 1996; White 1992), warfare and competition (Wilcox and Haas 1994), warfare and social stratification (LeBlanc 1999), and intimidation and dominance by non-Pueblo outsiders (Turner and Turner 1999) have been developed, emphasizing and incorporating select data from the osteological record. Christy G. Turner II and Jacqueline A. Turner (1999) have focused exclusively on disarticulated human remains, that is, human bones located in non-burial contexts.

Collectively, the archaeological data on fortification and strategic location and the osteological data on victims and mass graves suggest that fighting in the form of ambushes, raids, skirmishes, or attacks by a group of aggressors may have been the status quo in many parts of the precontact Southwest. Jonathan Haas (1990), Haas and Winifred Creamer (1995), and David Wilcox and Haas (1994) provide detailed overviews of archaeological data that demonstrate evidence of sustained intervillage conflict (including fortifications, palisades, towers, communities positioned in strategic locations, walled villages, and sites burned at the time of abandonment). The authors of these studies conclude that violent interactions between groups increased over time, starting around AD 1150 and continuing through the 1400s. The building of defensive architecture and the strategic location of sites by the Pueblo people there is compelling circumstantial evidence to suggest that people were in a mode of constant vigilance.

In summary, the osteological evidence for violence is highly varied. Steven LeBlanc (1999:83–90) and Signa Larralde (1998:20–21) provide overviews of human remains found in numerous contexts suggestive of different kinds of violence. In particular, they present reviews of the skeletal evidence for perimortem fractures, embedded stone points, burials with unusual mortuary treatment, and trophy skulls. Turner and Turner (1999) present seventy-six sites that show signs of interpersonal violence and ritual destruction of bodies. These include disarticulated, broken, and burned human remains. Thus, a wide variety of forms of violence as interpersonal strife, as performative rituals, and as endemic warfare and raiding were intrinsic to Pueblo cultures prior to contact. These kinds of violence have not been considered when forms of violence introduced by the Spanish are discussed.

The bioarchaeological data present a complex picture for the existing Pueblo communities on the eve of contact. Mass slayings, individual dismemberments, burning, possible cannibalism, scalping, intentional injury, witch execution, raiding for captives, and hand-to-hand combat have been documented on the human skeletal remains from the Southwest. However, the relationship of these signs of trauma and violence on the bodies to other political, economic, and ideological currents has not been fully examined. These cases of violence may represent a more large-scale and integrated system of power dynamics and forms of social control in addition to performances meant to intimidate, shows of force, aspects of coercion, or even conflict resolution.

## Complexities at Contact

The long history of human occupation in the Southwest is defined simultaneously by change and resiliency, and persistence and continuity. Thomas Sheridan and Nancy Parezo (1996:xxvi) state that for the people of the Southwest, it is the "persistence of ethnic identity in the face of constant change [including] . . . conquest, persecution, exile, and in some cases attempted genocide" that is unique and remarkable. There is a striking degree of biological and cultural continuity among many indigenous groups still living in these regions. For example, the Hopi people and their ancestors have lived on Black Mesa, Arizona, since AD 200 (Powell 1983). Hopi communities have very strong ties to their ancestral homelands, and they use information derived from archaeology, ethnohistory, and interviews with elders to identify ancestral sacred sites and locations (Ferguson et al. 1993).

The Southwest in general was a challenging place to live. Bioarchaeological data combined with archaeological patterns of movement and settlement suggest that droughts punctuated various times and regions particularly severely. Yet at the time of contact, there were large settlements along the Rio Grande to the east and in the northern and central parts of Arizona. Without even bringing in the stresses of contact, on the eve of contact there were signs of increasing disease stress and violence along with increasing population size, intensification of agricultural practices, greater emphasis on public architecture and trade, and the appearance of large regional systems (Wilcox and Haas 1994).

Spanish exploration and colonization of New Mexico led to profound disruptions, as Pueblo land, labor, and other resources were usurped and the Pueblo economy and culture were threatened by new invaders and by the introduction of Old World diseases—smallpox, measles, and other epidemic diseases (Kessell 1979; Reff 1991:228–30, 1993; Schroeder 1972; Simmons 1979; Snow 1981; Upham 1982; Wilcox 1981).

Whatever the range of reasons for Pueblo migration in the precontact periods, Spanish colonization of New Mexico in 1598 clearly added new and in many ways terrifying dimensions to the process of site abandonment. Before colonization in 1598 there were seventy-five to ninety occupied pueblos in the Rio Grande drainage; by 1643 only forty-three remained (Schroeder 1972:48, 55). Even those pueblos that persisted (welcoming immigrants from elsewhere) experienced population losses. As example, the population of Pecos declined by 40 percent between 1622 and 1641 (Kessell 1979:170).

Although it has been hypothesized that diseases like smallpox reached the Pueblo region before or shortly after European contact in 1539 (Dobyns 1983; Upham 1986), a stronger case is made for the introduction of disease following Juan de Oñate's founding of the first Spanish colony in New Mexico in 1598 (Reff 1991:102–3, 167). The spread of epidemic disease after this date over hundreds of miles via Native populations is indicated in Jesuit missionary documents from northern and western Mexico (Reff 1987a, 1987b, 1991). Epidemics are also noted in the missionaries' burial books, reports, and chronicles from the 1600s and 1700s (Kessell 1979:378; Reff 1991:230–31; Stodder 1990; Stodder and Martin 1992).

The relatively high incidence of cranial trauma following European contact is consistent with archaeological and historical evidence of warfare and violence, including increased warfare among the Pueblo people themselves and with their Athapaskan and Plains neighbors (Riley 1975:185), all of whom found their lives transformed by epidemic diseases, guns, horses, and massive economic disruption. The Spanish explorers and missionaries wrote about (and took advantage of) the relative wealth of the large villages like Hawikku and San Cristobal with their fields of corn and cotton. While they often misunderstood and misrepresented the Native peoples and their political and religious systems (Reff 1999, 2009), these early visitors left accounts that are

unanimous in their glowing commentary on the wealth and quality of
life enjoyed by the Pueblo people (Riley 1986:184, 232). They did not
write about Natives of the Greater Southwest as sickly, starving, and
barely able to survive to adulthood; rather, they described strong, agile,
and corpulent people who lived into older adulthood. Considering the
historical record, one could argue that warfare, famine, disease, and environmental degradation were more of a problem in sixteenth-century
Europe than in the communities encountered by the Spanish in the
Southwest (Sale 1991:28–36, 75–90, 134).

The earliest epidemic mentioned in written records for New Mexico
occurred in the 1630s, which is well after contact. Henry Dobyns (1983)
has argued that disease spread as far north from the Basin of Mexico to
the various pueblos as early as the 1520s. He suggests that there were at
least two major waves of epidemic diseases prior to Marcos de Niza's
expedition to Zuni in 1539 and Coronado's expeditions in 1540 (Stodder
and Martin 1992:55). Daniel Reff's (1991) careful reconstruction of six-
teenth- and seventeenth-century epidemics in what was called "Northern New Spain" include a smallpox pandemic (1520–24), measles and
smallpox (1593–97), and smallpox epidemics (1601–2, 1604, 1607–8,
1612–13, 1615, 1623–25, 1635, 1645–47, and 1652).

Embedded in this narrative of the constancy of epidemics is also
a range of things that do not fit the pattern. E. Charles Adams (1981)
demonstrates that the Hopis were not subject to any sustained contact until after the Pueblo Revolt in 1680. The Zunis put up a relatively successful resistance to Coronado and his army, and Zuni was
not in contact with the Spanish until 1629, when missions were built
(Ferguson 1981). By 1630 there were almost a hundred churches that
had been built in pueblos in the Southwest, but the actual number of
priests and colonists remained low in the 1620s but escalated as more
colonists steadily arrived. Some of the epidemics noted above in the
seventeenth century were likely the result of demographic disturbances
ranging from complete abandonment of some pueblos to the migration
of individuals and families. Diseases would have easily spread during
these interactions with the Spanish and internal movement within and
between Native communities. Looking to the bioarchaeological record
for the larger protohistoric sites of San Cristobal and Hawikku as well
as Pecos Pueblo, Ann Stodder and I (Stodder and Martin 1992:67) argue

that epidemics were actually only part of a suite of existing and new conditions that people were reacting and responding to.

## Pueblo Resilience

The complicated and entwined forces at work in the years leading up to contact and then throughout the period of colonial expansion can best be described as creeping genocide. But it is misleading to characterize epidemics as the leading reason for the depopulation of Pueblo groups in some of the regions. While epidemics were horrifying and caused untold thousands of deaths, the relentless domination and subjugation of the Pueblo people was likely much more of a factor in explaining the impact of contact on biological and cultural adaptation. The Spanish needed labor and resources in their quest to conquer and colonize, and so the forces that produced morbidity and mortality in Pueblo groups were a formulation of many injustices, including coercion and mistreatment. In contrast to the myth of the disease-free paradise, the syntheses of bioarchaeological data from the Southwest reveal high levels of biological stress prior to contact and especially in early historic populations (Martin 1994, 1997; Reff 1991, 1993; Stodder 1994, 2012; Stodder and Martin 1992).

The indigenous peoples of the Southwest have always been in a state of growth, migration, decline, and movement. The themes of migration, movement, and hardship tempered with a respect for the challenges of nature and climatic events in their everyday lives are strongly entwined in their oral narratives. Long-term cultural longevity cannot be understood on the basis of data reduced to events such as epidemics or counts of skeletal pathologies. The archaeological and historical records of the Pueblo Southwest and the Native peoples' histories document a persistent hold on traditional values and a commitment to "place" and land along with a resiliency and flexibility in adapting to novel and challenging ecological, political, and cultural conditions (Brown 2013). That the combined forces of creeping genocide did not completely undermine Pueblo peoples' capacity for resilience in the face of enormous odds is nothing short of remarkable. There are lessons to be learned from these groups because although they have carried a morbidity burden that appears to be unparalleled in the Western Hemisphere (see Stodder et al.

2002), they remain vibrant and viable cultures today. Demographically, their numbers have continued to rise and may currently be at sizes replicating those at contact (Sheridan and Parezo 1996).

## References

Adams, E. Charles. 1981. The view from the Hopi mesas. *In* The Protohistoric Period in the North American Southwest, AD 1450–1700, edited by David R. Wilcox and W. Bruce Masse, 321–35. Anthropological Research Papers 24. Tempe: Arizona State University.

Baker, Brenda J., and Lisa Kealhofer, eds. 1996. Bioarchaeology of Native American Adaptation in the Spanish Borderlands. Gainesville: University Press of Florida.

Barrett, Elinor. 2004. Conquest and Catastrophe: Changing Rio Grande Pueblo Settlement Patterns in the Sixteenth and Seventeenth Centuries. Albuquerque: University of New Mexico Press.

Baustian, Kathryn M., Ryan P. Harrod, Anna J. Osterholtz, and Debra L. Martin. 2012. Battered and abused: Analysis of trauma at Grasshopper Pueblo (AD 1275–1400). International Journal of Paleopathology 2(2–3):102–11.

Bellesiles, Michael. 2004. Western violence. *In* A Companion to the American West, edited by William Deverell, 162–78. New York: Blackwell.

Billman, Brian R., Patricia M. Lambert, and Banks L. Leonard. 2000. Cannibalism, warfare, and drought in the Mesa Verde region in the twelfth century AD. American Antiquity 65:1–34.

Brooks, James F. 2002. Captives and Cousins: Slavery, Kinship, and Community in the Southwest Borderlands. Chapel Hill: University of North Carolina Press.

Brown, Tracy L. 2013. Pueblo Indians and Spanish Colonial Authority in Eighteenth-Century New Mexico. Tucson: University of Arizona Press.

Cajete, Gregory A. 2010. A Pueblo perspective of the history of Santa Fe. *In* White Shell Water Place: An Anthology of Native American Reflections on the 400th Anniversary of the Founding of Santa Fe, New Mexico, edited by F. Richard Sanchez, 19–37. Santa Fe, NM: Sunstone Press.

Cordell, Linda S., and Maxine E. McBrinn. 2012. Archaeology of the Southwest. 3rd ed. Walnut Creek, CA: Left Coast Press.

Diamond, Jared. 1997. Guns, Germs, and Steel: The Fates of Human Societies. New York: W. W. Norton.

Dobyns, Henry F. 1983. Their Number Become Thinned: Native American Population Dynamics in Eastern North America. Knoxville: University of Tennessee Press.

Ferguson, T. J. 1981. The emergence of modern Zuni culture and society: A summary of Zuni tribal history, AD 1450–1700. *In* The Protohistoric Period in the North American Southwest, AD 1450–1700, edited by David R. Wilcox and W. Bruce Masse, 336–53. Anthropological Research Papers 24. Tempe: Arizona State University.

Ferguson, T. J., Kurt E. Dongoske, Leigh Jenkins, Michael Yeatts, and Eric Polingyouma. 1993. Working together: The roles of archaeology and ethnohistory in Hopi cultural preservation. CRM: The Journal of Heritage Stewardship 16:27–37.

Finzsch, Norbert. 2008. "[ . . . ] Extirpate or remove that vermine": Genocide, biological warfare, and settler imperialism in the eighteenth and early nineteenth century. Journal of Genocide Research 10(2):215–32.

Gutiérrez, Ramón A. 1991. When Jesus Came, the Corn Mothers Went Away: Marriage, Sexuality, and Power in New Mexico, 1500–1846. Stanford: Stanford University Press.

Haas, Jonathan. 1990. Warfare and the evolution of tribal polities in the prehistoric Southwest. *In* The Anthropology of War, edited by Jonathan Haas, 171–89. Cambridge: Cambridge University Press.

Haas, Jonathan, and Winifred Creamer. 1993. Stress and Warfare Among the Kayenta Anasazi of the Thirteenth Century A.D. Chicago: Field Museum of Natural History.

———. 1995. A history of Pueblo warfare. Paper presented at the 60th Annual Meeting of the Society of American Archaeology, Minneapolis, MN.

———. 1996. The role of warfare in the Pueblo III period. *In* The Prehistoric Pueblo World, A.D. 1150–1350, edited by Michael A. Adler, 205–13. Tucson: University of Arizona Press.

Habicht-Mauche, Judith. 2000. Pottery, food, hides, and women: Labor, production, and exchange across the protohistoric Plains-Pueblo frontier. *In* The Archaeology of Regional Interaction: Religion, Warfare, and Exchange Across the American Southwest and Beyond, edited by Michelle Hegmon, 209–31. Proceedings of the 1996 Southwest Symposium. Boulder: University Press of Colorado.

Hackett, Lewis Wendell. 1937. Malaria in Europe: An Ecological Study. Oxford: Oxford University Press.

Harrod, Ryan P. 2012. Centers of control: Revealing elites among the Ancestral Pueblo during the "Chaco Phenomenon." International Journal of Paleopathology 2(2–3):123–35.

Kantner, John. 2004. Ancient Puebloan Southwest. Cambridge: Cambridge University Press.

Kessell, John L. 1979. Kiva, Cross, and Crown: The Pecos Indians and New Mexico, 1540–1840. Washington, DC: Western National Parks Association.

Kohler, Timothy A. 2010. A new paleoproductivity reconstruction for southwestern Colorado, and its implications for understanding thirteenth-century depopulation. *In* Leaving Mesa Verde: Peril and Change in the

Thirteenth-Century Southwest, edited by Timothy A. Kohler, Mark D. Varien, and Aaron M. Wright, 102–27. Tucson: University of Arizona Press.

Kohler, Timothy A., Mark D. Varien, and Aaron M. Wright, eds. 2010. Leaving Mesa Verde: Peril and Change in the Thirteenth-Century Southwest. Tucson: University of Arizona Press.

Kuckelman, Kristin A., Ricky R. Lightfoot, and Debra L. Martin. 2002. The bioarchaeology and taphonomy of violence at Castle Rock and Sand Canyon Pueblos, southwestern Colorado. American Antiquity 67:486–513.

Larralde, Signa. 1998. The context of early Puebloan violence. In Deciphering Anasazi Violence: With Regional Comparisons to Mesoamerican and Woodland Cultures, edited by Peter Y. Bullock, 11–33. Santa Fe, NM: HRM Books.

Larsen, Clark Spencer, ed. 2001. Bioarchaeology of Spanish Florida: The Impact of Colonialism. Gainesville: University Press of Florida.

Larsen, Clark Spencer, and George R. Milner, eds. 1994. In the Wake of Contact: Biological Responses to Conquest. New York: Wiley-Liss.

LeBlanc, Steven A. 1999. Prehistoric Warfare in the American Southwest. Salt Lake City: University of Utah Press.

Lekson, Stephen H. 1999. The Chaco Meridian: Centers of Political Power in the Ancient Southwest. Walnut Creek, CA: AltaMira Press.

———. 2002. War in the Southwest, war in the world. American Antiquity 67(4):607–24.

———. 2012. Chaco's hinterlands. In The Oxford Handbook of North American Archaeology, edited by Timothy R. Pauketat, 597–607. Oxford: Oxford University Press.

Levene, Mark. 1999. The Chittagong Hill Tracts: A case study in the political economy of "creeping" genocide. Third World Quarterly 20(2):339–69.

Liebmann, Matthew J., and Robert W. Preucel. 2007. The archaeology of the Pueblo Revolt and the formation of the modern Pueblo world. Kiva 73(2):195–217.

Limerick, Patricia Nelson. 1987. The Legacy of Conquest. New York: W. W. Norton.

Malville, Nancy J. 1989. Two fragmented human bone assemblages from Yellow Jacket, southwestern Colorado. Kiva 55:3–22.

Martin, Debra L. 1994. Patterns of health and disease: Health profiles for the prehistoric Southwest. In Themes in Southwest Prehistory, edited by George J. Gumerman, 87–108. Santa Fe, NM: School of American Research Press.

———. 1997. Violence against women in the La Plata River valley (A.D. 1000–1300). In Troubled Times: Violence and Warfare in the Past, edited by Debra L. Martin and David W. Frayer, 45–75. Amsterdam: Gordon and Breach.

Martin, Debra L., Nancy J. Akins, Alan H. Goodman, and Alan C. Swedlund. 2001. Harmony and Discord: Bioarchaeology of the La Plata Valley. Vol. 5 of Totah: Time and the Rivers Flowing; Excavations in the La Plata Valley. Santa Fe: Museum of New Mexico, Office of Archaeological Studies.

Martin, Debra L., Alan H. Goodman, George J. Armelagos, and Ann L. Magennis. 1991. Black Mesa Anasazi Health: Reconstructing Life from Patterns of Death and Disease. Carbondale: Southern Illinois University Press.

Martin, Debra L., Ryan P. Harrod, and Misty Fields. 2010. Beaten down and worked to the bone: Bioarchaeological investigations of women and violence in the ancient Southwest. Landscapes of Violence 1(1):Article 3.

Morgan, Michele E. 2010. A reassessment of the human remains from the upper Pecos valley. In Pecos Pueblo Revisited: The Biological and Social Context, edited by Michele E. Morgan, 27–42. Papers of the Peabody Museum of Archaeology and Ethnology 85. Cambridge, MA: Harvard University.

Nelson, Ben A., Debra L. Martin, Alan C. Swedlund, Paul R. Fish, and George J. Armelagos. 1994. Studies in disruption: Demography and health in the prehistoric American Southwest. In Understanding Complexity in the Prehistoric Southwest, edited by George J. Gumerman and Murray Gell-Mann, 59–112. Reading: Addison-Wesley.

Nickens, Paul R. 1975. Prehistoric cannibalism in the Mancos Canyon, southwestern Colorado. Kiva 40(4):283–93.

Pérez, Ventura R. 2012. The taphonomy of violence: Recognizing variation in disarticulated skeletal assemblages. International Journal of Paleopathology 2(2–3):156–65.

Powell, Shirley. 1983. Mobility and Adaptation: The Anasazi of Black Mesa, Arizona. Carbondale: Southern Illinois University Press.

Rabasa, José. 1993. Inventing America: Spanish Historiography and the Formation of Eurocentrism. Norman: University of Oklahoma Press.

Reff, Daniel T. 1987a. The introduction of smallpox in the Greater Southwest. American Anthropologist 89(3):704–708.

———. 1987b. Old World diseases and the dynamics of Indian and Jesuit relations in northwestern New Spain, 1520–1660. Ejidos and Regions of Refuge in Northwestern Mexico 46:85-88.

———. 1991. Disease, Depopulation, and Culture Change in Northwestern New Spain, 1518–1764. Salt Lake City: University of Utah Press.

———. 1993. An alternative explanation of subsistence change during the early historic period at Pecos Pueblo. American Antiquity 58(3):563–64.

———. 1999. In the shadow of the saints: Jesuit missionaries and their New World narratives. Romance Philology 53(1):165–82.

———. 2009. Saints, witches and go-betweens: The depiction of women in missionary accounts from the northern frontier of New Spain. Colonial Latin American Review 18(2):237–60.

Riley, Carroll L. 1975. The road to Hawikuh: Trade and trade routes to Cibola-Zuni during late prehistoric and early historic times. Kiva 41(2):137–59.

———. 1986. An overview of the Greater Southwest in the protohistoric period. *In* Ripples in the Chichimec Sea, edited by Frances Joan Mathien and Randall McGuire, 181–234. Carbondale: Southern Illinois University Press.

Sale, Kirkpatrick. 1991. The Conquest of Paradise: Christopher Columbus and the Columbian Legacy. New York: Alfred A. Knopf.

Schroeder, Albert H. 1972. Rio Grande ethnohistory. *In* New Perspectives on the Pueblos, edited by Alfonso Ortiz, 41–70. Albuquerque: University of New Mexico Press.

Sheridan, Thomas E., and Nancy J. Parezo. 1996. Introduction. *In* Paths of Life: American Indians of the Southwest and Northern Mexico, edited by Thomas E. Sheridan and Nancy J. Parezo, xxiii–xxxiii. Tucson: University of Arizona Press.

Simmons, Marc. 1979. History of Pueblo-Spanish relations to 1821. *In* Handbook of North American Indians, vol. 19: Southwest, edited by Alfonso Ortiz, 236–55. Washington, DC: Smithsonian Institution Press.

Snow, David H. 1981. Protohistoric Rio Grande Pueblo economics: A review of trends. *In* The Protohistoric Period in the North American Southwest, AD 1450–1700, edited by David R. Wilcox and W. Bruce Masse, 354–77. Anthropological Research Papers 24. Tempe: Arizona State University.

Spielmann, Katherine A., Tiffany Clark, Diane Hawkey, Katharine Rainey, and Susan K. Fish. 2009. ". . . Being weary, they had rebelled": Pueblo subsistence and labor under Spanish colonialism. Journal of Anthropological Archaeology 28(1):102–25.

Stodder, Ann L. W. 1990. Paleoepidemiology of Eastern and Western Pueblo Communities. PhD diss., Department of Anthropology, University of Colorado, Boulder.

———. 1994. Bioarchaeological investigations of protohistoric Pueblo health and demography. *In* In the Wake of Contact: Biological Responses to Conquest, edited by Clark Spencer Larsen and George R. Milner, 97–107. New York: Wiley-Liss.

———. 1996. Paleoepidemiology of Eastern and Western Pueblo communities in protohistoric and early historic New Mexico. *In* Bioarchaeology of Native American Adaptation in the Spanish Borderlands, edited by Brenda J. Baker and Lisa Kealhofer, 148–76. Gainesville: University Press of Florida.

———. 2012. The history of paleopathology in the American Southwest. *In* The Global History of Paleopathology: Pioneers and Prospects, edited by Jane E. Buikstra and Charlotte A. Roberts, 285–304. Oxford: Oxford University Press.

Stodder, Ann L. W., and Debra L. Martin. 1992. Native health and disease in the American Southwest before and after Spanish contact. *In* Disease and

Demography in the Americas, edited by John W. Verano and Douglas H. Ubelaker, 55–73. Washington, DC: Smithsonian Institution Press.

Stodder, Ann L. W., Debra L. Martin, Alan H. Goodman, and Daniel T. Reff. 2002. Cultural longevity in the face of biological stress: The Anasazi of the American Southwest. *In* The Backbone of History: Health and Nutrition in the Western Hemisphere, edited by Richard H. Steckel and Jerome C. Rose, 481–505. Cambridge: Cambridge University Press.

Thornton, Russell. 1987. American Indian Holocaust and Survival: A Population History Since 1942. Norman: University of Oklahoma Press.

Turner, Christy G., II, and Jacqueline A. Turner. 1999. Man Corn: Cannibalism and Violence in the Prehistoric American Southwest. Salt Lake City: University of Utah Press.

Upham, Steadman. 1982. Polities and Power: An Economic and Political History of the Western Pueblo. New York: Academic Press.

———. 1986. Smallpox and climate in the American Southwest. American Anthropologist 88(1):115–28.

Verano, John W., and Douglas H. Ubelaker, eds. 1992. Disease and Demography in the Americas. Washington, DC: Smithsonian Institution Press.

Voss, Barbara L. 2008. The Archaeology of Ethnogenesis: Race and Sexuality in Colonial San Francisco. Berkeley: University of California Press.

White, Tim D. 1992. Prehistoric Cannibalism at Mancos 5MTUMR-2346. Princeton: Princeton University Press.

Wilcox, David R. 1981. Changing perspectives on the protohistoric Pueblos, AD 1450–1700. *In* The Protohistoric Period in the North American Southwest, AD 1450–1700, edited by David R. Wilcox and W. Bruce Masse, 378–410. Anthropological Research Papers 24. Tempe: Arizona State University.

Wilcox, David R., and Jonathan Haas. 1994. The scream of the butterfly: Competition and conflict in the prehistoric Southwest. *In* Themes in Southwest Prehistory, edited by George J. Gumerman, 211–38. Santa Fe, NM: School of American Research Press.

Wilcox, Michael V. 2009. The Pueblo Revolt and the Mythology of Conquest: An Indigenous Archaeology of Contact. Berkeley: University of California Press.

# 5

# Identity Erasure and Demographic Impacts of the Spanish Caste System on the Indigenous Populations of Mexico

*Gerardo Gutiérrez*

The Spanish caste system should be understood as an ideology/practice that created hierarchical categories of people to discriminate against individuals based on fictions of "purity of blood," genealogy, religion, class, and occupation (Martínez 2009). Marital and extramarital interracial unions in Spanish America led to the emergence of an admixed population that the colonial system attempted to monitor and control through the creation of racial labels. In this chapter I analyze the unstated rules governing the Spanish caste system and their long-term demographic and social impacts on the indigenous populations of Mexico. Beyond germs, guns, and steel, there were culturally constructed principles of exclusion based on folk racial concepts (especially those associated with phenotypic expressions such as skin color, facial structure, and hair texture) that began operating in the earliest stages of the Spanish colonial system, a process that eventually placed the vast majority of the Indian population in the lowest status of the colonial caste system.[1] Despite the abolition of the caste system in 1822, the pervasive ideology of allocating political and economic opportunities based on phenotypic characteristics continued to operate strongly, upholding the permanence of stigmatized groups (Wolf 1982:380–81). These cultural practices promoted the erasure of indigenous identity and rejection of the Amerindian phenotype (Aldama 2001).

This chapter examines the negotiated identities of race, class, and status in Mexico since the colonial period and argues that people phenotypically and culturally regarded as Indian were subjected to social and legal discrimination that have kept the indigenous groups in a state of structural poverty, affecting their socioeconomic status, well-being, and health. Moreover, admixture became a process through which the progeny of indigenous individuals were assimilated into the dominant Spanish system. Interracial unions contributed to an apparent decrease in indigenous population numbers due to changes of identity and erasure, a variable that is not fully considered in normal demographic studies. Throughout this chapter, I refer to "race" as a cultural construct that uses phenotypic and cultural variability to socially create discrete classes of people on which social advantages or prejudices are imposed (Marks 1996; Wagley 1965).

## Rules and Principles of the Spanish Caste System

In the Spanish language of the colonial period, *caste* referred to a lineage of descendants from known parents and the conflating belief that gentry/villainy and phenotypic and behavioral traits passed from parents to children through the "blood" (*Diccionario de Autoridades* 2002:219–20, *s.v. casta*).[2] Beginning in the medieval period, a hierarchical system of social status was practiced in Spain around the concept of *limpieza de sangre*, or "purity of blood," in which the genealogical line of each family was carefully and sometimes legally monitored, with the ultimate goal of preventing marriage and procreation between people of different estates, particularly between nobles and commoners or between Christians and non-Christians (Martínez 2008). These ideas on the segregation of different estates and religions were brought to the New World and adapted to the colonial reality, an arena where people of three different "races" met and interacted in ways never seen before in Europe (Comaroff 1987; Elliott 1998; Horowitz 1985:26–30).

The Spanish colonial caste system rested on the simplistic notion that the noblest people of the realm were those who could trace their ancestry to Christian families of the northern Iberian kingdoms who fought in the Reconquista or wars to recover regions under the control of the Muslim caliphates. Individuals from these families were called *hijosdalgos* (literally, the "sons of somebody"), and their blood was considered "pure"—without the "taint" of commoners, Jews, or Muslims (Martínez 2009:26). After arriving on the shores of America, all Spaniards immediately claimed *hidalguía*, or noble status, and believed themselves to be "pure bloods," regardless of their former status in Spain. Furthermore, all indigenous people of the Americas were reduced to a unique group label, "Indian," which ignored and erased pre-Columbian distinctions or self-identities. Through an aggressive evangelization program, most indigenous people in contact with the Spaniards became Christians, and because Indian blood was considered to be "untainted" by African or Moorish ancestry, their descendants had the potential to be transformed into Europeans after three generations of consecutive marriages with Spaniards. And so, Spanish imperial ambitions included not only policies of religious indoctrination and replacement of Native cultures but also bureaucratic and legal mechanisms for biological "promotion" and "demotion." As long as Spaniards married with Spaniards and Indians married with Indians, the system was quasi-neutral, in the sense that marriage considerations were based on the wealth and status of the participant families. Demotion mechanisms operated primarily on Mestizos (or Euro-Mestizos) whenever any of these individuals decided to marry or procreate children outside of the Spanish group. If Mestizos decided to marry with Indians, the process of demotion was reversible, and mixed-heritage descendants could again start moving toward the idealized goal of becoming European by marrying continuously with Spaniards. In contrast, caste demotion became quasi-permanent when any individual of Spanish, Indian, or Mestizo heritage decided to marry or procreate with African partners. The colonial bureaucracy soon recognized a Castizo caste, consisting of individuals resulting from the union of Mestizos with Spaniards.[3] If a Castizo married another Spaniard, the offspring of that couple was legally recognized as Spaniard. This designation was necessary for inheritance purposes, since many Spanish conquistadors and colonists legally recognized some of their Mestizo children. This practice also increased the number of "Spanish" people, which was always numerically low in comparison with either the surviving Indian or the imported African population.

The introduction of African slaves in Mexico produced the Mulatto caste (Spanish-African or Afro-Mestizo). Further accommodations were required to address the admixture of an African and Indian, which came to be known as "Lobo," and the admixture of an African with a Mestizo, reported in the eighteenth century as either "Mulato Torna Atras" or "Lobo Tente en el Ayre."[4] The stigma of marrying or having sexual intercourse with an individual of African descent seemingly emerged from the condition of slavery to which African populations were subjected during Portuguese expansion into western Africa in the early fifteenth century, as well as centuries of constant skirmishes and captive-taking between Mediterranean Europeans and dark-complexioned practitioners of Islam from northern Africa (Mörner 1967:14; Wolf 1982:380). This stigma profoundly impacted the choice of marrying with an African, because this act could "taint" the blood of one's descendants, condemning them to those castes that could never achieve limpieza de sangre and effectively curtailing their offspring's access to positions of political and economic power (Martínez 2009:30). Nevertheless, recent historical studies have shown how some African descendants in Mexico and Latin America resisted and coped with the most oppressive features of Spanish colonialism, gaining special status above that assigned to Indian populations through work as overseers or in the militia (see Landers and Robinson 2006; Restall 2005; Vinson 2001). After the War of Independence, the admixed African population, *pardos* or *morenos*, managed to blend into the emerging mestizo culture of Mexico, mitigating the stigma of slavery. At the same time, the culturally and phenotypically Indian groups became the center of political argument as they were identified as the population that was impeding the "progress" of the new republic.

## The Visual Expression of the Spanish Caste System

By the early eighteenth century, the caste system had created a convoluted typology difficult to explain or manage through verbal means. Moreover, judging from the long lists presented by José Pérez de Barradas (1976 [1948]:232–38), it is obvious that many labels are confusingly repetitive, with the use of the same name to describe different combinations or using different names to describe the same interracial combination. This indicates that if such categories were used, they were applied unsystematically and opportunistically, perhaps more to offend "equals," mock "superiors," or exercise power over "lesser" castes with denigrating labels. Hence, the caste paintings of late colonial Mexico may be considered the materialization through visual means of the racial values that had emerged after two centuries of Spanish rule and intensive interracial unions. These paintings were designed to reduce the complexity of a diverse and heterogeneous population into compartmentalized racial categories based on the concept of limpieza de sangre. They also represented an attempt to justify the colonial status quo of socioeconomic inequalities that allocated special privileges to Spanish colonists, together with a handful of Indian and African allies, while forcing the rest of the populace to submit to exclusionary policies. As an artistic genre, caste painting seems to have appeared almost spontaneously in 1711; it consists of sets of sixteen or twenty canvases depicting scenes of quotidian life of intercaste couples, usually with one of their offspring (figure 5.1) (Córdova and Farago 2012; Katzew 1996b:9, 14). Diverse landscapes, tools, dress, and social activities are used to highlight slight variations in skin color, facial features, and hair texture of the individuals portrayed as representative of their castes. Beyond racial diversity, the visual representations of castes and their verbal labels capture the *doxa*, or the self-evident, unquestioned, and undisputed "natural order" of the Spanish caste system and its ideology of imperial domination (following Bourdieu 2000:164–68). Therefore, the caste paintings of the eighteenth century should be analyzed not only as artwork created for powerful patrons but also as the product of two centuries of European colonialism in which new racial values had achieved maturity (Deans-Smith 2009; Katzew 1996a). For the first time, close contact between all humans in a spatial context of multicontinental empires created hybrid individuals who escaped early sixteenth-century boundaries of white, black, red, and yellow designations for people (Stoler 1995:30). It is not a celebration of plurality, however, but rather a lamentation of the unintended consequences of imperial expansion—a situation no one wanted to occur but that no authority or formal institution could prevent, despite very vocal opposition to interracial unions from the beginning of the Spanish imperial quest (Aguirre 1946:261; Mörner 1967:38, 65).

It has been argued that the caste paintings represent a failed attempt to organize the new complexity of colonial interraciality, with people bypassing categories through economic achievements (Klor de Alva 1996; Taylor 2009). Indeed, many individuals managed to outmaneuver the system, but to date no one has attempted to quantify the number of individuals who escaped the exclusions of the caste system through personal success. There were always legal loopholes allowed by colonial

Figure 5.1. *Casta* categories (detail), eighteenth century. Museo Nacional del Virreinato, Tepotzotlán, Mexico. (Photo courtesy of Art Resource.)

authorities, depending on political circumstances and economic convenience, but such loopholes could always be closed if so desired by
a vengeful bureaucrat or a jealous neighbor. As modern scholars, we
may find it easy to opine that the caste system was failing by the end of
the colonial period. Nonetheless, those who painted these caste scenes
and their patrons were living their own present, and in their lifetimes
the racial organization of the colonial society was the normal order of
things. Caste paintings not only highlighted the exclusionary practices
associated with colonial racial values but also promoted the permanence
of the system and its strong regulation to prevent racial mixtures perceived as socially dangerous, especially those composed of Indians and
Africans and, even worse, those who had blood of all three racial groups!
Caste paintings depict what made sense to the artists and the unquestioned world in which they lived, which is why they provide rare access
into the core of racial values and attitudes forged in Spanish America.

In addition, these paintings encapsulate a veritable handbook of
marriage strategies indicating the right steps for Indian and Mestizo
parents to take for their progeny to become legally Spaniard or how
they could stay or revert to the Indian estate, a strategy for some descendants of Indian rulers (caciques), who had to remain legally "Indian" to continue enjoying special privileges (Aguirre 1946:280; Haskett
1988). Caste paintings also present the dire consequences of incorporating suspicious "blood" into the family genealogy. Interestingly, colonial people had an alchemical notion of how blood "mixed," which
depended on the number of marriages that a family line had made with
other castes (Deans-Smith and Katzew 2009:1). Such genealogical ac-
counting became the province of elders who helped police the caste
system and its associated socioeconomic rewards and punishments. The
reappearance of undesired phenotypic traits supported the practice of
long-term "blood purification" through well-designed marriage patterns. Of course, this process required Spanish blood, and there was
always a scarcity of Spanish fiancés and fiancées in the geographical
vastness of the empire to fuel a "virtuous" cycle of caste promotion.
Thus, the system was always at risk of being engulfed by Indian and
African blood. The only option available for most well-to-do families
in the colonies was to recruit light-skinned Mestizos into the formation
of the so-called Spanish group (Aguirre 1946:251). Legal artifices were

also put into place to maintain the system for the not-so-rare situation of two seemingly "pure blood" Spanish parents procreating a child with a strong recessive Indian or African phenotype (literally a *tornatrás*, or "return backwards"). In those situations, such individuals underwent a bureaucratic process to obtain a certificate of "purity of blood," guaranteeing for all legal purposes that such person was to be considered a Spaniard (Martínez 2008). This legal procedure was popularized by the phrase *que se tenga por español* (take him/her for a Spaniard) (Pérez de Barradas 1976 [1948]:213).

To facilitate the identification and understanding of the most typical folk racial labels found in the surviving caste paintings (Katzew 1996a), I summarize them in table 5.1 (note, however, that typologies had regional and chronological variations, as did documentary sources). The "percentages of blood" in table 5.1 refers to the number of grandparents from the three parental populations: thus, 100 percent equals 4 grandparents from the same parental population, without mixture; 50 percent means 2 grandparents out of 4 from a particular parental population in the first generation of mixture; 25 percent is 2 grandparents out of 8 in the second generation of mixture; 12.5 percent represents 2 grandparents out of 16 in the third generation; 6.25 percent represents 2 grandparents out of 32 in the fourth generation; 3.125 percent is 2 grandparents out of 64 in the fifth generation; 1.5625 percent is 2 grandparents out of 128 in the sixth generation; 0.78125 percent represents only 2 grandparents of a specific parental population out of 256 in the seventh generation; and so on.

It is interesting to assess some of the patterns in eighteenth-century caste typology as depicted in the caste paintings by plotting the "percentage" of parental blood for each category in a ternary chart (figure 5.2). The first thing to note is that castes are closed groups that represented discrete categories, as opposed to the range of phenotypic variability of actual individuals. This closed categorization effectively reduced individuals into idealized groups often subjected to social and legal discrimination. The only two explicit exemptions to these discrete categories are seen in cases of "promotion" or "return" to the Spanish or Indian groups. This transformation was technically permitted only to Mestizos after two generations marrying consecutively with Spaniards or Indians. In theory, after reaching 87.5 percent of "blood" of a specific parental group (fourteen grandparents out of sixteen), those individuals were considered "pure bloods" again. These spaces provided the much-needed escape valves to allow the game of "passing," in which some individuals, especially bicultural Mestizos with the right phenotypes, could be considered "Spaniards" or "Indians" (Martínez 2009:33). Surprisingly, the variability along the Spanish-African axis offered fewer defined castes than along the Spanish-Indian axis, perhaps because once a Mulatto married another African their children automatically reverted to Africans.[5] Actually, things were not much different if Mulattoes married with Spaniards, because in the fourth generation, strong African phenotypic features were believed to reappear, which would lead to classifying those children as a "Negro return backwards." This suited the caste system by keeping most individuals of African descent in servitude to Spaniards, without regard for Spanish grandparents, based on the belief that Spanish blood was lost in that racial mixture (Martínez 2009:39).

Along the Indian-African axis, there is another gap in caste representation in the space between Lobo and African categories; again, any offspring of these two classes was most likely to be considered African. Curiously, the continuous mixtures of Lobo descendants with Indians were tracked until the seventh generation; perhaps this was a scare tactic to prevent Indians from marrying with Africans. Those individuals in the Tente en el Ayre (hold yourself in midair) category theoretically had 127 Indian grandparents and only 1 African. As long as racial mixture involved only two parental groups, things were relatively easy to follow, and even the seventh-generation Tente en el Ayre category was generally understood. Complexity ensued when individuals of the Mulatto, Mestizo, Lobo, and their related mixed castes began to intermarry. These castes mixed three different types of "blood" and required special knowledge to crack the "alchemical" numbers. The mathematical challenges of estimating the participation of each parental population in their blood (and the racial uncertainty this engendered) undoubtedly aided in the stigmatization of these castes. Frustration and mockery toward these "low castes" is expressed with labels like "I-Don't-Understand-You" (also known as Genizaro), which involved the mixture of 1 Indian and 1 African to produce a Lobo offspring, who married an Indian and had an Albarazado, who married a Mulatto to produce a Barcino, who

**Table 5.1.** The most typical caste labels found in paintings of the eighteenth century

| # | Parental groups | Parents | Percentage of parental blood | | | | |
|---|---|---|---|---|---|---|---|
| | | | Spanish | Indian | African | Perception |
| 1 | Indian (I) | I,I | 0 | 100 | 0 | "Pure" |
| 2 | Spanish (S) | S,S | 100 | 0 | 0 | "Pure" |
| 3 | African (A) | A,A | 0 | 0 | 100 | Stigmatized |

*Caste or racially mixed group*

| # | Indian-European axis | Parents | Spanish | Indian | African | Perception |
|---|---|---|---|---|---|---|
| 4 | Mestizo (M) | S,I | 50 | 50 | 0 | Demotion |
| 5 | Castizo (Cz) | S,M | 75 | 25 | 0 | Promotion |
| 6 | Mixed Spaniard (MS) | S,Cz | 87.5 | 12.5 | 0 | Promotion |
| 7 | Chamizo (Chm) | I,Cz | 62.5 | 37.5 | 0 | Demotion |
| 8 | Coyote (Cy) | I,M | 25 | 75 | 0 | Demotion |
| 9 | Mixed Indian (MI) | I,Cy | 12.5 | 87.5 | 0 | Promotion |

| # | African-European axis | Parents | Spanish | Indian | African | Perception |
|---|---|---|---|---|---|---|
| 10 | Mulatto (ML) | S,A | 50 | 0 | 50 | Demotion |
| 11 | Morisco (Mor) | S,ML | 75 | 0 | 25 | Demotion |
| 12 | Albino (Ab) | S,Mor | 87.5 | 0 | 12.5 | Demotion |
| 13 | Negro Torna Atras (Nta) | S,Ab | 93.75 | 0 | 6.25 | Demotion |
| 14 | Grifo (Grf) | ML,Ab | 68.75 | 0 | 31.25 | Demotion |

| Indian-African axis | Parents | Spanish | Indian | African | Perception |
| --- | --- | --- | --- | --- | --- |
| 15 Lobo (L) | I,A | 0 | 50 | 50 | Demotion |
| 16 Sambaiga (Sb) | I,L | 0 | 75 | 25 | Demotion |
| 17 Albarazado (Abz) | I,Sb | 0 | 87.5 | 12.5 | Demotion |
| 18 Chamizo-Indio (ChmI) | I,Abz | 0 | 93.75 | 6.25 | Demotion |
| 19 Cambujo (Cbj) | I,ChmI | 0 | 96.875 | 3.125 | Demotion |
| 20 Lobo Torna Atras (Lta) | I,Cbj | 0 | 98.4375 | 1.5625 | Demotion |
| 21 Tente en el Ayre (Tay) | I,Lta | 0 | 99.21875 | 0.78125 | Demotion |

| Indian-African-European spectrum | Parents | Spanish | Indian | African | Perception |
| --- | --- | --- | --- | --- | --- |
| 22 Mulato Torna Atras (Mlta) or Lobo Tente en el Ayre (Ltay) | ML,M | 50 | 25 | 25 | Demotion |
| 23 Barcino (Bar) | ML,Abz | 25 | 43.75 | 31.25 | Demotion |
| 24 Chino (Chn) | ML,Bar | 40.625 | 37.5 | 21.875 | Demotion |
| 25 Genizaro (Gn) | I,Chn | 18.75 | 60.9375 | 20.3125 | Demotion |
| 26 Gibaro (Gb) | ML,Gn | 9.374 | 55.47 | 35.156 | Demotion |
| 27 Calpamulato (CML) | ML,Sb | 25 | 37.5 | 37.5 | Demotion |
| 28 Mulato-Indio (MLI) | I,ML | 25 | 50 | 25 | Demotion |
| 29 Zambo (Z) | A,MLI | 12.5 | 25 | 62.5 | Demotion |

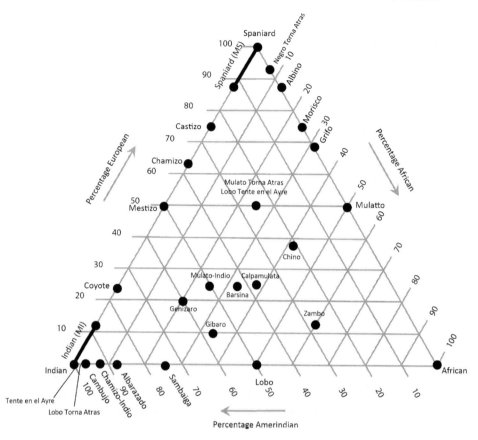

**Figure 5.2.** Distribution of caste labels according to the "percentage" of parental blood.

married a Mulatto to produce a Chino, who then married an Indian to produce a Genizaro! Not surprisingly, most of these categories have been lumped as "other castes" and grouped under the labels of Afro-Mestizo (Aguirre 1946) or *pardo* (Cook and Borah 1974) by scholars.

Despite the fact that the caste system was legally eliminated after the War of Independence with the passing of the Law of September 17, 1822, Mexican society remained in a state of denial about exclusionary practices from the colonial period and their reinforcement during the late nineteenth and early twentieth centuries, including the introduction of "scientific" racism that arrived with a new cycle of economic dependency on Europe and the United States (Deans-Smith and Katzew 2009:12). Indeed, during this period, Nordic and northern European appearances replaced Spanish as ideal and desirable phenotypes. Moreover, the Liberal Republican period of the second half of the nineteenth century witnessed the enforcement of even more exclusionary policies and negative attitudes toward Native populations. Many Liberal politicians demanded the eradication or complete acculturation of indigenous people. Although the labeling system was forbidden and church records ceased recording caste information, Mexicans continued to be brought up with these "normative" values and associated attitudes about variations in skin color, hair texture, and facial features. Unfortunately, anthropological studies in Mexico continue to find a direct correlation between structural poverty and the condition of being Indian, as currently defined by language, cultural practices, and a high percentage of Amerindian genetic markers expressed in the phenotype of individuals (Nutini 1997, 2004, 2005; Nutini and Isaac 2009).

## Population Changes in Colonial Mexico

Perhaps we will never know the actual size of the indigenous population of central Mexico on the eve of the Spanish conquest (for discussions on paleodemography in North America, see Swedlund, chapter 6, and Milner, chapter 2, this volume). Nonetheless, Sherburne Cook and Woodrow Borah (1971:viii) estimated that the preconquest indigenous population of central Mexico decreased by 95.7 percent from 1518 to 1605 (table 5.2) (but see methodological criticism in Henige 1998 and Zambardino 1980). If this was the case, it would be simplistic to blame merely germs and war for the assumed demographic collapse of the first century of Spanish presence in central Mexico (Wolf 1982:134–35). The first conquistadors and colonizers in a handful of urban centers demanded both a significant amount of Indian labor and scarce material resources from geographically extensive hinterlands. The removal of Indian workers from their communities during key moments of the agricultural cycle necessarily affected food production negatively, while tributary demands subtracted valuable economic resources from all communities, increasing the vulnerability of the affected populations and leading to economically induced famine. Weakened individuals

**Table 5.2.** Estimated size of indigenous
population during the early colonial period

| Year | Indigenous population (millions) | Percentage of population decline |
|------|----------------------------------|----------------------------------|
| 1518 | 25.2  | 0.0  |
| 1532 | 16.8  | 33.3 |
| 1548 | 6.3   | 75.0 |
| 1568 | 2.65  | 89.5 |
| 1585 | 1.9   | 92.5 |
| 1595 | 1.375 | 94.5 |
| 1605 | 1.075 | 95.7 |

*Source:* Data from Cook and Borah 1971:viii.

suffering from losses of up to 20 percent of their body weight were easy prey for epidemics, like *cocolitzi*, a hemorrhagic fever disease caused by an unidentified pathogen, which resurged repeatedly from 1545 to 1576 (Acuña-Soto et al. 2000). At the same time, Catholic religious rules forbade Indian males from practicing polygamy, preventing demographic recovery from these repeated cycles of epidemics.

Parallel to the collapse of the Native population, interracial unions began and some practices of the caste system also developed, influencing the way people married and reproduced. Legal marriages between the daughters of Native caciques and Spaniards are known to have taken place from the beginning of the conquest; however, many more women were taken by force. Perhaps the first large-scale event of this nature was the capture of the wives and daughters of Mexica warriors during the siege of Tenochtitlan. These women were immediately subjected to concubinage and produced the first large cohort of Mestizo children in 1522, with some Spaniards bragging that they had had dozens of children with these Indian women (Díaz del Castillo 2008:121, 310).

The scarcity of European women in New Spain required the Spaniards to depend predominantly on Indian women for partners, and then later on Mestizo women (for an in-depth analysis on women captives, see Cameron, chapter 7, and Martin, chapter 4, this volume). Some indigenous women had phenotypic features similar to those of

Spaniards and were particularly targeted as concubines. The defeated Aztecs painfully described how during the abandonment of Tenochtitlan, the Spaniards posted themselves along the few causeways leaving the island and were selecting and seizing all women of "yellow bodies" (Sahagún 1975:122). The phrase that some women were "very beautiful for an Indian" is recurrent in the accounts of the conquest and indicates the practice of selecting Native American phenotypic traits similar to European ones (Díaz del Castillo 2008:83, 236; Landa 1982:27). This in turn created a pool of phenotypically light-skinned Mestizos who were easily assimilated into the Spanish group. Spaniards born in America were self-conscious about their mixed heritage and were the ones who worked the hardest to "purify their blood." Toward this end, successful Spanish families of New Spain literally embarked on "importing" bridegrooms from the Iberian peninsula for their daughters, creating a society in which European phenotypes were highly appreciated and promoted. The traveler Gemelli Carreri observed this situation in 1697, noting that wealthy families from Mexico City paid large dowries to marry their daughters with Spaniards from Spain, even if those individuals were poor (Carreri 1983 [1700]:45).

The above-mentioned practices indicate that demographic figures for Mestizo individuals according to Aguirre (1946:237) and Cook and Borah (1974:197) greatly underestimate the actual numbers (see table 5.3). Not only were the Spaniards relying on Mestizo individuals for partners, but it is also apparent that Indian males and females began doing the same. I suspect that the Mestizos reported in table 5.3 are those whom no one wanted to claim and were considered illegitimate by both Spaniards and Indians. The continuation of this process in other regions subtracted many fertile indigenous women from the pool of available marriage partners for indigenous males, immediately affecting demography and provoking changes in the genetic and phenotypic composition of indigenous populations. Indeed, genetic samples of nine self-identified Indian groups in Mexico present admixtures with Europeans that range from 8.8 percent for the Huicholes to 37.3 percent for the Huaxtecs, indicating that there are no "pure" Indian populations in Mexico (Bonilla et al. 2005; Lisker and Babinsky 1986:145; Lisker et al. 1996:395). Table 5.3 demonstrates that regardless of the collapse of the indigenous population, the Native group continued to be the largest

**Table 5.3.** Population by caste in New Spain

| | Absolute numbers | | | | |
|---|---|---|---|---|---|
| Year | Spaniards | Africans and descendants | Mestizos | Total non-Indians | Indians |
| 1570 | 17,711 | 23,006 | 2,435 | 43,152 | 2,650,000 |
| 1646 | 182,348 | 151,618 | 10,9042 | 443,008 | 1,269,607 |
| 1742 | 401,326 | 286,327 | 249,368 | 937,021 | 1,540,256 |
| 1793 | 685,362 | 375,890 | 418,568 | 1,479,820 | 2,319,741 |
| 1810 | 1,107,367 | 634,461 | 704,245 | 2,446,073 | 3,676,281 |

| | As percentage of non-Indians | | |
|---|---|---|---|
| Year | Spaniards | Africans and descendants | Mestizos |
| 1570 | 41.04 | 53.31 | 5.64 |
| 1646 | 41.16 | 34.22 | 24.61 |
| 1742 | 42.83 | 30.56 | 26.61 |
| 1793 | 46.31 | 25.40 | 28.29 |
| 1810 | 45.27 | 25.94 | 28.79 |

| | As percentage of total population | | | | |
|---|---|---|---|---|---|
| Year | Spaniards | Africans and descendants | Mestizos | Indians | Non-Indians |
| 1570 | 0.66 | 0.85 | 0.09 | 98.40 | 1.60 |
| 1646 | 10.65 | 8.85 | 6.37 | 74.13 | 25.87 |
| 1742 | 16.20 | 11.56 | 10.07 | 62.18 | 37.82 |
| 1793 | 18.04 | 9.89 | 11.02 | 61.05 | 38.95 |
| 1810 | 18.09 | 10.36 | 11.50 | 60.05 | 39.95 |

*Source:* Data from Aguirre 1946:237.

*Note:* Colonial demographic figures cannot be taken at face value, and their absolute numbers are tentative; I provide them above only as an indication of major demographic trends. Here, I have relied on the statistics of Aguirre (1946), as do Cook and Borah (1974:180–269), because he presents statistics on caste demography for the entire colonial period. I have simplified Aguirre's classification of Euro-Mestizo, Afro-Mestizo, and Indo-Mestizo, as do Cook and Borah, by combining the Euro-Mestizo group (legitimate Mestizos) with the Spanish group and merging the African and Afro-Mestizo groups into a single category of Africans and their descendants. The Indo-Mestizo group (illegitimate Mestizos) was left simply as Mestizos. I used Cook and Borah's (1971:viii) 1570 Native population estimates (see table 5.2).

demographic group of New Spain in absolute numbers; however, one does see a dramatic increase in the relative number of Spaniards, Mestizos, and Africans and their related castes during the seventeenth century—to a point that in the mid-eighteenth century the non-Indian population was approaching 40 percent of the total population. The number of Mestizos finally caught up with the African castes by the second half of the eighteenth century, which suggests that the Spanish group became more closed and selective in the acceptance of newly created Mestizos. When the Spanish and Indian groups ceased absorbing Mestizos, the Mestizo population grew rapidly, surpassing the African group. The consolidation of the Mestizo group seems to have lowered the population number of the Indian group. Demographically speaking, any Indian marrying outside the group would be counted as a permanent loss, since technically that individual, together with his/her children, would add to the number of mixed-heritage people. And so, even when the Indian group grew in absolute terms, it still consistently lost its percentage of demographic dominance, a pattern that has continued until the present day. In the year 2000, their number (based on the capacity to speak a Native language) was estimated to be 6,044,547 people, but their demographic participation in the total population was only 7.1 percent (INEGI 2004:4). These numbers represent the demography of erasure, meaning that even though phenotypically Mexico continues to be strongly indigenous, beginning early in the colonial era an indigenous identity was often not beneficial, so people would use interracial unions to transform the identity of their children or sometimes even themselves by adopting the identity of their partner.

## Marriage Strategies and the Long-Term Impacts of the Caste System on the Economic Status of Individuals

The caste values that emerged during the sixteenth and seventeenth centuries were materialized in the caste paintings of the eighteenth century, and the associated linguistic and visual media helped to promote and re-create a racially oriented society that has continued impacting the well-being of those groups and individuals with strong indigenous cultures and phenotypes. The unfolding impacts of these racial values and practices on the marital patterns of the late colonial period can be observed by studying the census of 1777, taken at the height of the popularity of the caste paintings. Cook and Borah (1974:240) used this census to show that while the colonial castes were not monolithic, they were neither porous nor breached easily. Marriage in colonial Mexico was not random but carefully planned following well-known caste divisions.

Cook and Borah (1974:251) supported their argument by formulating the following hypothesis: "In late colonial Mexico, the sole factor which determined the ethnic character of a marital or reproductive union was random propinquity or contact between individuals in an unrestricted environment." They then proceeded to test it by generating expected numbers of unions for specific parishes given the stated total number of individuals of each sex and caste and the probability that the combinations occurred from random propinquity alone. The expected numbers were compared to the observed numbers, and Cook and Borah measured the degree of the observed from the expected by taking the ratio of the two magnitudes (observed/expected). If the ratio equaled 1.0, then the unions were the result of random propinquity; if the ratio was larger or smaller than 1.0, other factors besides randomness explained the unions. In their experiment, Cook and Borah found that intragroup marriages always occurred at ratios two to three times larger than 1.0, meaning that the observed number of intragroup marriages was much higher than those expected under the random hypothesis. They also found that the ratio for extragroup marriages was always smaller than 1.0, meaning that the observed number of extragroup marriages was less than expected under the condition of random propinquity (sometimes ten times less). Here, I reproduce their matrix for Antequera (Oaxaca City), since the situation there was typical for many other locales (see table 5.4).

The general findings show that in 1777 only 9.047 percent of males and 9.029 percent of females married outside their caste group. This result indicates that no universal, consistent bias referable to sex appears to have existed and that with every caste group, the proportion of intragroup unions exceeds that of any extragroup combination. Therefore, the universal tendency in 1777 was for more men and women of every caste type to choose a legal spouse within the same group rather than

**Table 5.4.** Matrix for intragroup and extragroup marriages in 1777 Antequera (Oaxaca City)

| | E(m) | M(m) | P(m) | I(m) | Total female |
|---|---|---|---|---|---|
| E(f) | 725 (314) 2.308 | 165 (238) 0.693 | 90 (167) 0.54 | 25 (286) 0.087 | 1,005 |
| M(f) | 142 (199) 0.714 | 307 (150) 2.048 | 104 (105) 0.991 | 81 (180) 0.451 | 634 |
| P(f) | 72 (157) 0.457 | 127 (119) 1.068 | 257 (83) 3.096 | 45 (142) 0.317 | 501 |
| I(f) | 47 (316) 0.149 | 148 (240) 0.617 | 72 (168) 0.429 | 744 (287) 2.592 | 1,011 |
| Total male | 986 | 747 | 523 | 895 | 3,151 |

*Source*: Data from Cook and Borah 1974:242.
*Note*: In each square are three numbers. The first (top) is the observed number, as derived from the census records, for the combination indicated. The second (in parentheses) is the number expected under the hypothesis of random propinquity. The third is the ratio of the observed to the expected number.
*Abbreviations*: (m) = male; (f) = female; E = Español; M = Mestizo; I = Indian; P = Pardo, a generic term referring to an individual in the African castes.

intermarry with another group (Cook and Borah 1974:251). The other interesting finding is that when Spaniards could not marry within their group, they tended to seek Mestizos rather than Mulattoes or Indians as marital partners. When Indians, Mulattoes, and Mestizos married outside their groups, they did not manifest any marked selectivity in the choice of spouse belonging to a particular caste. Unfortunately, the census does not provide clues as to extramarital patterns of individuals, because only legal unions were counted. Nonetheless, we can glean some information on illegitimate offspring from baptismal records of some parishes. Church documents from the early eighteenth century report that 17 percent of baptized children were illegitimate. Also noteworthy in the baptismal records is that all caste groups had similar proportions of illegitimate children (Rabell 1994). I assume that this was an open arena wherein interracial reproduction continued, despite the strict caste restrictions of the eighteenth century.

The use of caste categories was forbidden after 1822; still, the quantification of the Native population was reintroduced in 1895.[6] There is a significant change when comparing the last colonial tally of 1810 (3.6 million Indians, representing 60 percent of the total population) to the census of 1895 (2.03 million Indians, representing only 16.1 percent of the total population). First, beyond any normal error in counting methodologies, it is difficult to explain the decrease in the Native population without taking into account the likely change of identity by significant numbers of individuals who possessed both the cultural and phenotypic characteristics to join the Mestizo group. This reinforces the idea that many individuals who used to be counted as Indians during the colonial period were actually Euro-Mestizos and Afro-Mestizos. Native groups under the colonial regime received certain protections and access to communal lands, and many poor Mestizos and mixed Africans found it convenient to pass as Indians. This changed substantially with the Liberal governments that ruled Mexico during the nineteenth century, when laws were passed to seize communal lands and being an Indian became the most negatively stigmatized status in society. Thus, these factors need to be considered when evaluating the dramatic increase of the non-Indian population from 2.4 million to 10.5 million people between 1810 and 1895.[7] The prerogatives and legislation put in place by the colonial regime to protect the communal holdings of the indigenous communities were seen as impediments to the full integration of the indigenous population into the Mexican state and were systematically dismantled during this period. In practice the independent Republic of Mexico condemned all those who refused to abandon their indigenous identity. The continuation during the nineteenth and twentieth centuries of many of the exclusionary practices that emerged in the colonial period has reinforced patterns of structural poverty within the indigenous population. Poverty, hunger, and deprivation are directly associated with debilitating maladies and immunological deficiency that increase mortality rates (for study cases in North America, see Larsen, chapter 3, Kelton, chapter 8, and Hull, chapter 9, this volume). This was obvious during the last epidemic of cholera occurring in the transition period of the Colonial regime to the Independent period (1813–33), when the disease decimated the poor of Mexico, who happened to be predominantly identified with the disenfranchised castes (Márquez 1994).

This state of structural poverty and its associated diseases endures today. Genetic studies performed in Mexico over the past thirty years have identified that socioeconomic factors play a large role in the variation of ancestry informative markers (AIMs) in the population of the country, wherein low-income individuals and those from the lower middle class have higher percentages of indigenous AIMs, while individuals from the high-income class (plutocracy, political echelon, and prestige upper middle class) present a high percentage of European AIMs (Garza-Chapa 1983; Nutini and Isaac 2009). Genetic studies are inadvertently corroborating what folk wisdom and socioeconomic studies were already demonstrating: social class in Mexico is directly correlated with gene frequency distribution, such that individuals with high percentages of Amerindian AIMs and strong Indian phenotypes are usually poorer than those with higher European AIMs (Lisker et al. 1995:216; Nutini 1997). Studies of *mestizaje* demonstrate how Mexico's elites try to maintain or acquire more European phenotypic traits by attempting to marry their children with individuals exhibiting a more European phenotype. Interestingly, this process socially operates as intergenerational group selection, since grandparents and parents promote the acquisition of such traits by investing in sending their children to private schools in Mexico or abroad, where they are more likely to find European-like partners. Competition arises between siblings and close relatives to acquire and "bank" partners with the most European phenotypic traits, because extended family networking gains social prestige as more of the younger members marry into the "right" phenotype (Garza-Chapa 1983; Lisker et al. 1995:216; Nutini 1997). Popular

magazines depicting the lifestyles of Mexican elites, including their visits to exclusive resorts, malls, private schools, and hospitals of Mexico,
the United States, and Europe, show that indeed they look European,
and they enhance such looks through the conscious manipulation of
their phenotypes to "correct" any trace of Indian somatic traits by dye-
ing their hair, using "whitening" cosmetics, wearing cosmetic contact
lenses, or subjecting themselves to plastic surgery (Nutini 1997). This
conscious and subconscious erasure and denial of the indigenous identity sheds light on the obsession and struggles of past and present-day
Mexican elites to distance themselves from their Indian/African female
ancestors by the creation of strict and artificial somatic labels and clas-
sifications. Because phenotype plays such a critical role in the actual opportunities that any individual will have in his/her lifetime, the unequal
distribution of wealth affects the indigenous groups who continue to
be the poorest and most marginalized of all social segments of Mexican
society according to the official statistics of the Mexican government
(CEFP 2008; CONEVAL 2005; INEGI 2004; Serrano 2006).

## The Tyranny of *Pigmentocracia*

The above described patterns created a system that has been called *pig-
mentocracia* in Latin America, or the political and economic system in
which the allocation of wealth and political positions is based on slight
variations of skin color and phenotypic features, whereby European features enjoy the highest status, followed by light-skinned Mestizos, while
those with African and Indian features occupy the lowest status (Pérez
de Barradas 1976 [1948]:213; Wolf 1982:380). As we have seen in colonial
demographic studies of the Mexican population in the eighteenth century, there was a conscious effort to create and maintain rules of exclusion based on folk racial categories known as the Spanish castes. Despite
the genealogical fictions depicted in the caste paintings of this period,
they nonetheless provide access to the core beliefs, values, and practices
of the racial system imposed by European expansion on Amerindian
groups. Even if in the long run mestizaje has come to dominate the
identity of Mexico, caste discrimination in the colonial period did affect
the demographic health of indigenous groups due to the *opportunity cost*
of removing a significant number of indigenous females of reproductive

age, which prevented demographic recovery from the overall effects of Spanish colonialism. These women and their offspring were permanently lost to the Indian group. Among the long-term impacts of exclusionary policies associated with the caste system were major changes in the erasure of identities, when most of the mixed people, given the opportunity, chose to be associated with the Spanish group more than with the Indian. This in turn has promoted a conscious process of trying to acquire European phenotypic traits to be passed on to the subsequent generation. With the rejection of the Native phenotype, Indian and dark-skinned Mestizo individuals have been deprived of economic and social opportunities during their lifetimes, subsuming them and their descendants into structural poverty. At the same time, economic opportunities have primarily been offered to individuals of European phenotype—a situation that created a ruling and plutocratic class phenotypically more European but still mixed that continues the relentless pursuit of becoming more "white." According to popular lore, just a few more marriages would do it! Still, the problem remains: how to find partners of European descent in a country where twenty-five generations ago, a thousand Spanish males decided to create a "New Spain" but forgot to bring their wives with them. It is time for Mexican society to confront veiled racial practices if the country aspires to improve its social and economic standing. It is time for Mexico to eliminate its pervasive colonial mentality.

## Notes

1. Current anthropological literature approaches the study of caste based on the British colonial experiences with the *jātis* of the Indian subcontinent. The jātis are categories of related persons that supposedly share the same physical and moral substance. According to Brahmin scripts, people are categorized according to a fourfold social division based on a spiritual hierarchy and occupation, atop which is the *brahmana* (Brahmin), followed by the *ksatriya* (warrior/king); these two have the privilege of enforcing the brahminical law over the *vaiśya* (merchant) and *śudra* (laborer) (Dumont 1980). The current practice of caste politics in the Republic of India is a product of its British colonial history (Dirks 2001) and is different from the *casta* practices in the Spanish colonies, which were based on the procreation patterns of individuals of Spanish, African, and Amerindian origins, as discussed in this chapter.

2. The difficulty in studying the Spanish caste system is the conflation of core beliefs within a folk system that attempted to create and reproduce social inequality based on inherited and achieved status, religious creeds, cultural practices, identity, marriage regulations, and the reproductive system of individuals and groups. Folk systems tend to reduce this complexity to a small number of variables: fictitious genealogies and religion were the norm in the Iberian Peninsula. In the colonies, however, phenotype, wealth, and the practice of a European versus an indigenous culture became the norm. Because wealth was predominantly restricted to the European segment of the population, phenotypic and cultural selection of spouses has had a direct impact on the genotype of different social estates and classes in colonial Latin America. Nonetheless, the structuration of cultural practices and institutions is the primary driver of the Spanish caste system.

3. A Castizo was a Spanish-Indian individual with "blood" from six European grandparents out of eight.

4. The English spelling of "Mulatto" will be used throughout the text except where it appears as part of the colonial Spanish term; in these instances the Spanish spelling (Mulato) will be retained.

5. There are verbal categories in this gap between Mulattoes and Africans, but they are very rare and specialized (see Pérez de Barradas 1976 [1948]:232–38).

6. Mexican censuses of indigenous people ask for the number of individuals in a household who are older than five years of age and can speak a Native language.

7. The census of 1895 estimated that only 48,000 foreigners resided in Mexico. This was a small percentage of the total population.

## References

Acuña-Soto, Rudolfo, Leticia Calderón Romero, and James H. Maguire. 2000. Large epidemics of hemorrhagic fevers in Mexico, 1545–1815. American Journal of Tropical Medicine and Hygiene 62(6):733–39.

Aguirre Beltrán, Gonzalo. 1946. La población negra de México, 1519–1810: Estudio etnohistórico. Mexico City: Fondo de Cultura Económica.

Aldama, Arturo. 2001. The Chicana/o and the Native American "other" talk back: Theories of the speaking subject in a (post?) colonial context. *In* Disrupting Savagism: Intersecting Chicana/o, Mexican Immigrant, and Native American Struggles for Self-Representation, edited by Arturo Aldama, 3–33. Durham, NC: Duke University Press.

Bonilla, Carolina, Gerardo Gutiérrez, Esteban J. Parra, Christopher Kline, and Mark Shriver. 2005. Admixture analysis of a rural population of the state of Guerrero, Mexico. American Journal of Physical Anthropology 128:861–69.

Bourdieu, Pierre. 2000. Outline of a Theory of Practice. Cambridge: Cambridge University Press.

Carreri, Gemelli. 1983 [1700]. Viaje a la Nueva España. Vol. 2. Mexico City: Jorge Porrúa.

CEFP. 2008. Distribución del ingreso y desigualdad en México: Un análisis sobre la ENIGH, 2000–2006. Mexico City: Centro de Estudios de las Finanzas Públicas de la Cámara de Diputados.

Comaroff, John. 1987. Of totemism and ethnicity: Consciousness, practice and the signs of inequality. Ethnos 52(3–4):301–23.

CONEVAL. 2005. Mapas de pobreza y rezago social: Nacional. Mexico City: Consejo Nacional de Evaluación de la Política de Desarrollo Social.

Cook, Sherburne F., and Woodrow Borah. 1971. Essays in Population History: Mexico and Caribbean. Vol. 1. Berkeley: University of California Press.

———. 1974. Essays in Population History: Mexico and Caribbean. Vol. 2. Berkeley: University of California Press.

Córdova, James M., and Claire Farago. 2012. Casta paintings and self-fashioning artists in New Spain. In At the Crossroads: The Arts of Spanish America and Early Global Trade, 1492–1850, edited by Donna Pierce and Ronald Otsuka, 129–54. Papers from the 2010 Mayer Center Symposium at the Denver Art Museum. Denver, CO: Denver Art Museum.

Deans-Smith, Susan. 2009. "Dishonor in the hands of Indians, Spaniards, and blacks": The (racial) politics of painting in early modern Mexico. In Race Classification: The Case of Mexican America, edited by Ilona Katzew and Susan Deans-Smith, 43–72. Stanford: Stanford University Press.

Deans-Smith, Susan, and Ilona Katzew. 2009. Introduction: The alchemy of race in Mexican America. In Race Classification: The Case of Mexican America, edited by Ilona Katzew and Susan Deans-Smith, 1–24. Stanford: Stanford University Press.

Díaz del Castillo, Bernal. 2008. The History of the Conquest of New Spain. Edited by David Carrasco. Albuquerque: University of New Mexico Press.

Diccionario de Autoridades. 2002. Diccionario de autoridades de la Real Academia Española. 3 vols. Madrid, Spain: Editorial Gredos.

Dirks, Nicholas B. 2001. Castes of Mind: Colonialism and the Making of Modern India. Princeton: Princeton University Press.

Dumont, Louis. 1980. Homo Hierarchicus: The Caste System and Its Implications. Chicago: University of Chicago Press.

Elliott, John H. 1998. The Old World and the New: 1492–1650. Cambridge: Cambridge University Press.

Garza-Chapa, Raul. 1983. Genetic distances for ABO and Rh(D) blood groups in the state of Nuevo León, Mexico. Biodemography and Social Biology 30:24–31.

Haskett, Robert S. 1988. Living in two worlds: Cultural continuity and change among Cuernavaca's colonial indigenous ruling elite. Ethnohistory 35(1):34–59.

Henige, David. 1998. Numbers from Nowhere: The American Indian Contact Population Debate. Norman: University of Oklahoma Press.

Horowitz, Donald L. 1985. Ethnic Groups in Conflict. Berkeley: University of California Press.

INEGI. 2004. La población indígena en México. Mexico City: Instituto Nacional de Estadística, Geografía e Informática.

Katzew, Ilona, ed. 1996a. New World Orders: Casta Paintings and Colonial Latin America. New York: Americas Society Art Gallery.

———. 1996b. Casta paintings: Identity and social stratification in colonial Mexico. *In* New World Orders: Casta Paintings and Colonial Latin America, edited by Ilona Katzew, 9–29. New York: Americas Society Art Gallery.

Klor de Alva, Jorge J. 1996. Mestizaje from Spain to Aztlán: On the control and classification of collective identities. *In* New World Orders: Casta Paintings and Colonial Latin America, edited by Ilona Katzew, 58–71. New York: Americas Society Art Gallery.

Landa, Diego de. 1982. Relación de las cosas de Yucatán. 12th ed. Introduction by Angel Garibay K. Mexico City: Editorial Porrúa.

Landers, Jane G., and Barry M. Robinson, eds. 2006. Slaves, Subjects, and Subversives: Blacks in Colonial Latin America. Albuquerque: University of New Mexico Press.

Lisker, Rubén, and Victoria Babinsky. 1986. Admixture estimates in nine Mexican Indian groups and five east coast localities. Revista de Investigación Clínica 38:145–49.

Lisker, Ruben, Eva Ramírez, and Victoria Babinsky. 1996. Genetic structure of autochthonous populations of Meso-America: Mexico. Human Biology 68(3):395–404.

Lisker, Rubén, Eva Ramírez, Clicerio González-Villalpando, and Michael P. Stern. 1995. Racial admixture in a Mestizo population from Mexico City. American Journal of Human Biology 7:213–16.

Marks, Jonathan. 1996. Science and race. American Behavioral Scientist 40(2):123–33.

Márquez, Morfín Lourdes. 1994. La desigualdad ante la muerte en la ciudad de México: El tifo y el cólera (1813–1833). Mexico City: Siglo XXI.

Martínez, María Elena. 2008. Genealogical Fictions: *Limpieza de Sangre*, Religion, and Gender in Colonial Mexico. Stanford: Stanford University Press.

———. 2009. The language, genealogy, and classification of "race" in colonial Mexico. *In* Race Classification: The Case of Mexican America, edited by Ilona Katzew and Susan Deans-Smith, 25–42. Stanford: Stanford University Press.

Mörner, Magnus. 1967. Race Mixture in the History of Latin America. Boston: Little, Brown.

Nutini, Hugo G. 1997. Class and ethnicity in Mexico: Somatic and racial considerations. Ethnology 36(3):227–38.

———. 2004. The Mexican Aristocracy: An Expressive Ethnography, 1910–2000. Austin: University of Texas Press.

———. 2005. Social Stratification and Mobility in Central Veracruz. Austin: University of Texas Press.

Nutini, Hugo G., and Barry L. Isaac. 2009. Social Stratification in Central Mexico, 1500–2000. Austin: University of Texas Press.

Pérez de Barradas, José. 1976 [1948]. Los mestizos de América. Madrid, Spain: Espasa-Calpe.

Rabell, Cecilia. 1994. Matrimonio y raza en una parroquia rural: San Luís de la Paz, Guanajuato. In Historia y población en México (Siglos XVI–XIX), edited by Thomas Calvo, 163–204. Mexico City: El Colegio de México.

Restall, Mathew. 2005. Beyond Black and Red: African-Native Relations in Colonial Latin America. Albuquerque: University of New Mexico Press.

Sahagún, Bernardino. 1975. Florentine Codex: General History of the Things of New Spain. Book 12: The Conquest of Mexico. Translated by Arthur J. O. Anderson and Charles E. Dibble. Santa Fe, NM: School of American Research.

Serrano, Carreto Enrique, ed. 2006. Regiones indígenas de México. Mexico City: Comisión Nacional para el Desarrollo de los Pueblos Indígenas and Programa de las Naciones Unidas para el Desarrollo.

Stoler, Ann Laura. 1995. Race and the Education of Desire: Foucault's "History of Sexuality" and the Colonial Order of Things. Durham, NC: Duke University Press.

Taylor, William. 2009. Preface. In Race Classification: The Case of Mexican America, edited by Ilona Katzew and Susan Deans-Smith, ix–xviii. Stanford: Stanford University Press.

Vinson, Ben, III. 2001. Bearing Arms for His Majesty: The Free Colored Militia in Colonial Mexico. Stanford: Stanford University Press.

Wagley, Charles. 1965. On the concept of social race in the Americas. In Contemporary Cultures and Societies of Latin America, edited by Dwight B. Heath and Richard N. Adams, 531–45. New York: Random House.

Wolf, Eric R. 1982. Europe and the People Without History. Berkeley: University of California Press.

Zambardino, Rudolph. 1980. Mexico's population in the sixteenth century: Demographic anomaly or mathematical illusion? Journal of Interdisciplinary History 11(1):1–27.

# Contagion, Conflict, and Captivity in Interior New England

**6**

## Native American and European Contacts in the Middle Connecticut River Valley of Massachusetts, 1616–2004

*Alan C. Swedlund*

Most of us are familiar with the story of Governor Bradford and his fellow passengers settling in 1621 at Patuxet—to be named Plymouth by the English—and encountering their first Natives. Samoset, a northern Abenaki, enters their encampment, addresses them in English, and informs them that he will return with the more fluent Tisquantum—"Squanto"—who is a Native of Patuxet. By this time, both men have traveled widely along the Eastern Seaboard, and Squanto, all the way to Spain and England.[1]

This story, told in countless varying and undoubtedly inaccurate ways to schoolchildren and scholars alike, uncovers several themes of this book. Although American history textbooks often begin their section on New England with the Pilgrims and Indians at Plymouth, colonial historians have long known that by 1621 we are already several pages into the metaphorical chapter of Native-English encounters in New England. Conflict, captivity, enslavement, devastating disease, and displacement had all been in process for some time (see Jones 2004). Native communities from Maine to Long Island Sound had expanded on their traditional patterns of settlement rounds, interaction, and linguistic skill to include a new and more threatening group than they ever could have anticipated, and over the next several years their lives would be irrevocably changed. By 1629 the Massachusetts Bay Colony had been established, and by the early 1630s English fur traders were moving up the Connecticut River, leapfrogging the Dutch at Hartford into present-day Massachusetts. The great smallpox epidemic of 1633–34 brought European diseases inland, spreading westward through what is now New York and beyond. The stage for a full catastrophe, or what Russell Thornton (1987) and David Stannard (1992) have called the American Holocaust, was now in place in the Northeast.

In this chapter, after some brief remarks on European settlement of the Massachusetts coast, I focus attention westerly, away from the New England coast to interior New England, specifically, the middle Connecticut River valley, homeland of the Pocumtucks, Agawams, Norwottucks, Woronocos, and Sokokis, at times all lumped together as Pocumtuck. These loosely confederated bands and communities were Algonquian speaking, and they were closely related to the Nipmucks to the east and the Abenakis to the northeast. To the west and northwest—between the Connecticut and Hudson Rivers—were the Mahicans, also Algonquian speakers, and farther to the west, the Mohawks and other Iroquoian speakers. To the south were the Mohegans and Pequots in what is present-day Connecticut and the Narragansetts of Rhode Island (see figure 6.1). At the edges of the core area of any of these groups, identities were more fluid and could shift or blend together in the 1600s and before, so the Native community of Squakheag—where the town of Northfield, Massachusetts, is today, for example—has been variously identified historically as Pocumtuck, Nipmuck, and Sokoki-Abenaki (e.g., Johnson 1999; Salisbury 1982; Thomas 1979).

The Connecticut River, with its headwaters on the Canadian border and its endpoint in Long Island Sound, is the longest, largest river in New England. It served as a major north-south transportation route for Native Americans for over six thousand years and continues in that capacity to this day. In the center of the Pocumtuck homeland, at the confluence of the Deerfield and Connecticut Rivers, is the intersection of a major east-west route going back many centuries: the Mohawk Trail. Though buffered somewhat from the initial European invasion by the English along coastal New England, the French to the north and along the St. Lawrence, and the Dutch in the area of Long Island and New York, the middle Connecticut valley was heavily impacted by European trade, disease, and occupation in a few short years. It may be true, as several have noted, that the epidemic of 1616–17 did not penetrate this far into the interior, but the great smallpox epidemic of 1633–35—affecting all of New England, New York, and adjoining Canadian provinces—greatly impacted groups in the region (Bradford in Thomas

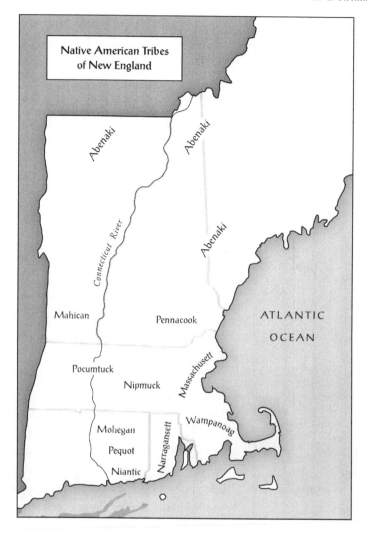

**Figure 6.1.** Approximate tribal locations in New England circa 1620. (Map by Jack Harrison.)

1979). The purpose of this chapter is not, then, to find some area and population that can serve as a case study of isolation, independence, or control, but rather to look at a highly connected and integrated subregion of New England that was perhaps spared the first epidemic wave but was already enmeshed in dense intertribal relations and very quickly into the processes of European colonialism, with all its consequences.

A purpose of this chapter, in addition to recounting a case study of contact, contagion, conflict, and captivity in one region, is to redress traditional narratives and offer some examples of more-recent narrative styles and epistemologies. The middle Connecticut valley was a very important site of conflict during and around the time of King Philip's War (1675–76), but its most well-known moment in contact period history is the famous—and some have claimed infamous—French and Indian raid on English settlers in Deerfield in 1704. The raid on Deerfield, and its subsequent captive-taking, is an emblematic example of the complex interrelations among Native and colonial settlements at this point in the history of the Northeast.

The complexity of this period in the Connecticut valley's history is easily subverted when attempting a narrow argument, and also the argument can easily become a gross oversimplification. I believe a more complete understanding comes from consideration of the multiple forces impacting the region and alternative ways of thinking about them. This would include consideration of ideas coming from some areas of postcolonial theory, which offer additional ways of understanding the history of contact and colonialism in America and which complement the rigorous historical and biocultural analyses recently offered by scholars (many of whom are represented in this book). Specifically, these have to do with notions of epidemics and plague as categories, with embodiment of race and disease in Native peoples, and with narratives of erasure of colonized people. These allow us to step outside of our usual epistemological boundaries when talking about disease and to find new ways to unravel and better interpret the colonial-Native experience. A few Euro-American and Native American scholars of the region have drawn our attention to how contact narratives have often overlooked or erased a more accurate and comprehensive Native history and point to the persistence and resiliency of Native Americans in New England to the present day. My argument, then, is that Native depopulation in New England can only be understood as a multicausal process, involving many factors of colonial occupation of a region inhabited by indigenous people, and that the narrative arc by which we historicize this encounter has often obscured the underlying processes involved.

## Numbers and Nosologies

Of those millions of indigenous people inhabiting North America prior to contact, perhaps 350,000 resided in the Northeast, according to Douglas Ubelaker (1992:173), and the numbers for New England range from a low of approximately 60,000 (Cook 1976:84) to over 100,000 (e.g., Thomas 1979). Neal Salisbury (personal communication, 2012) now estimates approximately 100,000 for southern New England alone, which I regard as reasonable. The vast majority of New England Natives were concentrated in southern New England, where a more temperate climate permitted agriculture and more-productive foraging. The Pocumtucks, depending on how they are defined, have been estimated at a low of 2,500 (Cook 1976) to 15,200 (Snow 1980:40; see also Snow and Lanphear 1988:24).[2]

If these numbers can be accepted as rough approximations for the region in 1600, then we can reduce them by at least 50 percent, and some would argue as much as 90 percent in some locales, for the Native population of New England by 1700. If I understand him correctly, Ubelaker (1992:173) would place the percentage reduction at about 58 percent of the total in 1600 for the Northeast as a whole, and this is well below historical estimates that often claimed as much as a 95 percent drop. Dean Snow and Kim Lanphear (1988:24) estimated losses of 80–90 percent in New England, with a 95 percent mortality rate for the Pocumtucks. These wide-ranging numbers leave much to be desired in terms of trying to assess actual population change resulting from early European contact in the Americas. While suggestive, they are inadequate to the task of making rigorous conclusions about the true magnitude of depopulation in the region.

The study of human remains has a long-standing tradition in the history of health, but it is also fraught with political and ideological minefields. As is well known, thousands of burials were unceremoniously excavated and pillaged in the past without permission from or in consideration of Native descendants. Furthermore, at least until the 1980s, the study of human remains by physical anthropologists had much more to do with a vulgar and simplistic study of human racial typology than with serious questions about Native American health (e.g., see critical reviews in Gould 1986 [1981] and Armelagos and Van

Gerven 2003). Small wonder, then, that there is great resistance among Native Americans to the use of human remains for determinations of health status.

In recent years there are growing numbers of anthropologists who have renounced past practices and have worked in collaboration with Native representatives to study health in the past; a few anthropologists of these are themselves of Native ancestry. Paleopathology, sexing, and aging performed on a large skeletal series absent of historical documentation can provide a considerable amount of information on the overall health of a community and indications of average age at death. However, it must be added that in the Northeast, remains useful for assessment of past health are rare owing to poor preservation in the acidic soils of New England and New York.

Postcontact information on actual human remains is similarly limited, although one skeletal series from Rhode Island, site RI1000 (see Rubertone 2001), dated approximately to the mid-1600s and conducted in collaboration with the Narragansetts, provides a small glimpse of health at this time. There are fifty-six individuals, but the remains are skewed heavily to subadults and young females. Researchers reported a high number of infectious lesions, many suggesting tuberculosis, as well as frequent dental caries and some enamel hypoplasias (see Baker 1994; Carlson et al. 1992). These indicators are difficult to generalize from, given the small sample size and the nature of the evidence, but they are consistent with a population that was under severe duress from colonial disruption.

The lack of good direct physical evidence on the history of the health of New England's Native population brings researchers back to the historical reports (problematic as they are) and documentation of European explorers, Native oral traditions, fishermen, traders, settlers, and those who studied them. As anecdotal as these sources are, they generally report healthy and robust individuals at the time of earliest contact (e.g., summaries in Jones 2004 and Salisbury 1982), but encounters shortly thereafter famously report empty villages and sickly or dying survivors.

One of the most difficult contact epidemics to name was the one first reported, that of 1616–17. Before contact, the Native population of northern New England assuredly would have faced periodic, seasonal food shortages and would have been challenged by the long New England winters. Natives to the south would have fared better, no doubt, but New England winters even on Cape Cod and in Narragansett Bay can be harsh. When food shortages did occur, as they did from the outset for the Plymouth settlers, dietary stress and nutritionally related diseases would have been somewhat common before the Pilgrims arrived, but this leaves a very different morbidity and mortality profile from that of a severe epidemic. In addition, the alliances and networks established among Native communities helped ensure that scarce resources would be shared and starvation usually averted (e.g., Brooks 2008).

The epidemic of 1616–17 was a different matter. Although smallpox is believed to have been present in Newfoundland at least as early as 1610 (Marshall 1981, cited in Waldram et al. 2006), medical historians reviewing early reports of the 1616–17 epidemic tended not to regard it as smallpox. Possibilities have included "plague," yellow fever, chicken pox, hepatitis, and other diseases, the latest suggestion being "leptospirosis accompanied by Weil syndrome" (Marr and Cathey 2010:281). Regardless of the microbe involved and the name of the disease, it devastated the coastal areas of New England and led to numerous reports by explorers, fishermen, and prospective settlers up and down the coast about abandoned villages and dead being left unburied and lying aboveground. Yet there is virtually no evidence that it moved very far inland. The frequency of contacts with Europeans or other Indians from coastal settlements was apparently too low or the contacts too sporadic for the infection to spread; possibly lower population densities also reduced the spread, as did the transmissibility and incubation time of the pathogen.

The epidemic of 1633–34 was more extensive geographically. The Connecticut valley was very much involved, as was all of interior New England, and there is no debate that the disease was smallpox. It was noted among the English in Plymouth in the summer of 1633 and caused deaths, but most recovered. The same was not true for Natives. Governor Bradford reported that it "swept away many of the Indians from all the places near and adjoining" and that the Indians were unable to bury all their dead (Jones 2004:31).

Bradford also reported that when smallpox came into the Connecticut River valley in the winter of 1633–34, it caused "such a mortality that of a thousand [who contracted the disease,] above nine and a half hundred of them died, and many of them did rot above ground for want of burial" (Bradford 1976:270).[3] Bradford described the presence of a Dutch trading party (Bradford 1976:270), who probably introduced the epidemic into the valley (Duffy 1953:43). Similar reports came from throughout interior New England, as well as from Natives in New York and the eastern provinces of Canada.

Many agree that the 1633–34 epidemic was probably the most devastating of all those in the seventeenth century, but there were other severe epidemics in New England of smallpox and other diseases that would have acted to further depress the Native population and their ability to make a strong and sustained recovery. Recurring outbreaks of smallpox were the major problem. John Duffy records the occurrence of smallpox epidemics in 1648–49, 1666, around the time of King Philip's War, again in 1677–78 and 1689, and a major outbreak in New England and Canada in 1701–3 (Duffy 1953:44–50). There was a major influenza outbreak in 1647 and again in 1675 (Duffy 1953:186–87). These would have been accompanied by numerous local and regional outbreaks of measles, scarlet fever, and dysenteries including typhoid and the more common microbial causes.

The epidemics also persisted into the eighteenth and early nineteenth centuries, afflicting Native and English populations alike in what is now Massachusetts, including Plymouth, the Massachusetts Bay towns, and the Connecticut valley. In George Sheldon's *History of Deerfield*, he mentions provisions for a smallpox hospital in July 1776 (Sheldon 1895–96:719). Allegedly, troops mustering in the area had brought the disease. In March 1793 the town also was asked to consider a smallpox "hospital"—which the town rejected—for inoculations because of cases in town (Sheldon 1895–96:767). In Stephen West Williams's 1842 address "Medical History of the County of Franklin" (which became the county where the center village of Pocumtuck was located, later named the town of Deerfield), he described the diseases and epidemics occurring to the English settlers of Deerfield from the late 1730s on. Among those he was able to document in the eighteenth century were scarlet fever epidemics in 1735 and 1740–41, measles in 1750, dysentery in 1751, canker rash (probably scarlet fever) in 1750, lung fever (pneumonia) in 1775, smallpox and dysentery in 1777, and canker rash again in 1792 and intermittently to 1795. Dysentery and scarlet fever epidemics were common throughout the period and well into the nineteenth century, often most affecting infants (dysentery) and children (scarlet fever) (Swedlund 2010).

Despite claims of 80–90+ percent fatality rates for the 1616–17 and 1633–34 epidemics, there are also claims of large settlements and populations of Native groups living along the coast and in the interior of Massachusetts after 1634. Some of this would be attributable to population recovery and some to the fact that those Natives in closest proximity to English settlements would have experienced the highest levels of mortality compared to those at farther distances and having less frequent direct contact. It is more reasonable to assume lower figures for the region as a whole, as has been suggested by several scholars, but also to acknowledge that depletion of the Native population remained quite high as a result not only of a series of epidemic and endemic diseases but also of the disruption and dislocation of traditional Native subsistence and residential practices. Malnutrition, relocation, disruption of community and family life, and depression of fertility, not to mention war and conflict, all came together to suppress the Native population of Massachusetts and New England until at least the mid-nineteenth century.

## Conflict and Captivity in the Connecticut Valley

If the 1616–17 epidemic permitted the English to gain a beachhead in coastal Massachusetts (Plymouth) by 1621, then it was similarly true that the smallpox epidemic of 1633–34 opened up similar possibilities in the Connecticut River valley. Early Dutch efforts to come up the Hudson and Connecticut Rivers initiated some early trade opportunities, but settlement was thwarted by a long-established and well-settled Native population (Thomas 1979). The Dutch trade in furs eventually allowed them to establish a trading post at Fort Orange at present-day Albany, New York. The French, coming through the Saint Lawrence River valley, by this time were well engaged in trade with Algonquian and Mohawk peoples. Traditional conflicts that erupted from time to time prior to European contact were exacerbated by issues over access to these trading partnerships with the Dutch and French by the mid-1620s, but the middle Connecticut River valley remained peripherally involved at most, primarily through connections with the Algonquian-speaking Mahicans to the west (e.g., Starna 2013:chap. 8; Thomas 1979:49).

In 1633, prior to the epidemic's arrival in the valley, Governor Winthrop of the Massachusetts Bay Colony declared the Connecticut valley "not fit for plantation, there being three or four thousand warlike Indians," and also because of the challenges of passage on the river (Winthrop 1908:103). By the winter of 1634, Bradford had made his observations (as discussed above) on the impact of the epidemic; however, settlement up the Connecticut River was immediate. By 1636 there were agreements between the Pequots and the Massachusetts Bay Colony to allow some English settlement in the lower valley. But growing tensions between the Pequots, English, Narragansetts, and Mohegans soon led to the devastating Pequot War of 1636–37. Primarily waged between the English and the Pequots, the results were many casualties and many Pequots taken captive and forced into personal service by the English or sold into slavery to the West Indies (e.g., Newell 2003:108–9). The treaty of Hartford, signed in 1638 (a treaty among the English, the Narragansetts, and the Mohegans), distributed some of the Pequot captives and granted the Pequot territory to the English of what had become Connecticut Colony (Pulsipher 2005:22–24; Thomas 1979).

Space does not permit a detailed discussion of the English-Native engagements that followed in the Connecticut River valley; a very superficial overview must suffice. In addition to the impacts of disease, conflict and captive-taking had risen to new levels once the English were fully involved. Competition for favorable trade relations with the Dutch and English resulted in very complex power relations among Native tribal groups, which were unstable and constantly shifting. Captive-taking was a tradition among and between Algonquian and Iroquoian speakers of the Northeast. This most often involved women and children and served to increase numbers as well as to create future kin and social alliances between the groups involved. The best known of these practices were the *mourning wars* of Iroquoian groups, who would capture individuals to ceremonially replace members of their own group who were lost to battle or sickness (Starna and Watkins 1991). With European trade, introduced diseases, and conflicts over territory, these captive-takings and other interactions were greatly intensified in the seventeenth and early eighteenth centuries (e.g., Snow 1994:110, 114). The English settlers moving into Native lands raised the level of killing and altered the prospects, outcomes, and probably gender ratios for Native captives.

In 1635 William Pynchon, a member of the Massachusetts Bay Colony and a founder of Roxbury, led an expedition to homelands of the Agawams in the southern part of the middle Connecticut valley to farm but also with the intention of establishing a fur-trading operation with Indians up the valley. Agawam became the town of Springfield in 1640, and Pynchon, as magistrate, was well situated between Albany and Boston, with a large area occupied by potential Native trading partners for furs, game, corn, and other commodities. The English towns of Northampton and Hadley soon followed, in 1654 and 1659, in the homelands of the Norwottucks. In 1667, a deed for a large parcel of Pocumtuck land was signed between the Pocumtuck sachem Chaulk (or Chaque) with John Pynchon, son of William, paving the way for an English settlement and fort. Three more deeds followed in the same year (Haefeli and Sweeney 2003:14–15; Sheldon 1895–96:8, 10).[4] There is a question whether Chaulk was in a position to sign on behalf of the Pocumtucks and even as to the nature of his affiliation with the Pocumtucks. His children were apparently taken captive by the Pocumtuck leader Onapequin years earlier (Bruchac 2011:44).

Chaulk was probably filling a vacuum in leadership and organization that had been created by events just a few years prior to 1667. In the 1640s the Pocumtucks had been allied with the Mohawks and Narragansetts in the fur trade and had been involved in wampum exchanges crossing through their territory. In 1663 a peace conference was held at Pocumtuck with English traders, Mahicans, Sokokis, and Iroquois from Kahnawake, near present-day Montreal. However, only a year later a peace delegation of Mohawks to Pocumtuck resulted in Mohawk deaths. While conflicts with the sachem Uncas and the Mohegans in Connecticut had involved the Pocumtucks and their former allies, conflict was now redirected toward these former allies. The 1665 attack on the Pocumtucks resulted in the destruction of their fort, numerous deaths, the taking of captives, and retreat of the survivors, possibly north, south, and east depending on where families had kin connections or other alliances. The Iroquois were now at war with the Natives in the whole area, and "where the Mohawk trail intersected the Connecticut River . . . [was] dangerous" (Haefeli and Sweeney 2003:15; see also Sheldon 1895–96:68–69; Starna 2013; Thomas 1979). The Pocumtucks were now quite dispersed, and while they were no doubt visiting and even temporarily residing in various parts of their homeland, the confluence of the Pocumtuck (Deerfield) and Quinetucket (Connecticut) Rivers was not only dangerous but also temporarily vacant and deemed abandoned by the English in 1667.

The Massachusetts General Court granted authority for the settling of Pocumtuck in 1669, and by 1675—the year commencing King Philip's War—there were approximately 200 English residents. In the war, the Pocumtucks aligned with the Wampanoag leader Metacom (King Philip), along with the Nipmucks, Narragansetts, and Abenakis. Indians from the Christianized "praying towns" like Natick joined the Mohegans and Pequots in siding with the English (e.g., Lepore 1998). In September 1675 a group of English troops—accompanied by 14 Deerfield men—were attacked by Metacom's forces south of the village. Casualties were high on both sides, including all of the men from Deerfield. The English abandoned Deerfield, and the Indians resettled and planted corn there the following spring. Successful raids on several middle valley towns, including Springfield, took place during that fall, though not each resulted in abandonment. Then, in May 1676, a company of 150 Englishmen attacked a large group of Natives encamped at Peskeompskut to fish at the falls, now named Turners Falls on the Connecticut River, after Captain Turner who led the expedition. As many as 300 Natives were killed, and they were reported mostly to be women, children, and the elderly (Haefeli and Sweeney 2003:21; Melvoin 1989; Sheldon 1895–96). The loss of women and children would be a crushing blow to the remaining Pocumtucks or any other Native group whose population was declining.

In June 1676 a large group of Englishmen searched both sides of the river, removing or pushing any remaining Indians farther north. The surviving Pocumtucks moved on to the mixed refugee settlement at Schaghticoke to the west, to the Pennacooks eastward, or to join other Native refugee groups in Canada (Haefeli and Sweeney 2003:21). A year later, 26 Pocumtucks under the leadership of Ashpelon came back to the area from their refuge in French Canada and attacked

Hatfield and Deerfield, killing several English settlers in Hatfield and 1 in Deerfield and taking several captives north, who were eventually released before reaching Canada (Haefeli and Sweeney 2003:21; Sheldon 1895–96:180–83).

Pocumtuck was again abandoned by the English until 1680, when it began to slowly rebuild and had a population of approximately 200 individuals by 1688 (Melvoin 1989:132). A decade of relative stability and growth shifted dramatically to one of alert in 1691 when about 150 Pocumtucks and possibly others arrived from Schaghticoke and established an encampment in the valley not far from Deerfield, while also moving from place to place, even returning to New York and back. Tensions increased again in 1694 and 1695 with minor attacks on Deerfield. In 1701 a smallpox epidemic "ravaged" the Saint Lawrence valley, including several Native Mohawk and Abenaki settlements. Then, in February 1704, the famous raid on Deerfield occurred by the French and their Indian allies, leading to over 40 English killed and 112 taken captive. It is estimated that of a raiding party that numbered more than 250, there were 48 French and Canadian troops and 200–250 from Native communities. These were primarily Mohawks, Hurons, and Abenakis but also included individuals and their descendants who were refugees from the Connecticut valley and elsewhere (Haefeli and Sweeney 2003; PVMA, 2004).[5]

From an English perspective, this is easily the most dramatic incident to occur in the history of conflict between Native groups and English in the Pocumtuck homeland, but it was not the last. Additional raids on Deerfield occurred with a French-Indian party in 1709 and as late as 1746, when 4 English were killed and 1 was taken captive at the Bars section of Deerfield. At the site, a captive's collar, or "prisoner's halter," of the Kahnawake Mohawks was found and retrieved; it is now part of the collection of the Memorial Hall Museum in Deerfield (figure 6.2; PVMA 1746).

In a close-up view of the history of conflict and captivity in the middle Connecticut valley, it is easy to lose focus on the broader context in which many of the examples described above took place. They were not in isolation from broader conflicts that were primarily the result of the series of French-Anglo, or "French and Indian," wars that were being fought both in Europe and in America in the contest for

**Figure 6.2.** Prisoner's Collar, Kahnawake Mohawk, circa 1746. (Courtesy Memorial Hall Museum, Pocumtuck Valley Memorial Association.)

territory in North America. Native populations were clearly caught in-between and formed alliances with the colonial power that they thought could best serve their own interests in trade and in the protection of their land. What could be considered raids or massacres or even battles up and down the Connecticut River valley would probably seem more like skirmishes when compared to the whole of King Philip's War, the Pequot War, or Queen Anne's War. And the ratcheting up of lives lost over prior, traditional conflicts between Native groups in New England is noteworthy.

Also, in this litany of conflict and captivity between 1635 and 1746 it is easy to overlook the fact that friendly contacts and even close familial connections existed over time among and between Native and English households. Our attention is easily drawn, as it should properly be, to the horrible treatment of the Natives of Massachusetts before and after King Philip's War. The numbers killed, sold, or made to serve as indentured servants, as well as the many who were sold into slavery to other colonies as far as the West Indies (e.g., Lepore 1998; Newell 2003; see also Cameron, chapter 7, this volume), form the overpowering image. Yet despite these atrocities committed, there is also evidence on the local level of more-friendly encounters and a persistence of Native Americans. There are numerous reports of visits between Pocumtuck descendants and those of other Native affiliations who were associated with the raid on Deerfield. Deerfield descendants who chose to stay in Canada and married into Native or French families made up a signifi-cant part of this periodic migration to Deerfield and the surrounding area. These sociable, and even familial, contacts recurred well into the nineteenth and early twentieth centuries and belie the sense of constant hostility and conflict represented by some of the early historical accounts. Recent research is greatly expanding our knowledge of these events (e.g., Bruchac 2007; Haefeli and Sweeney 2006). A tercentenary event commemorating the raid on Deerfield, held in 2004, punctuated this important dimension of the history of the Deerfield raid (see Haefeli and Sweeney 2006; PVMA 2004).

## Making Sense

Documentation of the disease history and the history of conflict in a region, while essential to the task at hand, does not in and of itself provide a self-explanatory resolution to deeper questions about "virgin soil" populations, European diseases, or war, conflict, and captivity as causal explanations for the impacts on and decline of Native populations in the Connecticut valley—or America, for that matter. Nor, after careful analysis, is there any way to apportion the relative effects of conflict, captivity, and disease in any rigorous or statistical sense. The difficulty of even measuring the magnitude of population at the time of contact and shortly thereafter underscores the challenges of estimation. And yet, in one sense, we have come to a general understanding of Native population decline in New England. It is all of those things. Like all complex problems, the causes are multifactorial and difficult to measure, but there are some strong signals.

We have been able to eliminate or greatly reduce the predicted effects of at least one variable as well. We no longer can make the case strongly that genetic or innate immunological deficiencies were key to the high death rates of Native populations at contact (e.g., Larsen 1994 and chapter 3, this volume; Jones 2003 and chapter 1, this volume). If lack of acquired immunity was a key factor, it was also exacerbated by the stress of malnutrition and inadequate opportunities for care of the sick.

This Connecticut valley example is useful from two perspectives. The first is the on-the-ground empirical evidence for population decline and displacement of the Pocumtucks and, by implication, other groups in western Massachusetts. The second is the erasure of that Native population in narratives of contact-period history that far exaggerate the demise—or even claims of extinction—of Native people beyond the actual case.

## Population

English population growth was a highly significant factor in dominating and displacing Native inhabitants (see Thornton 1997). In Massachusetts, English settlement (coupled with fertility and migration) is central to understanding the experience of the Native population. John Demos (1970) in Plymouth and Philip Greven (1972) in Andover showed us a long time ago the high fertility of colonial English families in Massachusetts. Households with completed fertility exceeding seven children were the average. Communities were capable of doubling in size approximately every twenty years or less. The rapid intrinsic growth, coupled with high rates of English immigration, flooded the region with families looking for more land. In the Connecticut valley, as in Deerfield, for example, mean completed family size was over seven as well, and this persisted well past the mid-1700s (e.g., Temkin-Greener and Swedlund 1978). As new young families sought settlement up the Connecticut valley, the "demand" for gaining "title" to Native lands was considerable. As Salisbury (1982:11) states, "[E]ach quest for land turned into a crusade against the 'savage' Indians." With each encroachment, the ability for Native settlements to maintain their own fertility and family structure was severely compromised.

Governor Bradford's accounts of abandoned communities along New England's shores and on the banks of the Connecticut River, with skeletons or corpses lying on the ground, were (at least partially) true, no doubt, but the obstacles to recovery for the Native population had less to do with their lack of immunity than the disruption and occupation of their settlements and foraging areas after these were occupied by the English.[6] And English settlements, too, had their bouts of epidemic disease, which could be quite serious.

In the middle Connecticut River valley, it is hard to make a strong case that disease was the predominant factor in Native population decline, and for the New England region as a whole, as a cause of overall mortality, disease may have been closer to 50–60 percent, certainly not 95 percent. Furthermore, to the extent that disease played a major role in population reduction—and it did—it had more to do with political and economic forces than the germs and diseases present. Despite the shift from marking disease as the major causal factor and instead making it only part of the equation, significant Native population decline is still not in dispute for New England and other colonial regions in North America. However, the losses at their worst also have been further exaggerated by conventions in recounting this history.

### Erasure and Persistence

Attempts to deny the presence of Native Americans in New England have a very long history. In some ways, one can say it began with the Separatists' and Puritans' first claims by Bradford and Winthrop that God had so favored the English that he had "consumed the natives with a miraculous plague wherby a great parte of the Country [was] left voyde of Inhabitantes" (quoted in Jones 2004:28; original spelling). Indians were everywhere in New England, and the earliest reports indicated that they were a strong and healthy "race," yet the claims of their demise were almost instantaneous and persistent. Numerous authors have pointed to the changing narratives over time to account for ongoing losses. For example, Salisbury (1982:3–6) tracks the shift from God's will to the descendants of the Puritans' claim in the nineteenth century that it was the "triumph of civilization over savagery and barbarism" to mid-twentieth-century claims of simple de facto cultural superiority over an inferior "race." In George Sheldon's (1895–96:74) *History of Deerfield*, the decline of the Pocumtucks is portrayed as the result of "the weaker race before the stronger" and attributable to the same causes that "have attended the march of civilization across the continent." By essentializing an inherent biological weakness in the Native American immune system—as some virgin soil proponents did—racialized explanations in one form or another persisted throughout the twentieth century.[7] But the tenacity of this argument is not the main point I wish to make here. The persistent claims of their demise have overshadowed the evidence for persistence of Native Americans.

There is a long tradition of regarding Massachusetts and the middle Connecticut valley as virtually devoid of an Indian presence after King Philip's War in 1677. Even though there was evidence to the contrary, and scholars from time to time made significant note of that fact, scholarship on Native persistence in New England coalesced beginning in the 1990s (e.g., Calloway 1990). This can be marked, for example, by the 1997 publication of Colin Calloway's book *After King Philip's War: Presence and Persistence in Indian New England* and perhaps also by some articles in the 1996 publication of a special issue of *William and Mary Quarterly* (e.g., Baron et al. 1996). Jean O'Brien dramatically enlarged on our recognition of the Native presence and persistence in the Northeast with her 2010 book, *Firsting and Lasting: Writing Indians out of Existence in New England.* Archaeologists (e.g., Bruchac and Hart 2012; Carlson 1997; Handsman 1992; Paynter 2001; Rubertone 2000, 2001; Silliman 2004, 2009) are also involved in rewriting the history of Native presence after contact in New England. As Rubertone (2000, 2001) has argued, by digging deeper into the historical archaeology and rich history of Native Americans, we are able to replace a narrative of colonized and marginalized peoples with one that renders them more visible. In the Connecticut valley, the recent research and collection by Evan Haefeli and Kevin Sweeney (2006) and Margaret Bruchac's 2007 dissertation and forthcoming book have gone a long way toward restoring a sense of ongoing connections and Native presence in the valley.

Already noted above were the occasional visits of Natives from the refugee communities at Schaghticoke, Kahnawake, and Odanak–St. Francis, where Pocumtucks fled at one time or another in the past and from where their own descendants lived and traveled. Space does not permit detailed examples here, but the excellent research of Abenaki scholars Lisa Brooks (e.g., 2008) and Margaret Bruchac (2007:esp. chaps. 4 and 7) on evidence in the historical record for Native families scattered throughout the valley through and beyond the nineteenth century are great testimonies to both the ongoing presence of Native Americans and also the erasure of that presence in the valley, and in New England in general, by so many scholars in the past.

Bruchac (e.g., 2007:chap. 5) and O'Brien (2010) also provide insightful and informative analyses of the various means of erasure that were practiced from the late seventeenth century on, including the tendency for newspapers and town histories of the nineteenth century to mold stories about the "last Indian" and the "vanishing Indian," referring to these tales as being part of a systematic "literary erasure" of the actual, physical presence of descendant Native families. In Robert

Paynter's (2002) work, he has been able to demonstrate how narratives created about Deerfield's colonial past have produced triumphalist allegories about the "bloody massacre" of 1704 and, almost simultaneously, the rise of a successful, iconic, and peaceful rural farming community. Through his analysis of material culture and the ethnohistorical record, Paynter (2001) also has shown how a "cult of whiteness" pervaded western New England and contributed further to the erasure of both Native and African Americans who lived in and around Deerfield and the middle valley.

Writing on the process of erasure of Native peoples (specifically, about the Pocumtucks of the middle Connecticut valley), Siobhan Hart (2012) argues that the production of historical narratives by a dominant group tends to elevate certain events, places, and pasts and marginalizes others. She adopts Michel-Rolph Trouillot's (1995:2) useful critique of historical production as the process by which the recording of "what happened" becomes "that which is said to have happened." Hart then proceeds to illustrate how this process has affected the history of the Pocumtuck homeland with specific reference to a particular archaeological site.

### Colonized Bodies

European exploration and colonial settlement in Africa and Asia in the past were usually narrated in medical-historical terms, as being about the fevers, plagues, and tropical diseases that afflicted the colonizers. America provided a counterexample, in that it tended to be narrated as a situation in which Europeans carried fatal diseases to a supposedly disease-free world. Both scenarios are exaggerated, of course, but in neither case do the Europeans get pathologized. The colonized were, in both cases. Asians and Africans were characterized as disease carrying and dangerous, their environments pathogenic. America's Natives were healthy in their Edenic "natural habitat," but they were unable to withstand the "diseases of civilization." Their "constitutions" were weak. They were not "fit." Eventually, it was concluded that their immune systems were "naïve." They were not genetically adapted to modernization.

Mary-Ellen Kelm has written extensively on how Canadian First Nations peoples' bodies were racialized and deemed unfit and unhealthy in the past (e.g., Kelm 1998, 2010). She argues that processes of colonization shaped aboriginal bodies as missionaries sought to reform bodily practices and nineteenth-century medical men studied their health "deficiencies" and racial characteristics. They were, after all, a "dying race" (Kelm 1998:xv). Of course, similar practices prevailed with the study of Native Americans by religious leaders, government officials, scientists, and physicians well into the twentieth century. Pathologizing Native people goes hand in hand with silences and erasures in the production of historical narratives.

## Native Numbers, Native Lives

It is a very long stretch from the Pocumtuck homelands in the middle Connecticut River valley to global proclamations about framing the history of disease in the Americas, but I cannot conclude this chapter without at least making reference to the fact that the discursive practices we employ to talk about the history of Native American health still often carry the echoes of past colonial studies. Fortunately, we are witnessing dramatic changes in the past several years by scholars who have examined those practices closely and opened our eyes to the ways in which indigenous bodies themselves have been colonized and scripted, the way plagues and epidemics have been used as means for blame and shame, and how increasing knowledge of genetics and immunity has reshaped our understanding of disease susceptibility and the nature of variation.[8] These understandings have resonance whether we are talking about New England, Mexico and the Southwest, the Northwest Coast, Canada, or elsewhere, and they need to increasingly become a part of our empirically based historical and prehistoric studies on aboriginal health.

Calloway (1990), Brooks (2008), Bruchac (2007), O'Brien (2010), and others have described the long-standing mobility of New England's Natives from very early times. Place-names in a Native language, like narrowly defined boundaries and tribal identities themselves, fail to capture the extended alliances and kin relations that varied but persisted for so many generations. But as the lucrative trade between New England's Natives and Europeans diminished in importance and the demand for land and English settlement increased, Indians were increasingly driven out of their homelands and deprived of the traditional economic means to thrive (e.g., Salisbury 1996). Forced relocations were greatly heightened by English and French occupation of homelands, especially after King Philip's War. This movement came with terrible hardship and was accompanied with significant losses caused by warfare and disease. However, the broad geographic dispersal of kin-based bands and communities—and their frequent movements—reinforced the perception that the decline from disease and hostilities was greater than actually may have been the case. Temporary and seasonal abandonments of core agricultural settlements also made it easier for the English to proclaim that epidemic disease had literally "wiped out" the inhabitants.

I open this chapter with mention of the story of Samoset and Squanto and will close with a brief recounting of the stories of Ashpelon and Wattanummon. Samoset and Squanto serve to point out the remarkable paths and mobility of two Native Americans who were among the first to establish contact with the leadership on the *Mayflower* in 1621. Wattanummon and Ashpelon illustrate the extensive travels, complex interactions, and varied identities of two Native Americans who were resident in the Connecticut Valley at one time or another.

Ashpelon was born at Norwottuck or Pocumtuck. He eventually found his way to a refuge in Canada. In the final throes of King Philip's War he returned to the Connecticut valley in 1677 and led raids on Hatfield and Deerfield, taking prisoners who were eventually released while heading northward through Vermont. Fifteen years later, Ashpelon returned to Deerfield in peace and was identified as a Schaghticoke leader (Haefeli and Sweeney 1994, 1995; Sheldon 1895–96:181–83, 231–32; Spady 1995). One can assume that he lived temporarily in several different Native communities from New York to Vermont to French Canada over his lifetime.

The even better documented Wattanummon was a member of the party that raided Deerfield in 1704. Variously identified as a Pennacook and a Pawtucket from the Merrimac River valley, he also was for a time a Pigwacket sachem and also lived at Cowassuck, Schaghticoke, and Odanak (Haefeli and Sweeney 1994).

Because Ashpelon's, Chaque's, and Wattanummon's names are known, historians and tribal elders are able to track some of their extensive travel and residential locations over their lifetimes, but they stand for others as representatives of the commonality and complexity of Native interactions in the seventeenth and early eighteenth centuries. These named individuals also remind us that the heavy losses of Native Americans in colonial encounters are not just numbers to be bandied about but the *lives* of thousands of resilient men and women in the face of disruption and dispossession.

## Acknowledgments

Without a wide circle of colleagues and friends in the Five College community and beyond, I would not have been able to write this chapter. I hope I have cited their groundbreaking research accurately. I thank Eric Johnson (University of Massachusetts, Amherst), Claire Carlson and David Bosse (Historic Deerfield), and Neal Salisbury (Smith College) for their careful reading and useful feedback on this chapter. I single out Robert Paynter (University of Massachusetts, Amherst), who has been a steady and always supportive colleague, providing many stimulating discussions, editorial suggestions, and sources for which I am most grateful. Also, Siobhan Hart, Ann Herring, Patricia Rubertone, William Starna, Dean Snow, and coeditors Cathy Cameron and Paul Kelton have provided insights and thoughtful suggestions to make this a better chapter, as did two anonymous reviewers.

## Notes

1. See Salisbury 1982 for details of this encounter.
2. Numbers vary significantly by how the middle Connecticut valley and the Pocumtucks are defined and the time period in question. I am reporting Sherburne Cook's estimate for the larger, "extended" definition (1976:58), which would include many band names in the middle valley. And for central and western Massachusetts together Cook gives a figure of 5,300 (1976:59). Dean Snow and Kim Lanphear (1988:24) revise the Pocumtuck figure to 18,400, but how they derived it is unclear.
3. These observations on smallpox deaths in the Connecticut valley were made in the Hartford-Windsor areas to the south of the Pocumtuck centers.
4. According to Margaret Bruchac (2007:22–23) and George Sheldon (1895–96:59), Chaque has been identified as a Podunk Indian from the Hartford area (the Podunks are a clan closely related to the Pocumtucks). This treaty retained rights of fishing, hunting, and gathering for the Pocumtucks, an important point related to future conflicts.

5. The raid on Deerfield is so well known that it is the subject of scores of articles and scholarly books, local histories, social histories of wide readership (e.g., Demos 1995), popular historical accounts (e.g., Williams and Williams 1853 [1707]), and stories for young readers (e.g., Smith 1939 [1904]; Steinmetz 2010). No justice can be given to it in the space permitted here; readers are referred to sources in the reference list.

6. Patricia Rubertone (2001) and others have suggested that the number of bodies unburied claimed by colonists could have been exaggerated to dehumanize Native Americans and make them seem more uncivilized.

7. Neal Salisbury himself was a proponent of the virgin soil explanation in his 1982 book *Manitou and Providence*; however, his argument did not contain the same biological and racial overtones that characterized others. In addition, Salisbury (pers. comm., 2013), while still acknowledging the importance of disease in New England Native population history, has modified considerably his view of the virgin soil model and today finds himself closer in agreement with Jones (2003; see also Jones, chapter 1, this volume).

8. References are too numerous to list, but I would include Anderson 2004, 2010; Arnold 1993; Comaroff 1993; Crawford 2003 and Crawford-O'Brien 2013; Jones 2004, 2006; Kelm 1998, 2010; Lux 2001; Mackenthun 1997; and the introduction and chapters in Herring and Swedlund 2010.

# References

Anderson, Warwick. 2004. Postcolonial histories of medicine. *In* Locating Medical History: The Stories and Their Meanings, edited by Frank Huisman and John Harley Warner, 285–306. Baltimore, MD: Johns Hopkins University Press.

————. 2010. From plague, an epidemic comes: Recounting disease as contamination and configuration. *In* Plagues and Epidemics: Infected Spaces Past and Present, edited by D. Ann Herring and Alan C. Swedlund, 251–67. Oxford, UK: Berg.

Armelagos, George J., and Dennis P. Van Gerven. 2003. A century of skeletal biology and paleopathology: Contrasts, contradictions, and conflicts. American Anthropologist 105(1):54–64.

Arnold, David. 1993. Colonizing the Body: State Medicine and Epidemic Disease in 19th Century India. Berkeley: University of California Press.

Baker, Brenda. 1994. Pilgrim's progress and praying Indians: The biological consequences of contact in southern New England. *In* In the Wake of Contact: Biological Responses to Conquest, edited by Clark Spencer Larsen and George R. Milner, 35–45. New York: Wiley-Liss.

Baron, Donna K., J. Edward Hood, and Holly V. Izard. 1996. They were here all along: The Native presence in lower-central New England in the eighteenth and nineteenth centuries. William and Mary Quarterly 53(3):561–86.

Bradford, William. 1976. Of Plymouth Plantation, 1620–1647: The Complete Text. Edited by Samuel Eliot Morison. 7th printing. New York: Alfred A. Knopf. Originally reprinted 1952.

Brooks, Lisa T. 2008. The Common Pot: The Recovery of Native Space in the Northeast. Minneapolis: University of Minnesota Press.

Bruchac, Margaret M. 2007. Historical Erasure and Cultural Recovery: Indigenous People in the Connecticut River Valley. PhD diss., Anthropology Department, University of Massachusetts, Amherst.

———. 2011. Revisiting Pocumtuck history in Deerfield: George Sheldon's vanishing Indian act. Historical Journal of Massachusetts 39(1–2):30–77.

Bruchac, Margaret M., and Siobhan M. Hart. 2012. Materiality and autonomy in the Pocumtuck homeland. Archaeologies: Journal of the World Archaeological Congress 8(3):293–312.

Calloway, Colin G. 1990. The Western Abenaki of Vermont, 1600–1800: War, Migration and the Survival of an Indian People. Norman: University of Oklahoma Press.

———. 1997. After King Philip's War: Presence and Persistence in Indian New England. Hanover, NH: University Press of New England.

Carlson, Catherine C., George J. Armelagos, and Ann L. Magennis. 1992. Impact of disease on the precontact and early historic populations of New England and the Maritimes. In Disease and Demography in the Americas, edited by John W. Verano and Douglas H. Ubelaker, 141–54. Washington, DC: Smithsonian Institution Press.

Carlson, Claire C. 1997. Native American Presences in Deerfield, Massachusetts: An Essay and Resource Guide. Research summary for the Pocumtuck Valley Memorial Association, Deerfield, MA.

Comaroff, Jean. 1993. The diseased heart of Africa: Medicine, colonialism and the black body. In Knowledge, Power and Practice: The Anthropology of Medicine in Everyday Life, edited by Shirley Lindenbaum and Margaret Lock, 305–29. Berkeley: University of California Press.

Cook, Sherburne F. 1976. The Indian Population of New England in the Seventeenth Century. University of California Publications in Anthropology 12. Berkeley: University of California Press.

Crawford, Suzanne. 2003. Body as Battleground: Health, Gender and Embodiment Among Native Communities of Washington State. PhD diss., Department of Anthropology, University of California, Santa Barbara.

Crawford-O'Brien, Suzanne. 2013. Coming Full Circle: Spirituality and Wellness Among Native Communities in the Pacific Northwest. Lincoln: University of Nebraska Press.

Demos, John. 1970. A Little Commonwealth: Family Life in Plymouth Colony. New York: Oxford University Press.

———. 1995. The Unredeemed Captive: A Family Story from Early America. New York: Vintage Paperback.

Duffy, John. 1953. Epidemics in Colonial America. Baton Rouge: Louisiana State University Press.

Gould, Stephen J. 1996 [1981]. The Mismeasure of Man. New York: W. W. Norton.

Greven, Philip. 1972. Four Generations: Population, Land, and Family in Colonial Andover, Massachusetts. Ithaca, NY: Cornell University Press.

Haefeli, Evan, and Kevin Sweeney. 1994. Wattanummon's world: Personal and tribal identity in the Algonquian diaspora. *In* Actes du vingt-cinquième congrès des Algonquinistes [Papers of the Twenty-Fifth Algonquian Conference], edited by William Cowan, 212–22. Ottawa, ON: Carlton University.

———. 1995. Revisiting the redeemed captive: New perspectives on the 1704 attack on Deerfield. William and Mary Quarterly 52(1):3–46.

———. 2003. Captors and Captives: The French and Indian Raid on Deerfield. Amherst: University of Massachusetts Press.

———, eds. 2006. Captive Histories: English, French, and Native Narratives of the 1704 Deerfield Raid. Amherst: University of Massachusetts Press.

Handsman, Russell G. 1992. Illuminating history's silences in the Pioneer Valley. *In* Native Peoples and Museums in the Connecticut River Valley—A Guide for Learning, edited by Dorothy Krass and Barry O'Connell, 7–28. Northampton, MA: Historic Northampton.

Hart, Siobhan M. 2012. Decolonizing through heritage work in the Pocumtuck homeland of northeastern North America. *In* The Archaeology of Colonialism in Native North America, edited by Maxine Oland, Siobhan M. Hart, and Liam Frink, 86–103. Tucson: University of Arizona Press.

Herring, D. Ann, and Alan C. Swedlund. 2010. Plagues and epidemics in anthropological perspective. *In* Plagues and Epidemics: Infected Spaces Past and Present, edited by D. Ann Herring and Alan C. Swedlund, 1–19. Oxford, UK: Berg.

Johnson, Eric. 1999. Community and confederation: A political geography of contact-period southern New England. In *The Archaeological Northeast*, edited by Mary Ann Levine, Michael S. Nassaney, and Kenneth E. Sassaman, 155–68. Westport, CT: Bergin and Garvey.

Jones, David S. 2003. Virgin soils revisited. William and Mary Quarterly 60(4):703–42.

———. 2004. Rationalizing Epidemics: Meanings and Uses of American Indian Mortality Since 1600. Cambridge, MA: Harvard University Press.

———. 2006. The persistence of American Indian health disparities. American Journal of Public Health 96(12):2122–34.

Kelm, Mary-Ellen. 1998. Colonizing Bodies: Aboriginal Health and Healing in British Columbia, 1900–1950. Vancouver: University of British Columbia Press.

———. 2010. Past into present: History and the making of knowledge about HIV/AIDS and aboriginal people. *In* Plagues and Epidemics: Infected

Spaces Past and Present, edited by D. Ann Herring and Alan C. Swedlund, 193–212. Oxford, UK: Berg.

Larsen, Clark Spencer. 1994. In the wake of Columbus: Native population biology in the postcontact Americas. Yearbook of Physical Anthropology 37:109–54.

Lepore, Jill. 1998. The Name of War: King Philip's War and the Origins of American Identity. New York: Alfred A. Knopf.

Lux, Maureen K. 2001. Medicine That Walks: Disease, Medicine, and Canadian Plains Native People, 1880–1940. Toronto: University of Toronto Press.

Mackenthun, Gesa. 1997. Metaphors of Dispossession: American Beginnings and the Translation of Empire, 1492–1637. Norman: University of Oklahoma Press.

Marr, John S., and John T. Cathey. 2010. New hypothesis for cause of epidemic among Native Americans, New England, 1616–1619. Emerging Infectious Diseases 16(2):281–86.

Melvoin, Richard I. 1989. New England Outpost: War and Society in Colonial Deerfield. New York: W. W. Norton.

Newell, Margaret Ellen. 2003. The changing nature of Indian slavery in New England, 1670–1720. In Reinterpreting New England Indians and the Colonial Experience, edited by Colin G. Calloway and Neal Salisbury, 106–36. Boston: Colonial Society of Massachusetts.

O'Brien, Jean M. 2010. Firsting and Lasting: Writing Indians out of Existence in New England. Minneapolis: University of Minnesota Press.

Paynter, Robert. 2001. The cult of whiteness in western New England. In Race and the Archaeology of Identity, edited by Charles E. Orser Jr., 125–42. Salt Lake City: University of Utah Press.

———. 2002. Time in the valley: Narratives about rural New England. Current Anthropology 43(supp.):S85–S101.

Pulsipher, Jenny H. 2005. Subjects unto the Same King: Indians, English, and the Contest for Authority in Colonial New England. Philadelphia: University of Pennsylvania Press.

PVMA. 1746. Prisoner's Halter. Image available at http://www.americancenturies .mass.edu/ collection/itempage.jsp?itemid=5689. Deerfield, MA: Pocumtuck Valley Memorial Association.

———. 2004. Raid on Deerfield: The Many Stories of 1704. Available at http:// www.1704.deerfield.history.museum/. Deerfield, MA: Pocumtuck Valley Memorial Association.

Rubertone, Patricia. 2000. The historical archaeology of Native Americans. Annual Review of Anthropology 29:425–46.

———. 2001. Grave Undertakings: An Archaeology of Roger Williams and the Narragansett Indians. Washington, DC: Smithsonian Institution Press.

Salisbury, Neal. 1982. Manitou and Providence: Indians, Europeans, and the Making of New England, 1500–1643. New York: Oxford University Press.

————. 1996. The Indians' old world: Native Americans and the coming of Euro-peans. William and Mary Quarterly 53(3):435–58.

Sheldon, George. 1895–96. A History of Deerfield, Massachusetts. 2 vols. Deerfield, MA: Pocumtuck Valley Memorial Association.

Silliman, Stephen. 2004. Social and physical landscapes of contact. *In* North American Archaeology, edited by Timothy R. Pauketat and Diana DiPaolo Loren, 273–96. London: Blackwell.

————. 2009. Change and continuity, practice and memory: Native American persistence in colonial New England. American Antiquity 74(2):211–30.

Smith, Mary P. Wells. 1939 [1904]. The Boy Captive of Old Deerfield. Boston: Little, Brown.

Snow, Dean R. 1980. The Archaeology of New England. New York: Academic Press.

————. 1994. The Iroquois. Oxford, UK: Blackwell.

Snow, Dean R., and Kim M. Lanphear. 1988. European contact and Indian de-population in the Northeast: The timing of the first epidemics. Ethnohistory 35(1):15–33.

Spady, James. 1995. As if in a great darkness: Native American refugees of the middle Connecticut River valley in the aftermath of King Philip's War, 1677–1697. Historical Journal of Massachusetts 23(2):183–97.

Stannard, David E. 1992. American Holocaust: The Conquest of the New World. Oxford: Oxford University Press.

Starna, William A. 2013. From Homeland to New Land: A History of the Mahican Indians, 1600–1830. Lincoln: University of Nebraska Press.

Starna, William A., and Ralph Watkins. 1991. Northern Iroquoian slavery. Ethnohistory 38(1):34–57.

Steinmetz, Karen. 2010. The Mourning Wars. New York: Roaring Book Press.

Swedlund, Alan C. 2010. Shadows in the Valley: A Cultural History of Illness, Death and Loss in New England, 1840–1916. Amherst: University of Massachusetts Press.

Temkin-Greener, Helena, and Alan C. Swedlund. 1978. Fertility transition in the Connecticut valley, 1740–1850. Population Studies 32(1):27–41.

Thomas, Peter A. 1979. In the maelstrom of change: The Indian trade and cultural process in the middle Connecticut River valley, 1635–1665. PhD dissertation, University of Massachusetts, Amherst.

Thornton, Russell. 1987. American Indian Holocaust and Survival: A Population History Since 1492. Norman: University of Oklahoma Press.

————. 1997. Aboriginal North American population and rates of decline, ca. A.D. 1500–1900. Current Anthropology 38(2):310–15.

Trouillot, Michel-Rolph. 1995. Silencing the Past: Power and the Production of History. Boston: Beacon Press.

Ubelaker, Douglas H. 1992. North American Indian population size: Changing perspectives. *In* Disease and Demography in the Americas, edited by

John W. Verano and Douglas H. Ubelaker, 169–76. Washington, DC: Smithsonian Institution Press.

Waldram, James B., D. Ann Herring, and T. Kue Young, eds. 2006. Aboriginal Health in Canada. 2nd ed. Toronto: University of Toronto Press.

Williams, John, and Stephen West Williams. 1853 [1707]. The Redeemed Captive Returning to Zion; or, A Faithful History of Remarkable Occurrences in the Captivity and Deliverance of Mr. John Williams . . . Northampton, MA: Hopkins, Bridgman.

Williams, Stephen West. 1842. A Medical History of the County of Franklin, in the Commonwealth of Massachusetts. Address to the Massachusetts Medical Society, Boston.

Winthrop, John. 1908. History of New England, 1630–1649. Edited by James Kendall Hosmer. Reprinted, New York: Barnes and Noble, 1959.

# 7

# The Effects of Warfare and Captive-Taking on Indigenous Mortality in Postcontact North America

*Catherine M. Cameron*

The size of the pre-Columbian indigenous population and the reasons for its decline were debated throughout the twentieth century by historians, anthropologists, physiologists, and other scholars, and most emphasized introduced disease as the major cause of population decrease (Crosby 1972; Dobyns 1966, 1983; Fenn 2001; Ramenofsky 1987). Critics of this explanation point to problems with estimating precontact population size and with evaluating the length of time over which decline occurred in specific parts of the New World, a lack of consideration of cultural factors that affect disease transmission (Baker and Kealhofer 1996), and a neglect of other factors that may have had a serious impact on Native health and mortality (Ubelaker 2006:699). I hope to contribute to this last topic by evaluating how European colonization transformed Native American practices of warfare, captive-taking, and enslavement and the impact of these changes on the size of North America's indigenous population. While not downplaying the effects of disease on Native mortality, I argue that indigenous captives acquired new values in international slave markets that led to a significant increase in the frequency and violence of warfare among indigenous groups to supply that market. Native Americans also fought one another over control of access to European goods and trading networks and fought with Europeans who were encroaching on the territory and resources they had traditionally used. Warfare caused many deaths, brutality toward captives shortened life spans, and the disruptions of war also increased mortality.

I use ethnohistoric and historic accounts to describe warfare, captive-taking, and enslavement among the indigenous people of three broad regions of the postcolonial North American continent. My goal is to evaluate the consequence of these practices on Native American health and mortality. In this overview, I do not attempt to be precise about the impact of warfare, captive-taking, and enslavement on indigenous population size. Instead, I use specific examples to show how the European intrusion transformed these practices, increasing the number of deaths and shattering indigenous societies (Ethridge and Shuck-Hall 2009). Mortality was caused not only by violence but also by the resulting social disruption that destroyed indigenous subsistence practices and the human community on which every individual relies.

## Indigenous Warfare and Captive-Taking: Before and After

The study of indigenous captive-taking and enslavement in the New World is a relatively new field, and most sources are less than a decade old (Brooks 2002; Cameron 2008a; Carocci and Pratt 2012; Ekberg 2007; Foster 2003; Gallay 2002; Rushforth 2003, 2012; Santos-Granero 2009; Snyder 2010; but see Bailey 1966; Lauber 1979 [1913]). Most scholars emphasize that warfare and captive-taking were common practices in small-scale societies of North America prior to the arrival of Europeans (as they were in most parts of the world [Cameron 2008a, 2011]). Archaeological evidence and the earliest historic accounts make it clear that precontact warfare could be violent and result in numerous deaths (Chacon and Mendoza 2007; Dye 2004; Keeley 1996:68). Archaeology also attests to the importance of captive-taking in precontact times (Alt 2008; Cybulski 1990, 1992; Keeley 1996:68; Martin 2008).

Both archaeological and early ethnohistoric accounts reveal selective aspects of captive-taking. Men were more often killed and women and children taken captive. For example, in the mid-sixteenth century, the French explorer René Laudonniére (2001:11) reported that among the indigenous people of coastal La Florida, "The kings make wars among themselves, always by surprise attack. They kill every male enemy they can. . . . They spare the enemy women and children, feed them, and retain them permanently among themselves" (see also DePratter 1991:50). In most groups, captives were incorporated into a variety of social locations. Some were maintained as slaves, while others became wives or were adopted. Regardless of the nature of incorporation, most captives remained in liminal positions in the society of their captors.

In precontact contexts, warfare was focused on male status-striving. Captives were an especially prized product of war that significantly boosted the captor's status. Captive-taking was often linked to an ideology that revered successful warriors (Rushforth 2012; Snyder 2010). Furthermore, captives who were made slaves became degraded individuals whose mere existence served to highlight the power of their owner. Captives often became retainers or personal servants, which resulted in a public and ongoing display of the wide gulf in status between owner and captive. In the kin-based societies on which this study focuses, captives increased the captor's group size, and larger group size translated into greater power. Female captives did not simply create an immediate increase in group size; in addition, their reproductive abilities promised future population increase. In the continuum of value that captives offered their captors, ranging from prestige good to labor machine, prestige was predominant. But captives also provided labor to their captors, and the product of their labor could enrich their masters.

As prestige goods, captives were often important items in alliance building between groups. In many parts of North America, warfare was one extreme of trading-and-raiding relationships, and captives taken during raids continued to be important actors after hostilities ceased. During times of peace, the exchange of women and material goods was framed within a prestational economy in which gift giving was a prerequisite for harmonious relations (Albers 1993; Rushforth 2003, 2012). Often multilingual and partly enculturated by their captors, captives/slaves offered in gift exchange had symbolic value that transcended that of ordinary goods (Cameron 2015). Across the Americas, the gift of a captive could signal an offer of friendship or an attempt to establish alliances with others. In efforts to establish peaceful relations, captives could be exchanged between combatants as replacements for people killed in war.

The role of warfare and captive-taking across Native North America was transformed by the entry of European colonists. Although captives were often traded (like other goods) along established trade routes in precontact times, they moved more often as prestige goods and much less frequently as units of labor. European demand for labor and the opening of the New World to international markets that specialized in human trafficking changed the value of the indigenous captive. Rather than serving as a prestige good or a nexus for intergroup interaction, the captive's most potent value was now as an item of commercial trade. Warfare among indigenous groups was reoriented to supply that market. This reorientation of indigenous warfare and captive-taking was compelled at least partly by Euro-American special interests that encouraged indigenous people to attack their neighbors and sell the captives they took (Bowne 2005; Gallay 2002; Hämäläinen 2008:116–17). From the Euro-American perspective, this policy had the felicitous outcomes of providing labor needed on plantations, in mines, and in European households and of destroying or scattering the Native societies whose land the colonists coveted.

The result of this change in the value of the captive was a dramatic increase in indigenous warfare and captive-taking and a repurposing of these activities in North American indigenous societies (Donald 1997:231–33; Ethridge 2009; Gallay 2002). No longer was warfare guided primarily by established tradition and ritual practice. The open market for slaves created other avenues for the acquisition of wealth and status for indigenous warriors. Alan Gallay (2002:296–97, also 23–39) illustrates poignantly the loss of tradition in an account of indigenous southeastern slavers who, in 1713, entered the village of one of the "petit nations" located south of New Orleans, saying they wanted to join these Chaoüachas people in singing the calumet of peace. Instead they killed the chief and enslaved his wife and ten other people. As Gallay (2002:296–97) notes, "[I]t is the scheme by which the slavers had captured their enemies that illustrates most pointedly how the English desire for slaves had so dramatically affected the culture of the region." The calumet ceremony, once a sacred way of uniting groups, could no longer be trusted.

The intensification of warfare and its focus on slaving had disastrous effects on indigenous population size across North America. In the Southeast, the English colonies often manipulated indigenous violence such that warfare caused deaths, enslavement, and the disappearance or transformation of many indigenous societies. To the north in the Pays d'en Haut, the "Upper Country" of New France, efforts by both the French and indigenous residents to control access to trade, as well as the threat of Iroquois raids, were similarly disastrous. In the Southwest Borderlands, slave raids killed many and sent thousands of indigenous people into the mines of New Spain and across the plains to the slave markets of the East or on to the plantations of the Caribbean. Indigenous identity was also lost as captives and their descendants became incorporated into Spanish households and interbred with the Spanish and other groups (see also Gutiérrez, chapter 5, this volume).

## The Native Southeast

The effect of the postcolonial slave trade on indigenous population size has perhaps been best studied in the Southeast (Bowne 2005; Ekberg 2007; Ethridge 2009, 2012; Ethridge and Shuck-Hall 2009; Gallay 2002; Kelton 2007; Ramenofsky 1987). Here, the English settled along the Atlantic coast and the French dominated the Mississippi valley. In La Florida, the Spanish established a system of missions and attempted to convert Native peoples but were less involved in the commercial and global ventures that preoccupied the English and French (Ethridge 2009:28–29; Gallay 2009:37). Indigenous societies along the Eastern Seaboard and beyond competed for access to European trade, resulting in hostility and aggression. The English needed Native American collaborators both as trading partners and as military allies to protect their interests in regions with only sparse European occupation (Gallay 2009:22). They also wanted the Indian slaves that warfare provided. To achieve these ends, they provided guns and other weapons and encouraged Native peoples to go to war against one another. The fifty years between 1670 and 1720 were catastrophic to Native Americans of the Southeast. Two episodes of warfare and captive-taking during this period provide a sense of the effect of these activities on population size: the Westo wars in the Carolinas and La Florida, and the 1704 destruction of the La Florida mission system by a joint English and indigenous army.

The transformation wrought by the European desire for labor is especially evident in accounts of the Westo slave raids of the latter half of the seventeenth century (Bowne 2005, 2009; Gallay 2002; Meyers 2009; Richter 2011). The Westos, an Iroquoian-speaking group, were a product of the disruptions caused by colonial intrusions into the

Northeast. Initially known as the Erie, they formed in the 1630s at the southern end of Lake Erie about the time of first European contact there (Bowne 2005). Because of conflicts with other Native groups, in 1656 they migrated to southwestern Virginia and before 1660 were attacking the coastal Cusabos people and raiding Indian settlements in north Florida. Slave raiding became their preferred form of subsistence (Gallay 2002:41), and they were the first indigenous society to sell Indian captives to Virginia settlers (Bowne 2009:105–6; Richter 2011:321). They had already acquired guns in the north and had a dramatic military advantage over southern groups, whom they systematically raided for captives and other goods (Bowne 2005, 2009:106–7). As early as 1659, the Westos were attacking other groups in the low country of the Carolinas and were raiding hundreds of miles south into La Florida, which was then thinly populated with Spanish missions surrounded by affiliated Christianized Indians (Meyers 2009:95). With regard to how they knew where to go to obtain slaves, Eric Bowne (2005:75) notes that "perhaps the Westos traveled to Spanish Florida on the advice and encouragement of the English in order to harass the missions and/or gather intelligence concerning their military strength." In other words, the Westos likely selected their targets in La Florida using knowledge gained from English colonists (see also Gallay 2002; Meyers 2009:95–96).

In the mid-1660s, the Westos moved farther south, to the Savannah River area, and continued their violent raiding. When the Carolina colony was established in 1670, local Indians in the area turned to the English for protection. By 1674, the English had arranged a trade agreement with the Westos that specified that only nonlocal Indians would be taken, not the local Indians (Bowne 2009:108). The lord proprietors and English colonists were often at odds with one another in determining who would control trade with Native Americans (Bowne 2005:5; Gallay 2002:48–56), however. Colonists profited by exploiting Indians. The lord proprietors not only had moral objections to this but also did not want to have to send troops to save colonists from wars the colonists had started for their own enrichment (Gallay 2002:58). The Westos captured and sold several thousand southern Indians between 1660 and 1680 and killed many others (Bowne 2009:111; Gallay 2002:295–96).

The ascendancy of the Westos was short. They were outsiders to the Southeast and had few local allies besides the British. Once the British realized that their interaction with the Westos limited their options for profitable trade with other groups, they withdrew their support (Gallay 2002:56–57). The Westos were largely destroyed by 1682 in a series of European-engineered attacks undertaken by Savannah (Shawnee) warriors, and shortly thereafter it was reported that fewer than fifty Westo remained (Gallay 2002:60; Meyers 2009:97). When the Savannahs occupied the territory from which the Westos had been routed, the Carolina colony complained that the Savannahs were not providing adequate beaver pelts for trade, so the colony encouraged them to undertake slave raids. Taking the initiative themselves, the Carolina colonists, under a manufactured pretext, began a war with another Native group, the Waniahs. The Savannahs captured the Waniahs and sold them to a trader, who shipped them to Antigua (Gallay 2002:60).

Attacks on the Indians and Spanish of La Florida continued to be devastating (Boyd et al. 1951; Gallay 2002:145–48). In 1704, raiders led by the former governor of Carolina, James Moore, included 50 whites and 1,500 Creek allies. This attack began the destruction of the Spanish mission system (which was completed in subsequent raids) and caused the death and enslavement of a significant proportion of the indigenous Apalachee population. Moore, whose main goal was slaves for his own enrichment, reported, "In this expedition I brought away 300 men, and 1000 women and children, have killed and taken as slaves 325 men and have taken [as] slaves 4000 women and children" (Boyd et al. 1951:94). Moore's claim that he enslaved 4,000 Native Americans has been questioned (those "brought away" apparently went willingly and were resettled), but Gallay's (2002:145–49) careful analysis suggests that 2,000–4,000 Apalachees were enslaved in the 1704 attacks, and he discusses "the destruction of the Apalachee province" (Gallay 2002:148). Following Moore's raids, even more Native Americans were killed, captured, and enslaved. A mission padre reported that attacks after 1704 resulted in the death or enslavement of more than four-fifths of the Christian Indians who had survived Moore's raids, but very likely many more non-Christian Indians were also killed or enslaved (Gallay 2002:295). As Gallay (2002:296) notes, by the early eighteenth century, Florida was nearly depopulated of Indians.

Warfare and slave raiding by the Westos and other Native American groups transformed the cultural and geopolitical landscape of the

Southeast. Fear of attack caused parts of the Southeast to be abandoned—to be later reoccupied by Europeans. Native societies decimated by war, slaving, and disease were forced to abandon their settlements to join other groups or seek protection from the English or Spanish. Some groups disappeared entirely, while others, such as the Creeks, Cherokees, and Choctaws, were created from the remnants of Mississippian chiefdoms that gathered together into new formations (Ethridge 2009). By the eighteenth century, some southeastern groups, such as the Cherokees, had become powerful slaveholders themselves of both indigenous and African people, although they were eventually dispossessed of both their southeastern land and their slaves by white intruders (Miles 2005).

Numbers provide a sense of the impact of violence on indigenous mortality. The Southeast may have been home to about 199,400 Native Americans in 1685. By 1715, the population had dropped more than 54 percent to 90,100 (Wood 1989:38–39). During this same interval (1685–1715), the English enslaved between 24,000 and 51,000 indigenous Americans, with most shipped to the West Indies (Gallay 2002:294–302). Robbie Ethridge (2009:15) estimates that in a simple chiefdom of 2,000–5,000 people, the capture of only 200–500 women and children would significantly depress fertility because of the loss of women of child-bearing age, eliminate a strata of young group members, and make population recovery almost impossible.[1] As Ethridge (2009:15) notes, "slaving was more than sufficient to stress a simple chiefdom beyond its breaking point[.]" Combined with disease, the effects could be overwhelming, and the first southeastern pandemic is argued to have occurred in 1696. Slaving is even indicted in disease transmission here, as smallpox apparently moved into the interior following trails of indigenous slavers (Kelton 2007).

## The Pays d'en Haut

The Pays d'en Haut included the lands upriver from Montreal around the Great Lakes. It extended west to the Minnesota River and south to the confluence of the Mississippi and Missouri Rivers (Rushforth 2012:20; White 1991). It included primarily Algonquian speakers (including the Kickapoos, Foxes, Sauks, Illinois, and Miamis), but also the Hurons, who were Iroquoian speakers, and on the west Siouan speakers. To the east was Iroquoia, the land of the Five Nations of the Iroquois League, whose violent raids affected a large part of eastern North America during the seventeenth century, including the Pays d'en Haut. During the early eighteenth century, the Pays d'en Haut was embroiled in the Fox wars. The causes of these wars have been variously explained, most recently as an attempt by Indian allies of the French to prevent a French-Fox alliance (Rushforth 2006, 2012). A significant toll of dead and captured resulted from Iroquois raids on the Hurons and from thirty years of war among the Foxes, the French, and the indigenous allies of the French.

The Five Nations of the Iroquois Confederacy have been described as the first militaristic slaving society of the postcontact era (Ethridge 2009:29). During the early seventeenth century, as a result of severe population decline due to European diseases, increasing opportunities for trade with Europeans (trade that focused primarily on beaver pelts), and the introduction of European weapons, Iroquois "mourning wars" were transformed from occasional revenge for the death of an Iroquois at the hands of an enemy to constant and violent attacks against increasingly distant targets (Richter 1983). During the course of the seventeenth century and into the eighteenth, the Iroquois raided throughout the Northeast and into parts of present-day Canada, into the Mississippi valley, and well into the Southeast (Ethridge 2009:30–31; Richter 2011:148–51). One goal of these wars was to reverse population losses by adopting captives as new group members. In the process, however, the Iroquois destroyed or displaced a significant proportion of the indigenous population of the Northeast and beyond.

An Iroquois attack on the Hurons in July 1648 provides a sense of the magnitude of population losses caused by the Iroquois, as well as further losses of population and social coherence that resulted from the disruptions triggered by warfare (Trigger 1976:751–54). In this event, several hundred Iroquois attacked one of the largest and best-fortified Huron settlements, Teanaostaiaé. Although numerous Hurons escaped, as many as seven hundred were captured or killed, representing over one-third of a population of two thousand. Ravaged Teanaostaiaé was abandoned, and the remaining displaced population was unable to clear and plant new fields so late in the season. As panic gripped Huronia, women became reluctant to work in their fields for fear of Iroquois attack. Surplus food was consumed, and the next winter the Hurons faced famine, doubtless resulting in further deaths. The following year, several other Huron settlements were attacked, and a further seven hundred Hurons were lost. Again, fields could not be planted, and the remaining Hurons burned their villages as clan segments, lineages, and families scattered to find refuge with other groups. Huronia was abandoned and the Huron people became defenseless refugees.

The Fox wars have been variously attributed to Fox belligerence, ineffective French mediation, and most recently, efforts by Pays d'en Haut tribes to manipulate French efforts to expand their trading network to the west (Rushforth 2006). The French and Foxes had long sought mutual alliance, but other groups detested the Foxes and resented French efforts to include them in the alliance. Rushforth (2006, 2012) argues that French allies—the Illinois, Ottawas, Ojibwas, and others—feared that as the French moved west, these allied tribes would lose their prominent positions in the French trade. The allied tribes intentionally drove a wedge between the Foxes and the French by capturing Fox people during battles and selling them to the French. French colonists profited from the lucrative slave trade and were happy to ignore French government efforts to bring the Foxes into a general alliance.

Serious war broke out when the allied tribes attacked Fox villages near Detroit in 1712, and violent battles continued at intervals until the late 1730s. The toll exacted by the Fox wars in dead and captured was significant. An estimated one thousand Foxes settled near Detroit in 1710; most of these were slaughtered during the war of 1712–13 (White 1991:158–59). Surviving Foxes retaliated violently, and warfare continued intermittently for almost three decades. By 1727, the Foxes and the French had abandoned all efforts at alliance, and the French gave orders to exterminate the Foxes, although this was modified by the request to bring women and children back as captives (Rushforth 2012:218). Captives were taken in large numbers, as indicated by the numbers of Fox slaves entering French settlements: eighty Fox slaves were registered in parish records in just three years (1713–16), and these were likely only a portion of the slaves held in the colony (Rushforth 2006:66). In following years, as the wars continued, Foxes captured in raids "continued to stream into Montreal" (Rushforth 2006:70). The Fox population, which had been several thousand in the early eighteenth century, was just a few hundred by the early 1730s (Rushforth 2006:76). Other tribes also suffered severe losses (White 1991:166).

## The Southwest

In the Southwest Borderlands, as in regions to the east, warfare, captive-taking, and enslavement were vastly amplified by access to European markets and European demands for labor. The remoteness of much of the region and a lack of resources to draw Europeans meant that the Southwest Borderlands remained free of strong European control until well into the nineteenth century. Still, the Southwest and its indigenous and small European populations were strongly affected by global commercial markets, and one of the region's most profitable products was slaves. For more than two centuries, the Comanches, Navajos, Apaches, Kiowas, and other indigenous groups engaged in raiding and trading across the Southwest, their networks extending well into Sonora and Chihuahua, north to Yellowstone, and east almost to the Mississippi, linking with commercial markets in Mexico City, New England, the Caribbean, and California (Brooks 2002:33). Indigenous groups became allies or enemies as expediency dictated, and the sedentary Pueblo peoples and small Spanish population similarly sought to improve their precarious hold on the region through strategic alliances with or attacks on their mobile neighbors (Brooks 2002; Hämäläinen 2008).

Thousands of indigenous people died during these centuries of struggle. Indigenous mortality and social disruption were fueled by occasional edicts from Mexico City that sought to stem Indian raids through programs of extermination. Many more indigenous people, primarily women and children, were taken captive. Captives might then vanish from indigenous populations in two ways. First, many captives became domestic slaves in Spanish households, and Spanish proclivities for incorporation meant that captives and their descendants disappeared into the Hispanic world, their indigenous origins forgotten (Brooks 2002:50–51; Brugge 1968, 1993:97–98; Gutiérrez 1991:151–56). Second, they might be sold on a continent-wide slave market and taken far from their borderlands homes. Still others were enslaved, married, or adopted by their indigenous captors. These captives actually replenished captor numbers, but this meant that Southwest Borderlands groups were an ethnic mélange. The following section provides a sense of the magnitude of loss of life and identity in this region by exploring the interactions of two Southwest Borderlands groups—the Comanches and the Apaches—and their relationship with the Spanish.

From the time of their initial colonization of the Southwest, the Spanish were involved in capturing and enslaving indigenous people. In one of the earliest documented raids, Juan de Oñate, leading the first Spanish colonists to settle in New Mexico, attacked Acoma Pueblo, killing more than eight hundred people. Of the five hundred Acoma people taken captive, all those over age twelve were enslaved for twenty years; of the captive children, girls were given to the missions, and boys to the sergeant major. Sixty or seventy girls were taken to Mexico City to become nuns (Brugge 1993; Schroeder and Stewart 1988:411). Spanish law prohibited enslavement of Indians, but the law was often ignored by the governors of New Mexico. The Spanish justified the practice of buying and selling captives by arguing that they were being "rescued" from heathen Indians who had captured them (Brooks 2002:123). Subsequent to the Acoma massacre, the Spanish did not frequently enslave Pueblo Indians, but they did work with indigenous allies to raid Apachean tribes, Plains Indians, the Utes, and others for the purpose of taking captives (Brugge 1993:96; Schroder and Stewart 1988:411). Slaves were one of the few sources of wealth in the region, and as Spanish governors had often paid more for their appointment than they would receive in salary, the slave trade was an opportunity for profit (Brugge 1993:96). Historian David Brugge (1993:97) calls the Spanish market for captives in colonial New Mexico "the strongest economic power in the region."

Most slaves were sold by indigenous captors to Spanish settlers as household servants. The wealthiest Spanish kept the largest number of slaves, but the majority of families had at least a few. Slaves were not only a source of wealth but also a status symbol for Spanish families (Brugge 1993:97). Following prehistoric patterns of Plains-Pueblo interaction, slaves and other goods were frequently exchanged at fairs held at pueblos that bordered the plains, especially Taos and Pecos. Here captives from many borderlands groups were bought and sold, although the Comanches likely supplied most of the captives from Plains tribes (Brugge 1993:98). Other captives were sold to markets outside of New

Mexico. The Comanches sold Apache women east to the French, and many were sent south to the mines at Parral in Chihuahua (Brugge 1993:98). Records from the 1710s, for example, report over four hundred captives taken in New Mexico. Some had been illegally taken, but by the time efforts were made to recover them, many had been sold away, died of smallpox, and or been baptized, meaning that they could not be returned to their non-Christian families (Brugge 1993:98).

Like the briefly ascendant Westos, some borderlands groups profited from European intrusion, and the Comanches were perhaps the most successful. Their efforts to engage Spanish markets and control trade across the region had serious consequences for other groups. A Shoshonean group originating in the Great Basin, the Comanches established themselves in the southern plains during the late seventeenth century and throughout the course of the eighteenth century became one of the most successful of the mobile raiding and trading groups. Adopting European technology, including horses, guns, and metal-tipped lances and arrows, they created what historian Pekka Hämäläinen (2008) has described as an "empire." The Comanchería eventually extended west nearly to Taos, north beyond the Big Timbers of the Arkansas, east almost to the junction of the Cimarron and Arkansas Rivers, and south to less than one hundred miles from San Antonio (Hämäläinen 2008:169). In the process of creating their empire, the Comanches repeatedly attacked and eventually dislodged the Apaches from the Great Plains south and west of the Rio Grande (Hämäläinen 2008:64). Allied with the Utes, Comanche warriors raided west into Navajo territory (Hämäläinen 2008:25) and attacked the Pawnees and Arapahoes to the north and the Osages to the east, in all areas killing and taking captives. They sold many captives at the fairs in Taos and kept many others. Success on their eastern front gave them access to markets in Louisiana controlled by the French, who were eager for slaves (Hämäläinen 2008:42–44). Meanwhile, the Comanches had alternately friendly and antagonistic relationships with the Spanish and frequently raided Spanish and *genízaro* (mixed indigenous and Spanish people [see Brooks 2009]) villages, killing and capturing many.

Comanche raids on their indigenous enemies caused significant mortality and social disruption. A Spanish expedition heading toward the Arkansas River valley in 1719 encountered the aftermath of a Comanche-Ute attack on Jicarillas and Sierra Blanca Apaches. One fleeing refugee group reported that the destruction of a single rancheria had resulted in 60 deaths and 64 women and children captured. As they entered the Arkansas valley, the Spanish found "a wasteland of deserted Apache villages and burned maize fields that the Comanche-Ute invasion [had] left in its wake" (Hämäläinen 2008:34). By 1724, the Comanches had expelled the Apaches from all lands north of the Canadian River. Between 1744 and 1749, the Comanches and Utes attacked Pecos and Galisteo Pueblos, killing at least 150 people (Hämäläinen 2008:44). On the eastern front, a 1751 attack on the Osages by allied Comanche and Taovayas warriors killed 22 Osage chiefs and untold others (Hämäläinen 2008:49). At about the same time, the Comanche began expanding south into Texas, systematically displacing the Lipan Apaches (Hämäläinen 2008:58–62). Spanish attempts to help the Apaches infuriated the Comanches, who with their allies "attacked Apache villages and Spanish settlements relentlessly, creating a broad, triangle-shaped shatterbelt extending from the San Sabá to San Antonio and Nueces missions" (Hämäläinen 2008:61). In the end, the Lipans were pushed south to the coastal Texas plain. The number of Lipan dead and captured was almost certainly large.

The Comanches attacked newly established Spanish towns, and some were abandoned. For example, a raid on Abiquiu in 1747 netted 23 women and children. In 1760, after a Spanish insult at the summer fair in Taos, Comanche raiders ravaged the Taos valley, burning and sacking local ranches. From one ranch for which records exist, they took 60 women and children (Hämäläinen 2008:51; see also Brooks 2002:64). After a brief peace in the early 1760s, Comanche attacks escalated dramatically, making the Rio Grande valley one of the most violent places in America. "Mixing small hit-and-run guerrilla raids with massive destroy-and-plunder operations [the Comanches] killed and captured hundreds of settlers . . . and left dozens of villages burned and abandoned" (Hämäläinen 2008:74).

Although the Comanches were most often the successful aggressors, they also occasionally sustained significant losses at the hands of the Spanish and their indigenous allies. In 1747 the Spanish, retaliating for attacks on their settlements in northern New Mexico, encountered a large camp of Utes and Comanches along the Chama River. The Spanish killed 107 Indians and took 206 captive (Hämäläinen 2008:42). Four years later in another success for the Spanish, 112 Comanches were killed on the Llano Estacado by a force retaliating for a Comanche raid on Pecos. Of the 33 Comanche survivors, 4 women were retained, but others sent back to their people as an offer of peace (Hämäläinen 2008:46). In 1761, in the aftermath of the Taos valley disaster, Comanches returned to Taos to attempt to reestablish trade relations with the Spanish. Negotiations failed, and while the Spanish chased Comanche warriors (killing more than 400), a group of Utes newly allied with the Spanish attacked the Comanche camp, taking more than 300 women and children captive (Hämäläinen 2008:52). Only 36 Comanches survived. Given an estimated 10,000 Comanches at their population peak, this must have been a significant blow to their numbers (Hämäläinen 2008:66). On the eastern front, the Spanish were also sometimes successful against the Comanches, reporting 50 killed and 149 captured in a 1758 retaliatory raid in Texas and "heavy casualties" in 1766 when the Spanish attacked a band of Comanches and their allies in the same region.

While the Comanches often had the upper hand in their interactions with the Spanish, other groups did not fare as well. Apachean groups (Apaches and Navajos) were frequent targets of raids, not only by the Comanches but also by the Spanish and other groups. A record of Spanish attacks on the Apaches during one year in the early eighteenth century is exemplary. In 1705, a newly appointed governor "took his time on the way to Santa Fe to campaign against Apache bands in the El Paso area" (Brugge 1979:108–9). In June, in a campaign against the Gilas and Chilmos, "the Spaniards claimed success in killing some warriors and capturing some of their families, causing the Apaches to flee into the mountains" (Brugge 1979:109). In September, a second campaign "wrought even greater destruction, again killing and capturing many, burning corn and homes, and bringing back as loot horses, sheep, goats, buckskins, baskets, and other items" (Brugge 1993:110). That same month, a different Spanish expedition was sent out to invade Hopi territory but "made an unprovoked attack on some Apaches to capture children" (Brugge 1993:111).

As the eighteenth century progressed, many Apache groups were pushed south and west by the Comanches into areas that are now part of northern Mexico. Apache groups that had occupied the relatively rich plains, where they had been buffalo hunters and part-time agriculturalists, entered the mountains and deserts of northern New Spain where obtaining a livelihood was more difficult. The original inhabitants of Chihuahua and Sonora had fought the Spanish, but by the early eighteenth century these groups had been devastated by Spanish punitive expeditions and disease, leaving the area open for the Apaches (Griffen 1988a:1–2). Apache raids on Spanish settlements and presidios were most intense in the early 1770s. Between 1771 and 1776 in Nueva Vizcaya (the modern Mexican states of Chihuahua and Durango), "1,674 Spaniards were killed, 154 were captured, over one hundred ranches were abandoned, and over sixty-eight thousand animals were stolen" (Griffen 1988b:33). Apache raids were obviously very effective.

But the small population of Apaches also suffered substantial casualties during this period, which must have significantly affected their numbers. A series of events reported by Griffen (1988b:30–33) lists Apache deaths and captives taken: in late 1770 near the Pecos River, 28 dead, 36 captured; in 1771 in the same area, 58 dead; in 1773, 45 dead and many wounded; in 1774 near Sierra de la Escondida, 4 dead; in 1774 in the Sierra del Hacha, 7 dead and 13 captured; in 1775 in the Sierra del Cobre, 20 captured; in 1775 east of the Rio Grande and in the Sacramento Mountains, 40 dead and 7 captured; in 1775 in the Mimbres-Mogollon-Gila country, 4 dead and 18 captured. Between October 1 and early November 1775, Spanish attacks on fifteen rancherias resulted in 132 Apaches dead and 104 captured (Griffen 1988b:33).

By the 1790s, Spanish pacification efforts had proved successful, and many Apaches settled near presidios, where they were provided with rations (Griffen 1988a:3). However, after Mexico won its war of independence in 1821, the resources of the new country were stretched thin. In 1831, the government quit supplying food to the Apaches, and they left the presidios and returned to raiding (Griffen 1988a:3–4). Mexico then fixed on a policy of extermination, "hiring paid killers and hit squads, frequently North Americans and other foreigners, to exterminate Apaches" (Griffen 1988a:6). They offered enormous sums for Apache scalps: 100 pesos for a male scalp, 50 pesos for those of women, and 25 pesos for a child's scalp (Bailey 1966:31–32). One scalp hunter arrived in Chihuahua City in 1845 with 182 scalps, 18 captives, and some Mexican women and children he had rescued. In response, the Apaches only intensified their raiding. They were finally subdued when Anglo-Americans took over much of the northern part of New Spain in 1848.[2]

Violence engendered by the Spanish entrada into the Southwest Borderlands resulted in the death of thousands of people from the sixteenth through nineteenth centuries, and many more indigenous people disappeared. Some were sold to the mines of southern Chihuahua (Bailey 1966:20; Brooks 2002:50–51; Hämäläinen 2008:27), and others were transshipped to the Caribbean, a Spanish practice since the earliest days of Spanish involvement in New Spain (Brooks 2002:61; Conrad, 2015). For example, during the last two decades of the eighteenth century, as many as five hundred Apaches were transported to the Caribbean, along with other groups (Conrad, 2015; Conrad describes the fate of Apaches who were sent to Havana in 1802). Countless captives simply disappeared from the rolls of indigenous people as they were absorbed into local Hispanic society. While the English in the eastern United States rapidly set about establishing racial boundaries between themselves and the African and indigenous people they enslaved, the Spanish incorporated indigenous people, albeit at the lowest rungs of their society. Early eighteenth-century baptismal records document Indians "adopted" or "redeemed" by the Spanish, although in fact these individuals became low-status domestic slaves in colonial households (Brugge 1968, 1993). As Brugge notes for New Mexico, "A typically New Mexican *casta* (class) became established as a result of the incorporation of these people into the society. Made up of captives and their descendants . . . they were collectively called genízaros. . . . Their numbers and specific ethnic origins fluctuated according to the wars fought, the vulnerability of the various tribes to raiding, and the availability of captives through trade" (1993:97; see also Brooks 2009; Gutiérrez 1991:151).

Although genízaros were part of an exploited class, James Brooks (2009:326) argues that "kinship was the route by which genízaros gradually influenced and became part of a larger Hispano identity group in northern New Mexico." Similar processes of incorporation also depleted or eliminated indigenous identities in what are now the states of northern Mexico (Gutiérrez, chapter 5, this volume).

As in the rest of North America, European diseases including smallpox and cholera killed many of the indigenous people who occupied the Southwest Borderlands, but warfare and captive-taking almost certainly had a significant effect on population levels. Both the Comanches and the Apaches were highly adaptable people who used both negotiation and aggression to better their place in the multiethnic postcolonial world they inhabited. Nevertheless, warfare caused by indigenous adoption of European technology, efforts to co-opt European trade, Spanish efforts to foment hostilities among indigenous groups and to commercialize captives, and occasional attempts at outright extermination by Spanish and subsequently Mexican governments all combined to take a severe toll on Native people and their traditional societies.

## Warfare, Captive-Taking, and Population Decline in North America

The size of the indigenous population of North America at the time of European contact has been a topic of scholarly study for almost two hundred years (Ubelaker 2006). Population estimates have always varied widely, which makes estimating the magnitude of population decline especially difficult. While there is no doubt that the introduction of European diseases had a significant effect on indigenous population size (Crosby 1972; Dobyns 1966, 1983; Fenn 2001; Kelton 2007; Ramenofsky 1987), scholars have begun to recognize that other causes, especially cultural disruption, also took a toll (Ubelaker 2006:699). This study attempts to evaluate one such factor: the increase in warfare and captive-taking as a result of the introduction of globalized European markets to North America. I argue that indigenous competition for access to European markets, the commercialization of captives/slaves, and European encouragement of indigenous conflict all served to increase warfare and raiding throughout Native North America. The result was a steep increase in deaths from violence that further reduced indigenous populations. Captives were taken and suffered a variety of fates that resulted in shortened life spans, reduced fertility, transshipment outside the region, and the erasure of indigenous identity.

The effects of European intrusion on indigenous warfare and captive-taking were evident in each of the three areas I examined: the Southeast, the Pays d'en Haut, and the Southwest Borderlands. Estimates of numbers of Native peoples killed or captured in raids and warfare are sketchy, although they have been best documented in the Southeast (Gallay 2002; Ethridge 2009) and based on these, warfare here seems to have been most devastating to indigenous populations. As Gallay (2002:299–308) shows, a large number of southeastern Native Americans were killed or sold off the continent. The Pays d'en Haut suffered violent wars for much of the seventeenth and eighteenth centuries, involving especially the Iroquois in the seventeenth century and the Foxes in the eighteenth century. Death and the dislocation suffered by captives decimated many groups there. In the Southwest Borderlands, many indigenous people were killed during the constant raiding carried out by the Spanish, Comanches, and Apaches, especially from the late seventeenth to early nineteenth centuries. Many captives were also sold out of the region to become part of the globalized market in slaves. Numerous others ended up as domestic slaves in Spanish households, where their indigenous origins and those of their descendants were erased through baptism, sexual appropriation, and separation from their Native society. Differences in the racialization practiced by the English in contrast to tendencies toward incorporation practiced by the Spanish affected outcomes in the two regions to some extent, although loss of indigenous identity also occurred in the East and in other parts of North America.[3]

What is especially difficult to assess is the degree to which social disruption arising from warfare and captive-taking caused ancillary deaths. In the Huron example above, historical accounts suggest that famine resulted after wars in which refugees had to flee their homes during the middle of the growing season. Comanche raids on Apache agricultural settlements similarly resulted in burned fields and refugees who were forced to adopt new means of survival. The aftermath of war, raiding, and captive-taking in many parts of North America must have frequently disrupted subsistence practices and led to famine or starvation. Even more difficult to reconstruct, but perhaps equally ruinous, may have been the interruption of social systems that had sustained indigenous people for centuries. Mortality rates from disease and injuries sustained in battle almost certainly increased as curers and curing methods were lost, families and caregivers separated, the enslaved denied treatment, and the ill left to die alone.

## Notes

1. The demographic effect of the death of women is, of course, far greater than the death of men, and the destruction of a way of life must also have significantly shortened indigenous life span in the region.

2. For a detailed study of the period 1831–48, including the numbers killed and captured on both the Indian and the Mexican sides, see DeLay 2008.

3. Among seventeenth-century Virginia Algonquian peoples, "Indians severed their bonds with tribal society, lived on English plantations, mixed with non-Indians, and gradually lost tribal and Indian identity, at least in the eyes of White observers" (Feest 1973:74, quoted in Ubelaker 2006:699).

## References

Albers, Patricia. 1993. Symbiosis, merger, and war: Contrasting forms of intertribal relationship among historic Plains Indians. *In* The Political Economy of North American Indians, edited by John H. Moore, 94–132. Norman: University of Oklahoma Press.

Alt, Susan. 2008. Unwilling immigrants: Culture, change, and the "other" in Mississippian societies. *In* Invisible Citizens: Captives and Their Consequences, edited by Catherine M. Cameron, 205–22. Salt Lake City: University of Utah Press.

Bailey, L[ynn] R[obison]. 1966. Indian Slave Trade in the Southwest. New York: Tower Publications.

Baker, Brenda J., and Lisa Kealhofer, eds. 1996. Bioarchaeology of Native American Adaptation in the Spanish Borderlands. Gainesville: University Press of Florida.

Bowne, Eric E. 2005. The Westo Indians: Slave Traders of the Early Colonial South. Tuscaloosa: University of Alabama Press.

———. 2009. "Caryinge awaye their corne and children": The effects of Westo slave raids on the Indians of the Lower South. *In* Mapping the Mississippian Shatter Zone: The Colonial Indian Slave Trade and Regional Instability in the American South, edited by Robbie Ethridge and Sheri M. Shuck-Hall, 104–14. Lincoln: University of Nebraska Press.

Boyd, Mark F., Hale G. Smith, and John W. Griffin. 1951. Here They Once Stood: The Tragic End of the Apalachee Missions. Gainesville: University Press of Florida.

Brooks, James F. 2002. Captives and Cousins: Slavery, Kinship, and Community in the Southwest Borderlands. Chapel Hill: University of North Carolina Press.

———. 2009. "We betray our own nation": Indian slavery and multi-ethnic communities in the Southwest Borderlands. *In* Indian Slavery in Colonial

America, edited by Alan Gallay, 319–52. Lincoln: University of Nebraska Press.

Brugge, David M. 1968. Navajos in the Catholic Church Records of New Mexico, 1694–1875. Research Reports 1. Window Rock, AZ: Research Section, Parks and Recreation Department, Navajo Tribe.

———. 1979. Early 18th century Spanish-Apachean relations. *In* Collected Papers in Honor of Bertha Pauline Dutton, edited by Albert H. Schroeder, 103–22. Albuquerque, NM: Albuquerque Archaeological Society Press.

———. 1993. The Spanish Borderlands: Aboriginal slavery. *In* Encyclopedia of the North American Colonies, edited by Jacob Ernest Cooke, 91–101. New York: Charles Scribner's Sons.

Cameron, Catherine M. 2008a. Captives in prehistory: Agents of social change. *In* Invisible Citizens: Captives and Their Consequence, edited by Catherine M. Cameron, 1–24. Salt Lake City: University of Utah Press.

———, ed. 2008b. Invisible Citizens: Captives and Their Consequence. Salt Lake City: University of Utah Press.

———. 2011. Captives and culture change: Implications for archaeology. Current Anthropology 52(2):169–209.

———. 2015. Commodities or gifts? Captive/slaves in small-scale societies. *In* The Archaeology of Slavery: A Comparative Approach to Captivity and Coercion, edited by Lydia Wilson Marshall, 24–40. Occasional Paper 41. Carbondale: Center for Archaeological Investigations, Southern Illinois University.

Carocci, Max, and Stephanie Pratt, eds. 2012. Native American Adoption, Captivity, and Slavery in Changing Contexts. Basingstoke, UK: Palgrave Macmillan.

Chacon, Richard J., and Rubén G. Mendoza, eds. 2007. North American Indigenous Warfare and Ritual Violence. Tucson: University of Arizona Press.

Conrad, Paul. 2015. Indians, convicts, and slaves: An Apache diaspora to Cuba at the start of the nineteenth century. *In* Linking the Histories of Slavery in North America and Its Borderlands, edited by James Brooks and Bonnie Martin. Santa Fe, NM: School for Advanced Research Press.

Crosby, Alfred W., Jr. 1972. The Columbian Exchange: Biological and Cultural Consequences of 1492. Westport, CT: Greenwood.

Cybulski, Jerome S. 1990. Human biology. *In* Handbook of North American Indians, vol. 7: Northwest Coast, edited by Wayne Suttles, 52–59. Washington, DC: Smithsonian Institution Press.

———. 1992. A Greenville Burial Ground: Human Remains and Mortuary Elements in British Columbia Prehistory. Hull, QC: Canadian Museum of Civilization.

DeLay, Brian. 2008. War of a Thousand Deserts: Indian Raids and the U.S.-Mexican War. New Haven, CT: Yale University Press.

DePratter, Chester B. 1991. Late Prehistoric and Early Historic Chiefdoms in the Southeastern United States. New York: Garland Publishing.

Dobyns, Henry F. 1966. Estimating aboriginal American population, 1: An appraisal of techniques, with a new hemispheric estimate. Current Anthropology 7:395–449.

———. 1983. Their Numbers Become Thinned: Native American Population Dynamics in Eastern North America. Knoxville: University of Tennessee Press.

Donald, Leland. 1997. Aboriginal Slavery on the Northwest Coast of North America. Berkeley: University of California Press.

Dye, David. 2004. Art, ritual, and chiefly warfare in the Mississippian world. *In* Hero, Hawk, and Open Hand: American Indian Art of the Ancient Midwest and South, edited by Richard Townsend and Robert Sharp, 191–206. New Haven, CT: Yale University Press.

Ekberg, Carl J. 2007. Stealing Indian Women: Native Slavery in the Illinois Country. Urbana: University of Illinois Press.

Ethridge, Robbie. 2009. Introduction. *In* Mapping the Mississippian Shatter Zone: The Colonial Indian Slave Trade and Regional Instability in the American South, edited by Robbie Ethridge and Sheri M. Shuck-Hall, 1–62. Lincoln: University of Nebraska Press.

———. 2012. The emergence of the colonial South: Colonial Indian slaving, the fall of the precontact Mississippian world, and the emergence of a new social geography in the American South, 1540–1730. *In* Native American Adoption, Captivity, and Slavery in Changing Contexts, edited by Max Carocci and Stephanie Pratt, 47–64. New York: Palgrave Macmillan.

Ethridge, Robbie, and Sheri M. Shuck-Hall, eds. 2009. Mapping the Mississippian Shatter Zone: The Colonial Indian Slave Trade and Regional Instability in the American South. Lincoln: University of Nebraska Press.

Feest, Christian F. 1973. Seventeenth century Virginia Algonquian population estimates. Quarterly Bulletin of the Archaeological Society of Virginia 28(2):66–79.

Fenn, Elizabeth A. 2001. Pox Americana: The Great Smallpox Epidemic of 1775–82. New York: Hill and Wang.

Foster, William H. 2003. The Captor's Narrative: Catholic Women and Their Puritan Men on the Early American Frontier. Ithaca, NY: Cornell University Press.

Gallay, Alan. 2002. The Indian Slave Trade: The Rise of the English Empire in the American South, 1670–1717. New Haven, CT: Yale University Press.

———, ed. 2009. Indian Slavery in Colonial America. Lincoln: University of Nebraska Press.

Griffen, William B. 1988a. Utmost Good Faith: Patterns of Apache-Mexican Hostilities in Northern Chihuahua Border Warfare, 1821–1848. Albuquerque: University of New Mexico Press.

———. 1988b. Apaches at War and Peace: The Janos Presidio, 1750–1858. Albuquerque: University of New Mexico Press.

Gutiérrez, Ramón. 1991. When Jesus Came, the Corn Mothers Went Away: Marriage, Sexuality, and Power in New Mexico, 1500–1846. Stanford, CA: Stanford University Press.

Hämäläinen, Pekka. 2008. The Comanche Empire. New Haven, CT: Yale University Press.

Keeley, Lawrence H. 1996. War Before Civilization: The Myth of the Peaceful Savage. Oxford: Oxford University Press.

Kelton, Paul. 2007. Epidemics and Enslavement: Biological Catastrophe in the Native Southeast, 1492–1715. Lincoln: University of Nebraska Press.

Lauber, Almon W. 1979 [1913]. Indian Slavery in Colonial Times Within the Present Limits of the United States. Williamstown, MA: Corner House Publishers.

Laudonniére, René. 2001. Three Voyages. Translated by Charles E. Bennett. Tuscaloosa: University of Alabama Press.

Martin, Debra L. 2008. Ripped flesh and torn souls: Skeletal evidence for captivity and slavery from the La Plata valley, New Mexico, AD 1100–1300. *In* Invisible Citizens: Captives and Their Consequences, edited by Catherine M. Cameron, 159–80. Salt Lake City: University of Utah Press.

Meyers, Maureen. 2009. From refugees to slave traders: The transformation of the Westo Indians. *In* Mapping the Mississippian Shatter Zone: The Colonial Indian Slave Trade and Regional Instability in the American South, edited by Robbie Ethridge and Sheri M. Shuck-Hall, 81–103. Lincoln: University of Nebraska Press.

Miles, Tiya. 2005. Ties That Bind: The Story of an Afro-Cherokee Family in Slavery and Freedom. Berkeley: University of California Press.

Ramenofsky, Ann F. 1987. Vectors of Death: The Archaeology of European Contact. Albuquerque: University of New Mexico Press.

Richter, Daniel K. 1983. War and culture: The Iroquois experience. William and Mary Quarterly 40(4):528–59.

———. 2011. Before the Revolution: America's Ancient Pasts. Cambridge, MA: Harvard University Press.

Rushforth, Brett. 2003. "A little flesh we offer you": The origins of Indian slavery in New France. William and Mary Quarterly 60(4):777–809.

———. 2006. Slavery, the Fox wars, and the limits of alliance. William and Mary Quarterly 63(1):53–80.

———. 2012. Bonds of Alliance: Indigenous and Atlantic Slaveries in New France. Chapel Hill: University of North Carolina Press.

Santos-Granero, Fernando. 2009. Vital Enemies: Slavery, Predation, and the Amerindian Political Economy of Life. Austin: University of Texas Press.

Schroeder, Albert H., and Omer C. Stewart. 1988. Indian servitude in the Southwest. *In* Handbook of North American Indians, vol. 4: History of Indian-White Relations, edited by Wilcomb E. Washburn, 410–13. Washington, DC: Smithsonian Institution.

Snyder, Christina. 2010. Slavery in Indian Country: The Changing Face of Captivity in Early America. Cambridge, MA: Harvard University Press.

Trigger, Bruce G. 1976. The Children of Aataentsic: A History of the Huron People to 1660. Montreal: McGill-Queen's University Press.

Ubelaker, Douglas H. 2006. Population size, contact to nadir. *In* Handbook of North American Indians, vol. 3: Environment, Origins, and Population, edited by Douglas H. Ubelaker, 694–701. Washington, DC: Smithsonian Institution.

White, Richard. 1991. The Middle Ground: Indians, Empires, and Republics in the Great Lakes Region, 1650–1815. Cambridge: Cambridge University Press.

Wood, Peter. 1989. The changing population of the colonial South: An overview by race and region, 1685–1790. *In* Powhatan's Mantle: Indians in the Colonial Southeast, edited by Peter H. Wood, Gregory A. Waselkov, and M. Thomas Hatley, 35–103. Lincoln: University of Nebraska Press.

# Remembering Cherokee Mortality
# During the American Revolution

*Paul Kelton*

# 8

On March 8, 1780, Cherokee warriors captured twenty-eight straggling travelers sailing down the Tennessee River and *might* have acquired something that they surely had not wished for: smallpox. The captives, all belonging to the Stuart family, were said to be "diseased with small-pox" at the outset of their journey. They departed from an upper tribu-tary of the river on December 22, 1779, and kept some distance from the larger flotilla commanded by John Donelson. Donelson aimed to keep the disease from spreading and even had to warn the distant Stuarts "each night when the encampment should take place by the sound of a horn." He appeared to have succeeded; he made no men-tion of smallpox spreading beyond the infected family in his journal, the only surviving written record of the voyage. Isolating the Stuarts, however, made them vulnerable to the Cherokees, or, more precisely, to a dissident faction of the indigenous nation known as the Chicka-maugas. This group remained allied with the British and refused to come to terms with the Americans, as had the majority of their nation. They found the Stuarts a tempting target. "The Indians," Donelson (1779[–80]) recorded, ". . . observing [Mr. Stuart's] helpless situation, singled off from the rest of the fleet, intercepted him & killed & took prisoners the whole crew, to the great grief of the whole Company." Fearing that the Chickamaugas would overtake the whole flotilla, the main group kept moving forward despite hearing the "cries" of those left behind. The Chickamaugas remained in possession of their captives

The original, expanded version of this chapter can be found in Paul Kelton's *Cherokee Medicine, Colonial Germs*. Copyright © 2015 by the University of Oklahoma Press, Norman, Publishing Division of the University. The author wishes to acknowledge the generous support of the University of Kansas, College of Liberal Arts and Sciences, for a General Research Fund Grant (#2301729) that funded the completion of this essay.

and their baggage while the rest of the Donelson party completed its circuitous route down the Tennessee and then up the Cumberland to settle near present-day Nashville (Donelson 1779[–80]).

What happened next to the Chickamaugas is not entirely clear. If any one of the Stuarts had at the time an active infection of smallpox, then the warriors may have become infected and an epidemic may have erupted. Descendants of those Tennessee pioneers seem to remember it that way, and scholars—historians, anthropologists, and others—have agreed. Some even conclude that not just the Chickamaugas but also the Cherokees as a whole suffered. But no written record that dates to 1780 confirms that the indigenous nation suffered a widespread outbreak of smallpox. Logic suggests a successful transmission of disease at least to some Chickamaugas, but hard evidence has yet to be found. So, if the evidence does not clearly reveal whether the Native captors of the Stuarts and their countrymen suffered from colonialism's most deadly disease, then what can this episode tell us? A great deal, as I argue in this chapter. First, it highlights the need for scholars to critically examine and carefully contextualize the evidence that is used when discussing colonial germs and their impact on indigenous peoples. Faulty memories and frontier mythology often contaminate the data we use for our analyses. Second, such problematic evidence supports conclusions in which germs are given more agency than they deserve in the depopulation and dispossession of indigenous peoples. Consequently, the actions of the colonizers in destroying the health and well-being of Natives become forgotten.

The suggestion that the Chickamaugas suffered an epidemic in 1780 first appeared in print in 1857, when John Carr, at the age of eighty-four, published his memoirs of early pioneer life in Tennessee. "Though but a small boy at the time," Carr (1958 [1857]:9) recollected "the reports of the great and terrible mortality which prevailed in the Cherokee Nation after the capture of Stuart's boat." He added, "Without doubt, the wretches paid dearly for their booty" (Carr 1958 [1857]: 9). There is some reason to question Carr's memory, however. Carr was a seven-year-old resident of Virginia at the time of the Donelson party's voyage; he did not participate in the voyage but went to Tennessee some years later. There, he may have heard tales from other settlers of smallpox avenging the deaths of the Stuarts, but in a letter to Lyman Draper in 1854, Carr does not refer to the Chickamaugas succumbing to the disease when discussing the Donelson party. His knowledge of this early attempt at white settlement in the Cumberland valley, moreover, appears to have come directly from the published accounts of Judge John Haywood (1823:85–96) and James G. M. Ramsey (1853:197–202). Neither of these authors concluded that the Chickamaugas in fact became infected and suffered an outbreak. It seems that between 1854 and 1857, then, Carr added an epidemic to his memory of events.

One can only speculate what triggered Carr to add "the great and terrible mortality" of the Chickamaugas to the events of the Donelson party's voyage. But a passage he includes just below his mention of the epidemic is suggestive. "It was said that, when they were attacked with the small-pox, and the fever was upon them," Carr (1958 [1857]:9) wrote about the Natives, "they took a heavy sweat in their houses for that purpose, and then leaped into the river and died by scores." Carr or someone whom he relied on for information had almost certainly read James Adair's *The History of the American Indians* (1776), a memoir written by a trader who lived and worked among the southeastern Indians for much of the eighteenth century and claimed to have observed Cherokee medical personnel attempting to deal with a smallpox epidemic in 1738. "When they found their theological regimen had not the desired effect, but that the infection gained upon them," Adair (2005 [1776]:252–53) wrote about Native medicine men, "they held a second consultation, and deemed it the best method to sweat their patients, and plunge them into the river,—which was accordingly done." The eighteenth-century trader concluded that such practices killed many people. "Their rivers being very cold in summer, by reason of the numberless springs, which pour from the hills and mountains—and the pores of their bodies being open to receive the cold, it rushing in through the whole frame, they immediately expired" (Adair 2005 [1776]:253). Settlers on their way to Tennessee would have had no knowledge of how the Chickamaugas responded, if indeed they had a need to respond at all to smallpox. The inclusion of Adair's account makes Carr's rendition appear even more fabricated. The Chickamaugas suffered doubly: once because of punishment for their attack on the Stuarts' boat and again because of their supposed ignorance in how to deal with a deadly disease.

Carr's memories of Chickamauga mortality received greater circulation when, two years later, Albigence Waldo Putnam included them in his *History of Middle Tennessee* (1859). Putnam reprinted Donelson's journal verbatim and then cited Carr and unnamed "others" as authorities on what happened to the Chickamaugas (Putnam 1859:69–75). "As the result of the capture of Stuart's boat and crew, in which were the cases of small-pox, Mr. Carr has stated, and others have affirmed the same, that 'great mortality' prevailed in the Cherokee nation afterwards. Without doubt the wretches paid dearly for their booty" (Putnam 1859:77). Putnam also included reference to smallpox-stricken Indians leaping into the river but added one more detail about their supposed demise that reveals James Adair's influence: "A large majority destroyed themselves, or died with the disease," Putnam claimed. Adair had indeed referred to mass suicide of Cherokee medical personnel for their failure to cure patients during the 1738 epidemic. "A great many killed themselves," the English trader wrote: "[S]ome shot themselves, others cut their throats, some stabbed themselves with knives, and others with sharp-pointed canes; many threw themselves with sullen madness into the fire, and there slowly expired" (Adair 2005 [1776]:253). Putnam went a step further and added what was standard Jacksonian rhetoric about the demise of American Indians being their own fault. The smallpox epidemic, mass suicide, "and other diseases and vices, raged among them, and so increased that the nation was hastening to extinction" (Putnam 1859:77). He concluded that in committing the murders of the Stuarts and other settlers, the Chickamaugas had invited the "judgment of heaven," which came in the form of smallpox that "destroyed hundreds of them" (Putnam 1859:309).

The Chickamaugas' supposed demise became written into an even more widely read narrative when Theodore Roosevelt (1889) included the anecdote in volume 2 of his four-volume series, *The Winning of the West*. Roosevelt narrated a version of the American past in line with prevailing Manifest Destiny ideology, wherein Providence destined an inferior race of indigenous peoples to disappear amid a tide of superior Euro-Americans who would spread civilization across the North American continent. The Donelson party received their due as part of this epic saga. The future president used the original manuscript of Donelson's journal and for the most part accurately summarized its contents. He referred to the family having smallpox, being kept at the rear of the larger group, and thus becoming vulnerable to attack. The future president, though, went off script and included the details that Carr had concocted and that Putnam later echoed. "But a dreadful retribution fell on the Indians," Roosevelt (1889:336–37) claimed, "for they were infected with the disease of their victims, and for some months virulent small-pox raged among many of the bands of Creeks and Cherokees." Then Roosevelt (1889:337) added Adair's information for more drama: "When stricken by the disease, the savages first went into the sweat-houses, and when heated to madness, plunged into the cool streams, and so perished in multitudes." While this is largely a summary of what Putnam had earlier published, Roosevelt added some interesting details. The epidemic raged for "some months," and the death toll involved "multitudes," a term that could easily mean that more Natives actually died than the "scores" that Carr and "hundreds" that Putnam suggested. More damaging is that germs became benighted actors in Roosevelt's grand and celebratory narrative of American expansion.

Roosevelt's scholarly legacy unfortunately persisted into the twentieth century. James Mooney drew upon *The Winning of the West* when writing the first professional historical and ethnographic account of the Cherokee people. A forerunner of today's ethnohistory, Mooney's *Myth of the Cherokees* (1900) utilized primary sources as well as ethnographic information that he garnered from Cherokee informants. But he barely scratched the surface of the documentary sources available and relied heavily on secondary work published in the nineteenth century. "As if in retributive justice," Mooney (1900:56) wrote while referencing Roosevelt, "the smallpox broke out in the Chickamauga band in consequence of the capture of Stuart's family, causing the death of a great number." A later and more fully documented treatment of Cherokee history perpetuated the tale of the 1780 epidemic. John P. Brown (1938:182n9) wrote as a matter of fact, "[T]he Chickamaugas contracted smallpox from the captives." Brown (1938:182n9) gave no reference to his source for this factual-sounding statement, but he had earlier cited the works of both Roosevelt and Putnam, from which he must have derived his estimate of "several hundred" Cherokees dying.

The two medical scholars E. Wagner Stearn and Allen E. Stearn helped perpetuate the story of the Chickamaugas' demise. In a coauthored work that offered the first scholarly treatment of smallpox's impact on American Indians, they sought to use the experiences of Indians to promote universal vaccination. They included the supposed infection of the Chickamaugas among the numerous anecdotes to make their case and did not deviate from previous accounts of the event. "The Cherokee Indians captured a boat on which were twenty-eight persons, among whom was a man named Stuart, and his family, who were infected with the smallpox," the Stearns (Stearn and Stearn 1945:46) wrote while citing Mooney's *Myths of the Cherokees.* "As if in retribution, smallpox broke out among the Chickamauga band, causing the death of many" (Stearn and Stearn 1945:46). To be fair, the Stearns referred to violent conflict, enslavement, and removals for causing Native population decline, but these other factors were mentioned only in passing, giving the reader the impression that smallpox acted as an independent agent. Indeed, as they stated in their preface, the virus acted "as a weapon in the hands of the white man, a weapon so powerful that it was feared by the red man much more than were bullets and swords." It was this disease above all other aspects of colonialism that had doomed indigenous peoples, and had it not been for vaccination, something they assert was made available through Euro-American benevolence, Indians would not have had "a chance for survival" (Stearn and Stearn 1945:8).

More-recent scholars have found it difficult to free their work from colonial narratives. The historian Peter Wood, for example, cites the supposed 1780 epidemic as a fact that helps explain the growing population disparity between indigenous peoples and Europeans and African Americans in the colonial South. "The disease quickly spread through the remote Indian settlement and, according to one authority, 'caused the death of several hundred Indians,'" Wood claimed, while citing Brown as the authority (Wood 1987:35). The sociologist Russell Thornton did not add much critical insight into the episode in his work on Cherokee demography. "[S]mallpox is said to have struck a dissident group of Cherokees, the Chickamaugas," Thornton (1990:34) passively asserts and then quotes the Stearns at length. He properly cites his source but unfortunately allows the information to stand without scrutinizing its validity (Thornton 1990:34). To be sure, both Wood and Thornton provide valuable works of scholarship that move us closer to understanding the full demographic impact of colonialism on indigenous peoples. They also do not entirely ignore other factors such as slavery, warfare, and theft of resources, but the perpetuation of a problematic assertion is troubling.

The same can be said of Elizabeth Fenn in her 2001 *Pox Americana: The Great Smallpox Epidemic of 1775–82*. Citing the Donelson journal as her only source, Fenn (2001:116) states as a matter of fact that while some Chickamaugas ventured into Georgia to help the British, "their families in the mountains of Tennessee had just picked up smallpox in an attack on some settlers."[1] She then concludes her discussion of Britain's Native allies in the South with an allusion to major population losses from disease: "For . . . the Cherokees . . . , the pox and the war were disastrous: Having chosen the losing side, the Indians soon had to face an onslaught of Anglo-American expansion with much-depleted numbers" (Fenn 2001:133). The war part of the equation, however, remains left out of the discussion. American military actions against Cherokees are only vaguely referenced in the pages of *Pox Americana*, which in the end echoes deterministic narratives of colonial germs rather than the colonizer's exercise of force ensuring Native depopulation and dispossession (e.g., Crosby 1972, 1976, 1986; Dobyns 1983). "*Variola* was a virus of empire," Fenn (2001:275) asserts. "[I]t made winners and losers, at once serving the conquerors and determining whom they would be." Fenn, to be sure, does not rely on the Cherokees' supposed infection in her skillful and eloquent reconstruction of smallpox's spread across North America, with southern Appalachia included as a leg on its journey. The capture of members of the Donelson party was a minor anecdote that a reader would hardly remember unless he or she was specifically interested in the Cherokees. If the author had omitted reference to the incident, the larger importance of the work would still stand: prior to *Pox Americana*, scholars knew only bits and pieces of what was in reality a massive continental epidemic.

Extreme violence and not the great smallpox epidemic of 1775–82 in fact figures prominently in the documentary record of the Cherokees' experience during the American Revolution. The contemporary scholars referenced above including Thornton, Wood, and Fenn, I am sure, would readily acknowledge the horror that the Cherokees faced amid brutal warfare waged against them, but the exclusive discussion of disease by scholars has occluded the violence and leads readers in a dangerous direction. One only has to make a brief examination of the Cherokees' experience during the American Revolution to see how the colonists' violent actions and not their germs did the most damage.

A major outbreak of hostilities with the settlers was hardly what the Cherokees needed in the 1770s. They were then recovering from the past traumas associated with colonialism. Smallpox certainly made a devastating visit in 1738–39 and may have struck at least twice before, once around 1698 and then again around 1711 (Kelton 2007:152–53, 175–76). The indigenous population in southern Appalachia prior to these epidemics cannot be known with certainty, but Peter Wood (1989:38, 63) makes a reasonable estimate of 32,000. By the 1750s, the population had shrunk to around 9,000. A war with the British that began in 1759 and ended in 1761 took its toll as well. British armies invaded three different times, resulting in numerous villages being burned, hundreds of people being driven into the woods to starve, and an outbreak of measles and smallpox that spread among the thousands of refugees. Cherokee population likely reached its nadir at 7,200 by the end of the war (Wood 1989:38, 63–65). The dire situation led at least one Cherokee leader to reveal that his people were consciously trying to increase their population. In 1762, the esteemed war leader Ostenaca had recently been in England and reported to the governor of South Carolina that he and his party found that the "number of warriors and people of one colour" they saw in England "far exceeded what [they] thought possible." He added, "Our women are breeding children night and day to increase our people and I will order those who are growing up to avoid making war with the English" (Ostenaca 1762). Actual population increase following the war with the British is impossible to calculate precisely, but Wood (1989:38, 65) again makes a reasonable estimate of some 8,500 Cherokees by the time of the American Revolution.

Cherokees certainly had the potential to increase their population during the first half of the 1770s. An epidemic of an unknown disease appears to have had some damaging impact, but no further outbreaks would be reported among any Cherokee groups until the supposed 1780 outbreak (Kittagusta 1766). Meanwhile, Cherokee subsistence practices remained stable. Maize, bean, and squash production provided a rich diet, and all indications are that cultivation of this triad flourished during the years before the Revolution. In addition, Cherokees increasingly turned to domestic livestock in the 1760s and 1770s. Women had begun to keep hogs and chickens sometime earlier in the eighteenth century, and their holdings of these animals increased in the early 1770s

(Hatley 1989). One would expect, then, that female fertility among the Cherokees remained relatively high, at least compared to hunting-and-gathering tribes whose constant movement, regular periods of deprivation, and high-protein, low-carbohydrate diets depressed female fertility. Conflict with other Natives also appeared to slacken and take less of a toll on their population. Cherokees were embracing a growing pan-Indian alliance that stretched from the Great Lakes to the Gulf of Mexico (Dowd 1992). According to one British agent, Cherokees had received the appeals of their former Shawnee enemies to halt "shedding the Blood of their Red Brothers" and had accepted "that it was time for them to unite and oppose the Progress of the White People as they undoubtedly intended to extirpate them from the face of the Earth" (Cameron 1774). The Cherokees listened to such appeals with approval and sent emissaries to the north to foster peace (Cameron 1774). Such acceptance did not automatically lead the Cherokees into the fight against the colonists. When Lord Dunmore and Virginia waged war on the Shawnees in 1774, Cherokees did not rush to aid their new Native friends. Nevertheless, they did not help the British king and his still-loyal subjects either, as they had during the early years of the Seven Years War (1754–63). Protecting their population from the harmful impact of war seemed paramount to many Cherokee leaders.

As the Americans began to sever their ties with the British, Cherokees grew more divided about what to do. Late in 1775, the British superintendent for Indian affairs in the South, John Stuart, gave a green light to his deputy, Alexander Cameron, and other British agents to supply Natives with provisions and military materials. He also sent antirebel talks to King George III's Native friends and encouraged them to act in concert with His Majesty's troops rather than attacking indiscriminately (O'Donnell 1973:33). In April 1776, the British delivered twenty-one wagon loads of ammunition to the Cherokee town of Chota. The more militant warriors led by Dragging Canoe did not want to wait for more detailed plans from the British and argued that settlers who had taken up residence nearest to their nation should be pushed back immediately. Women threatened the men not to go to war. Many males, Alexander Cameron learned, grew "very uneasie About their women and children, saying that [if] any rupture should happen between them and the white people the women would run to the wood and starve" (Cameron 1776). A decade of recovery was in danger should major conflict escalate.

And escalate it did. In late spring and into summer, Dragging Canoe's warriors joined with northern Natives—Shawnees, Delawares, and Mohawks—and launched multipronged attacks on backcountry settlers (O'Donnell 1973:42–43). Americans believed that Native attacks were precursors for a larger British invasion by sea, and hysteria reigned (Hatley 1995:192). Thomas Jefferson of Virginia ingrained such hysteria into the Declaration of Independence, including in the famous list of grievances against King George III the charge that he "has endeavoured to bring on the inhabitants of our frontiers, the merciless Indian Savages, whose known rule of warfare, is an undistinguished destruction of all ages, sexes and conditions." To a colleague back in Virginia, Jefferson (1776) explicitly expressed what ought to be done to those most involved in the raids on the southern colonies: "I hope that the Cherokees will be driven beyond the Missisipi & that this in future will be declared to the Indians the invariable consequences of their beginning a war." Such suggestion might correspond with how one today would define ethnic cleansing. One of the leading South Carolina patriots went even further. William Henry Drayton wrote to military commanders, "[I]t is expected you make smooth work as you go—that is you cut up every Indian corn field, and burn every Indian town—and that every Indian taken shall be the slave and property of the taker; that the nation be extirpated, and the lands become the property of the public" (quoted in Hatley 1995:192). Griffith Rutherford (1776:652), who would command North Carolinian forces, echoed such genocidal urges and called for "a Finel Destruction of the Cherroce Nation." Three of his fellow North Carolinians, then serving in the Continental Congress, sympathized with the homicidal desires of those whom they represented. "To extinguish the very race of them and scarce to leave enough of existence to be a vestige in proof that a Cherokee nation once was, would perhaps be no more than the blood of our slaughtered countrymen might call for," they exclaimed. Yet they urged their state's forces to act with some humanity: "But Christianity, the dear Religion of peace & mercy, should hold our conquering hands, & while we feel the resentment of Men, We ought not to forget the duties of the Christian. Women and Children are not a Conquest worth the American Arms." For Native men, however, there would be no holding back. "[M]ercy to the warriors is cruelty to ourselves," they concluded (Hooper et al. 1776:731).

What followed was total war on the Cherokees. Each of the four divisions of the nation—Lower, Middle, Valley, and Overhills—suffered. Andrew Williamson's South Carolinian troops converged on the lower towns in August 1776. One participant referred to the Cherokees as "game" but did not get much of a chance to hunt his prey, as Natives abandoned their towns on the approach of the Carolinians (Rockwell 1867:214). The same man was astonished by the bounty of Cherokee agriculture. "[T]hey were very well stored, far beyond our conception," he marveled (Rockwell 1867:214). The invaders carted off all the food they could and destroyed the rest. Every lower town lay in ruins, with the homes and public buildings of each put to the torch. In September, Williamson's forces converged with Rutherford's North Carolinians in the middle towns. The region's inhabitants fled in advance, setting the woods on fire to cover their escape, but the Americans caught a few stragglers and took them captive. An officer later claimed that he at first denied permission to the men to sell the prisoners into slavery but his men "Swore Bloodily that if they were not sold for Slaves upon the spot, they would Kill & Scalp them Immediately." The commander gave way on the issue and reported back to his superior that his men were "Very spirited & Eager for Action, and . . . Very Desirous that your Honnour would order them upon a second Expedition" (Moore 1776: 897).

The main damage to the Cherokees remained the scorched earth that Americans left behind. After torching the middle towns, the armies of the two Carolinas marched through the valley towns. There, Cherokees resisted in a two-hour battle and managed to kill or wound thirty-one of the invaders. In the end, Carolinians overwhelmed the warriors and forced them to retreat. Cherokees left supplies that they would need to survive the upcoming winter, including a large supply of "blankets, moccasins, boots, some guns, matchcoats, deerskins, &c, &c" (Rockwell 1867:219). After this brief fight, the total war continued. At the first valley settlement, the troops, according to one soldier, "spread through the town to destroy, cut down and burn all the vegetables belonging to our heathen enemies, which was no small undertaking, they being so plentiful supplied" (Rockwell 1867:219). The soldier also commented on the vast number of hogs that the Cherokees had, as well as "great apple trees, and, whiteman-like improvements." These were quickly destroyed. Most Cherokees again managed to escape before the troops arrived in their villages, but North Carolina's troops managed to surround one town before all of its inhabitants vacated and killed an unreported number of them (Rockwell 1867:219). Americans surprised another group and captured sixteen individuals, largely consisting of Tory traders, their wives, and bicultural children (Hamilton 1940: 256; Rockwell 1867:220). Most of these would later return to the Cherokee Nation, but an untold number of others were not so lucky. One soldier, for example, captured a lame woman and immediately killed her, while another soldier killed an "old Indian prisoner" that he had in his possession (Hamilton 1940:256; Rockwell 1867:219).

Meanwhile, Virginia's forces bore down on the Overhills. On October 18, Colonel William Christian and his forces of over one thousand men arrived on the Little Tennessee after having received conflicting messages about Cherokee intentions to resist. It turned out that he met with no opposition as he went through the first four towns along his path. "[T]he Indians had ran off hastily," Christian (1776:61) reported. "[S]ome of them had shut their doors and some had not: they had carried off their cloathes & best of their Household goods but took but little provisions." He continued, "[T]he greatest part of them I judged went off in Canoes down the Tenesee." The colonel found abandoned "Horses, Cattle, Dogs, Hogs, and Fowls"; remarked that "[t]he crops of Corn and sweet potatoes are very great"; and estimated that the residents of the Overhill towns must have left "between forty and fifty thousand bushels of Corn and ten or fifteen thousand Bushels of Potatoes" (Christian 1776:61). Unlike the Carolinians, the Virginians paused before commencing any destruction. They treated with relative kindness "an old woman and two children" by giving them food after they had been in the woods for six days and nights "without Fire or provisions other than Grapes and Hawes" (Christian 1776:61). They also took in "a young man who had lost his wife and was then in search of her." He told the Virginians that his people "were so much afraid that they would fly before [the Americans] wherever [they] went" (Christian 1776:62). The Overhills people had certainly learned the fate of their nation's other divisions and feared that they would end up enslaved or killed if they remained.

Christian made some effort to distinguish between hostile Cherokees and those who would agree to peace. The colonel suggested to
Governor Patrick Henry that such an effort would be a more honorable
course for their newly independent state. "I know six [Cherokee lead-
ers] that I could kill & take Hundreds of them, and starve hundreds by
destroying their corn," he reported, "but it would be mostly the women
and children as the men could retreat faster than I can follow and I am
convinced that the Virg'a State would be better pleased to hear that I
showed pity to the distressed and spared the suppliants; rather than I
should commit one act of Barbarity in the destroying [of] a whole nation of Enemies" (Christian 1776:62). Perhaps the Carolinians' prior efforts weighed a bit on the colonel's conscience? Christian sent a request
to the Raven of Chota to discuss terms, which above all else meant the
surrender of Alexander Cameron, the British agent whom settlers held
most responsible for instigating indigenous violence. The Virginians,
though, did not receive what they wanted and took punitive actions.
Joined by three hundred North Carolinians, Christian's forces spared
Chota and some other towns but destroyed the five towns perceived to
be most hostile (Williams 1776). The punishment was as severe as what
towns in the nation's other divisions faced. Joseph Williams, one of
Christian's officers, later recalled that the Overhills "had great numbers
of fat cattle and hogs, with poultry of every kind in abundance." The
soldiers consumed or drove off the livestock and either burned or destroyed the Natives' "immense quantities" of corn (Williams 1925:110–
11). Without their season's harvest, their livestock, shelter, clothing, and
bedding, many people of the Overhills found themselves in the same
situation as the vast majority of their countrymen in the other divisions.
Cherokees faced the ensuing winter of 1776–77 as a nation of starving
and exposed refugees.

They suffered additional violent assaults before their supposed experience with smallpox in 1780. The majority of their nation tried to come
to terms with the Americans. In 1777, they treated with representatives
from the southern states and surrendered substantial quantities of land
to their north and east (O'Donnell 1973:57–58). Dragging Canoe and
his faction wanted nothing to do with accommodating the Americans.
They rejected the land cessions, seceded from the larger nation, moved
south to the bend of the Tennessee River, and established several towns

on Chickamauga Creek, from which they received their name (C. Stuart 1777). The Chickamaugas continued to receive supplies from the British and raid Americans (J. Stuart 1778). In April 1779, two hundred Chickamaugas went to help the British in their attack on Savannah, but while they were away, nine hundred North Carolinians and Virginians under Colonel Evan Shelby destroyed all eleven Chickamauga towns. Dragging Canoe's warriors subsequently retaliated and courted another American invasion (Brown 1938:175). In the fall, Colonel Andrew Williamson pursued some of the Native raiders into northern Georgia. There, South Carolinians burned seven towns—some of which had been built by refugees from the 1776 invasion—at the height of harvest, bringing the residents another severe period of hunger. One British agent commented that these Cherokees were "living upon nuts & whatever they can get." He managed to purchase three hundred bushels of corn from other Cherokee divisions to alleviate their hunger (A. Cameron 1779c).

As Americans enacted another round of town burnings, the great smallpox epidemic of 1775–82 made its appearance in the South. Elizabeth Fenn is certainly correct to conclude that some Natives became infected. The Cherokees' southern Native neighbors, the Muskogees or Creek Confederacy, suffered a terrible outbreak (Fenn 2001:115). Transmission possibly occurred through trading or diplomatic engagement with the British at Pensacola, a place in which smallpox proliferated during the winter and spring of 1779. Muskogee warriors possibly could have also acquired the disease by way of infected American captives they brought back to their towns. In any event, the consequent epidemic became evident to the British. Alexander Cameron (1779b) reported to General Augustine Prevost that the Creeks "seem to be tired of War . . . besides the Small Pox has reduced them much, and those Towns who have not had it as yet, have fled with their Families into the Woods." Word of the outbreak reached the Americans. The *Pennsylvania Gazette* reported on October 27, 1779, "The smallpox, we are told, rages most violently among the Creek Indians at present, so that they will hardly be able to do any thing for their British brothers this campaign." Some Cherokees also became infected. In December 1780, the British commander at Augusta, Georgia, reported that smallpox had incapacitated 140 Creeks and Cherokees who were helping defend the city from the rebels. The commander added that the infected Natives were being nursed back to health and he expected them to recover (Brown 1780b). Still, neither he nor any other source suggested that the great epidemic made its way into the Cherokee Nation.[2]

Cherokees in fact were aware of smallpox's presence near them and tried to avoid it. At the same time that one party of Chickamaugas supposedly picked up the virus from the Stuarts, another group of their warriors begged out of helping the British for fear of the dreaded disease. "Having held a conference with the [Chickamauga] Indian chiefs on this subject," one British officer reported, "they told me, they were willing & ready to give every assistance in their power to the Great King & had come down from their nation for that purpose but that as the small pox (from a general inoculation being permitted by the civil authority) raged throughout the province, they would not be able to prevail on their young men & warriors to remain under their present apprehensions of receiving an infection from which their nation had on a former occasion sustained a loss of 2500 men" (Brown 1780a). The Cherokee leaders likely had the devastating 1738–39 epidemic in their minds, an event that they may have survived during their younger years or that they learned about from their elders. In any event, they fully knew the dangers of the disease and warned the British that "if only one of the party was infected the others would disperse & run into the woods" (Brown 1780a). The officer concluded "that it would be highly impolitic in the present juncture to hazard our Indian interest by exposing them to a contagion so fatal" (Brown 1780a). Cherokees consequently went away to "shun the smallpox," leaving it unknown to their British friends and posterity whether they took the virus with them (Prevost 1780).

Cherokees of course *could* have had a major smallpox epidemic in 1780. Chickamaugas perhaps did pick up the virus from the British near Savannah, despite their efforts to shun the disease. They perhaps could have taken the disease back to their villages by way of infected captives they took in Georgia or the Carolinas, or perhaps their capture of the Stuarts on the Tennessee River did in fact lead their warriors to contract the contagion. Nevertheless, one should not automatically jump to the conclusion that a successful transmission occurred or exaggerate the possible impact that this supposed transmission had. It may be the case that Cherokee warriors who were exposed to the disease were not susceptible.

Some of them may have been survivors of previous smallpox epidemics in 1738–39, 1749, and 1759–61 and thus had acquired immunity (Wood 1987:34). Younger warriors in their teens, of course, would have been vulnerable, but transmission was not certain simply because Indians were involved. The Stuarts, moreover, may not have been as viable of a vector as they first appear to be. Recall that the journey began on December 22 and the Chickamaugas captured them on March 8. Did the Stuarts maintain a chain of infection over this more-than-two-month period? By the time of the incident, smallpox may have run its course through them, unbeknownst to Donelson, who had limited contact with the stragglers as he kept them away from the larger group. Lastly, supposing that transmission occurred from an infected captive to a susceptible Chickamauga warrior, one should not assume that the disease inevitably spread. Cherokees had learned to quarantine infected patients and close off unexposed villages from outside contact when smallpox was suspected of spreading nearby. By the time of the American Revolution, in other words, they realized smallpox was an infectious disease, sought to avoid it, and tried to curtail its spread when it arrived (Kelton 2004). Of course, the war would have made it difficult to maintain such preventative measures, giving one more reason to believe that smallpox spread amid the chaos and upheaval that Cherokees faced.

Such speculation, however, detracts from the more potent and devastating aspect of colonialism that the American Revolution brought to the Cherokees. The extreme violence of the period predated their supposed infection and continued after. Americans again launched a massive assault on the Cherokee people not long after they supposedly contracted smallpox. Dragging Canoe planned to attack settlers in North Carolina during the fall of 1780, but other Cherokees worried that his activities would bring disaster on all of them. Led by the Beloved Woman Nanye-hi (known by the Americans as Nancy Ward), the peace faction warned the Americans of Dragging Canoe's plans and hoped they would be spared any retaliation. They were not. Late in 1780, John Sevier led 250 men into the Cherokee Nation, defeated a large body of warriors on the way, and killed 34 (Brown 1938:192–93). Sevier waited for Arthur Campbell's forces of 400 Virginians to join him, and when they arrived in late December, the Americans repeated what they had done in 1776 and 1779. They feasted on the food that Cherokees left behind and put three towns to the torch. At Hiwassee, Nanye-hi approached the troops and asked for peace, but instead they torched two more towns (Brown 1938:194–95). Campbell reported destroying fifty thousand bushels of corn along with countless other provisions before his and Sevier's forces left on January 1, 1781 (O'Donnell 1973:107). Sevier, though, returned in March. He burned fifteen middle towns, killed 29 Natives, and took another 9 prisoner (Brown 1938:196). Such actions left many Cherokees "perishing in the woods & eating roots" (Clanosee et al. 1781). The Raven of Chota later said of Campbell's and Sevier's actions that "they dyed their hands in the Blood of many [of] our Women and Children." He pled with the British for help, claiming, "[O]ur families were almost destroyed by famine this spring" (Raven 1781).

Cornwallis's surrender at Yorktown brought no respite to Cherokees. Dragging Canoe and the militants continued to seek vengeance against the Americans. But a series of small raids against South Carolinians late in 1781 provoked massive retaliation. Andrew Pickens's forces destroyed thirteen Cherokee towns, while Elijah Clarke's troops sacked another seven towns. In 1782, John Sevier returned, laid waste to some of the valley towns, and inflicted the most devastating assault on the Chickamaugas yet. He deliberately planned his invasion to occur after crops had ripened, and he consequently destroyed vast quantities of produce as well as all the livestock he could find (Sevier 1901). At least nine towns were destroyed in the process (Brown 1938:200). Pickens returned as well. His South Carolinians along with a force from Georgia rushed into the Cherokee Nation in September and October to force Lower, Middle, and Chickamauga Cherokees to surrender prisoners, horses, and loyalists (O'Donnell 1973:127). By the end of 1782, Colonel William Christian predicted that "hundreds" of Cherokees would die of starvation. They were "almost naked," he claimed, and "their corn and Potatoes, it is supposed will be all done before April. And many are already out, particularly widows and Fatherless Children" (Christian 1782). One Cherokee leader exclaimed to the departing British that he had lost "in different Engagements Six hundred Warriors" and in addition, his "towns [had] been thrice destroyed and [his] Cornfields laid waste by the enemy" (Cherokee Headmen 1783).

Even without a smallpox epidemic, then, the American Revolution proved to be an utter catastrophe for the Cherokee people. As in the other cases discussed in chapters in this volume (especially those by Larsen, Martin, Swedlund, Cameron, and Hull), colonialism escalated violence and created traumatic living conditions under which Cherokees found it difficult to recover from population losses. The Americans' scorched earth tactics caused immeasurable harm and led to numerous deaths from starvation and exposure. Such violence stifled a decade of recovery and according to Wood brought Cherokee population to 7,500, or only 300 above his estimate for its nadir after the 1759–61 British war (Wood 1989:38). Smallpox did infect at least a small number of Cherokees confined with the British at Augusta and may have been more widespread, but the Americans did not need to introduce the deadly disease, either wittingly or unwittingly, to produce a dire health crisis for Natives they sought to conquer. By waging a scorched earth policy, something completely intended, they purposely altered material conditions knowing that severe human suffering and fatalities would result. The chaos and upheaval of the war in fact may have been a necessary precondition for something like smallpox to spread widely and create extreme mortality rates among those who became infected.

That a frontier settler's memory of smallpox became written into the Cherokees' experience during the Revolutionary War further exemplifies something deeply problematic in the larger literature on the European introduction of novel germs. David Jones (chapter 1, this volume, and 2003) has eloquently and powerfully critiqued this literature, and to this critique one can add that many historians have been misled by unsubstantiated claims that have found their way into their analyses as fact. Perhaps it may be as Jones states that using "morally neutral biohistorical forces" has great interpretive appeal that has led both academics and a lay audience to accept with little question the works of Alfred Crosby (1976, 1986), Jared Diamond (1997), and Charles Mann (2005, 2011), but as this chapter shows, narratives of disease are anything but morally neutral. Non-Natives told stories of smallpox's impact on their indigenous adversaries for a reason, and scholars have been complacently uncritical about these stories. Narratives of disease thus continue to be told that obscure how colonialism—in all its manifold yet connected aspects—has negatively impacted indigenous health and well-being. Most troubling, and far from being morally neutral, such narratives silence Native voices—voices that with some research can be found in the historical record. Meeting with representatives from the state of Virginia at the end of the Revolution, for example, a Cherokee delegation sought peace and asked a question—a very important question that turns out to be central to this volume. "Look back and recollect what a numerous and warlike people we were, when our assistance [was] asked against the French on the Ohio—we took pity on you then, and assisted you," they began. "We have been continually since, decreasing, and are now become weak. What are the causes?" We would all do well to listen to their answer: "War, and succeeding invasions of our Country" (Cherokee Chiefs 1782).

## Notes

1. Fenn cites Donelson et al. 1964. This includes a verbatim transcript of Donelson's journal that is in the Tennessee State Library and Archives. There are no editorial footnotes added to the version Fenn cites, and thus no one other than the reader could make the inference that a successful transmission of smallpox from the captives to captors occurred.

2. Something other than smallpox may have caused significant mortality among Cherokees in 1779, but the evidence for this remains problematic. In 1804, Dr. Benjamin Smith Barton wrote that Cherokees suffered from what Euro-American traders called "the head-Pleurisy" that was "common along the low-grounds of the River Tennessee, and near stagnant waters." He claimed that "[i]n the course of a single week, in the summer of 1779, it carried off 350 of these Indians. Some of the sick died after an illness of less than twenty-four hours. The practice of sweating was thought to be one cause of the excessive mortality of the disease" (Barton 1804/1805:132–33). He acquired this information from an unnamed source. An examination of the entire Benjamin Smith Barton collections at both the American Philosophical Society and the Historical Society of Pennsylvania has not revealed any evidence of where Barton received this information. Alexander Cameron, who was among the Cherokees that summer, did not report any such epidemic, thus casting doubt on Barton's assertion (Cameron 1779a, 1779b, 1779c). In any event, the symptoms do not appear to be smallpox, and the mortality predated the Donelson voyage.

## References

Adair, James. 2005 [1776]. *The History of the American Indians*. Edited by Kathryn E. Holland Braund. Tuscaloosa: University of Alabama Press.

Barton, Benjamin Smith. 1804/1805. Miscellaneous facts and observations. Philadelphia Medical and Physical Journal 1:132–33.

Brown, John P. 1938. Old Frontiers: The Story of the Cherokee Indians from Earliest Times to the Date of Their Removal to the West, 1838. Kingsport, TN: Southern Publishers.

Brown, Thomas. 1780a. Letter dated March 18, 1780, to Lord George Germaine. Records of the British Colonial Office, class 5/81/225–26, transcript. Library of Congress Manuscript Division, Washington, DC.

———. 1780b. Letter dated December 17, 1780, to General Cornwallis. In Cornwallis Papers, edited by Ian Saberton, 3:295–97. East Sussex, UK: Naval and Military Press, 2010.

Cameron, Alexander. 1774. Letter dated June 18, 1774, to John Stuart. Thomas Gage Papers, vol. 120. William L. Clements Library, Ann Arbor, MI.

———. 1776. Letter dated May 7, 1776, to John Stuart. Records of the British Colonial Office, class 5, part 1, Westward Expansion, 1700–1784, microfilm reel 7. Frederick, MD: University Publications of America.

———. 1779a. Letter dated July 15, 1779, to Lieutenant Governor Henry Hamilton. Haldimand Papers: 1777–1783, Additional Manuscript 21777, microfilm. Manuscript Group, British Museum, London.

———. 1779b. Letter dated October 15, 1779, to General Augustine Prevost. Records of the British Colonial Office, class 5/182/268–69, transcript. Library of Congress, Manuscript Division, Washington, DC.

———. 1779c. Letter dated December 18, 1779, to Lord George Germain. Headquarters Papers of the British Army in America, microfilm reel 9. Library of Congress Manuscript Division, Washington, DC.

Carr, John. 1854. Letter dated October 10, 1854, to Lyman Draper. Draper Manuscripts, microfilm, reel 116, vol. 6, 20, p. 63. State Historical Society of Wisconsin, Madison.

———. 1958 [1857]. Early Times in Middle Tennessee. Nashville, TN: Parthenon Press. Reprint, Nashville, TN: Horsely and Associates.

Cherokee Chiefs. 1782. An address from the friendly chiefs of the Cherokees to the commissioners of the United States, April 29, 1782. In Calendar of Virginia State Papers and Other Manuscripts, 3:171–72. New York: Kraus Reprint, 1968.

Cherokee Headmen. 1783. Talk delivered at Picolata by the headman of the Cherokees as the representatives of his nation, enclosed in letter dated January 12, 1783, from Thomas Brown to Thomas Townsend. Records of the British Colonial Office, class 5/82/631, transcript. Library of Congress Manuscript Division, Washington, DC.

Christian, William. 1776. Letter dated October 15, 1776, to Patrick Henry. Virginia Legislative Papers. Virginia Magazine of History and Biography 17(1):60–62.

———. 1782. Letter dated December 16, 1782, to Governor Benjamin Harrison. In Calendar of Virginia State Papers and Other Manuscripts, 3:398. New York: Kraus Reprint, 1968.

Clanosee et al. 1781. Talk delivered by Clanosee or the Horse Leach & Aucoo, messengers sent by Oconostotee & some other chiefs of the Cherokee Nation on the 28th of April 1781. Draper Manuscripts, microfilm, reel 116, vol. 1, 20. State Historical Society of Wisconsin, Madison.

Crosby, Alfred W. 1972. The Columbian Exchange: Biological and Cultural Consequences of 1492. Westport, CT: Greenwood Publishing.

———. 1976. Virgin soil epidemics as a factor in the aboriginal depopulation in America. William and Mary Quarterly 33:289–99.

———. 1986. Ecological Imperialism: The Biological Expansion of Europe, 900–1900. New York: Cambridge University Press.

Diamond, Jared. 1997. Guns, Germs, and Steel: The Fates of Human Societies. New York: W. W. Norton.

Dobyns, Henry F. 1983. Their Number Become Thinned: Native Population Dynamics in Eastern North America. Knoxville: University of Tennessee Press.

Donelson, John. 1779[–80]. Diary. "Journal of a voyage, intended by God's Permission, in the good Boat Adventure, from Fort Patrick Henry on Holston river to the French Salt Springs on Cumberland River, kept by John Donaldson, Decem. 22, 1779." http://www.tn.gov/tsla/founding_docs/33635 _Transcript.pdf (accessed November 13, 2012). Tennessee State Library and Archives, Nashville.

Donelson, John, et al. 1964. Three Pioneer Documents: Donelson's Journal, Cumberland Compact, Minutes of Cumberland Court. Nashville: Tennessee State Historical Commission, 1964.

Dowd, Gregory Evans. 1992. A Spirited Resistance: The North American Indian Struggle for Unity, 1745–1815. Baltimore, MD: Johns Hopkins University Press.

Draper, Lyman Copeland. n.d. Draper Manuscripts. Microfilm edition. State Historical Society of Wisconsin, Madison.

Fenn, Elizabeth. 2001. Pox Americana: The Great Smallpox Epidemic of 1775–82. New York: Hill and Wang.

Hamilton, J. G. de Roulhac, ed. 1940. Revolutionary diary of William Lenoir. Journal of Southern History 6(2):247–59.

Hatley, M. Thomas. 1989. The three lives of Keowee: Loss and recovery in eighteenth-century Cherokee villages. In Powhatan's Mantle: Indians in the Colonial Southeast, edited by Peter H. Wood, Gregory A. Waselkov, and M. Thomas Hatley, 223–48. Lincoln: University of Nebraska Press.

———. 1995. The Dividing Paths: Cherokees and South Carolinians Through the Revolutionary Era. New York: Oxford University Press.

Haywood, John. 1823. The Natural and Aboriginal History of Tennessee: Up to the First Settlements Therein by the White People, in the Year 1768. Nashville, TN: George Wilson.

Hooper, William, et al. 1776. Letter dated August 7, 1776, to North Carolina Council of Safety. In The Colonial Records of North Carolina, edited by

William L. Saunders, 10:730–32. Raleigh, NC: P. M. Hale, Printer to the State, 1886. Documenting the American South, http://docsouth.unc.edu /csr/index.html/document/csr10-0321 (accessed January 15, 2013). University of North Carolina, Chapel Hill.

Jefferson, Thomas. 1776. Letter dated August 13, 1776. The Avalon Project: Documents in Law, History and Diplomacy, http://avalon.law.yale.edu/18th _century/let8.asp (accessed November 1, 2012). Lillian Goldman Law Library, Yale Law School, New Haven, CT.

Jones, David. 2003. Virgin soils revisited. William and Mary Quarterly 60:703–42.

Kelton, Paul. 2004. Avoiding the smallpox spirits: Colonial epidemics and southeastern Indian survival. Ethnohistory 51:45–71.

———. 2007. Epidemics and Enslavement: Biological Catastrophe in the Native Southeast, 1492–1715. Lincoln: University of Nebraska Press.

———. 2015. Cherokee Medicine, Colonial Germs: An Indigenous Nation's Fight Against Smallpox, 1518–1824. Norman: University of Oklahoma Press.

Kittagusta. 1766. Address to [Charles Greville Montagu,] September 22, 1766. In The Colonial Records of North Carolina, edited by William L. Saunders, 7:256–57. Raleigh, NC: P. M. Hale, Printer to the State, 1886. Documenting the American South, http://docsouth.unc.edu/csr/index.html/document /csr07-0137 (accessed January 15, 2013). University of North Carolina, Chapel Hill.

Mann, Charles. 2005. 1491: New Revelations of the Americas Before Columbus. New York: Alfred A. Knopf.

———. 2011. 1493: Uncovering the New World Columbus Created. New York: Alfred A. Knopf.

Mooney, James. 1900. Myths of the Cherokees. Washington, DC: Bureau of American Ethnology.

Moore, William. 1776. Letter dated November 17, 1776, to Griffith Rutherford. In The Colonial Records of North Carolina, edited by William L. Saunders, 10:895–98. Raleigh, NC: P. M. Hale, Printer to the State, 1886. Documenting the American South, http://docsouth.unc.edu/csr/index.html/document/csr10-0428 (accessed January 15, 2013). University of North Carolina, Chapel Hill.

O'Donnell, James H. 1973. Southern Indians in the American Revolution. Knoxville: University of Tennessee Press.

Ostenaca. 1762. Talk of Judd's friend to governor of South Carolina, South Carolina Council Journal, November 3, 1762. Records of the States of the United States of America, microfilm reel 8. Washington, DC: Library of Congress Photoduplication Service.

Pennsylvania Gazette. 1779. Philadelphia (Pennsylvania), October 27, 1779. http://www .accessible.com/accessible/docButton?AAWhat=builtPage&AAWhere= THEPENNSYLVANIAGAZETTE.GA1779102705.64850&AABeanName =toc3&AANextPage=/printBrowseBuiltPage.jsp (accessed March 5, 2015).

Prevost, Augustine. 1780. Letter dated March 19, 1780, to General Henry Clinton. Headquarters Papers of the British Army in America, microfilm reel 8. Library of Congress Manuscript Division, Washington, DC.

Putnam, A[lbigence] W[aldo]. 1859. History of Middle Tennessee; or, Life and Times of General James Robertson. Nashville, TN: privately printed.

Ramsey, J[ames] G[ettys] M[cGready]. 1853. The Annals of Tennessee to the End of the Eighteenth Century. Charleston, SC: John Russell.

Raven. 1781. Talk of Cherokee Nation delivered by the Raven of Chottee at Savannah, September 1, 1781. Records of the British Colonial Office, class 5/82/510, transcript. Library of Congress Manuscript Division, Washington, DC.

Rockwell, E[lijah] F[rink], ed. 1867. Parallel and combined expeditions against the Cherokee Indians in South and in North Carolina in 1776. Historical Magazine and Notes and Queries, n.s., 2:212–20.

Roosevelt, Theodore. 1889. The Winning of the West. Vol. 2. New York: G. P. Putnam and Sons.

Rutherford, Griffith. 1776. Letter dated July 5, 1776, to North Carolina Council of Safety. In The Colonial Records of North Carolina, edited by William L. Saunders, 10:651–52. Raleigh, NC: P. M. Hale, Printer to the State, 1886. Documenting the American South, http://docsouth.unc.edu/csr/index.html/document/csr10-0275 (accessed January 15, 2013). University of North Carolina, Chapel Hill.

Sevier, John. 1901. A memoir of John Sevier. American Historical Magazine 6:40–45.

Stearn, E. Wagner, and Allen E. Stearn. 1945. The Effect of Smallpox on the Destiny of the Amerindian. Boston: Bruce Humphries.

Stuart, Charles. 1777. Letter dated April 8, 1777, to John Stuart. Records of the British Colonial Office, class 5, part 1, Westward Expansion, 1700–1784, microfilm reel 7. Frederick, MD: University Publications of America.

Stuart, John. 1778. Letter dated March 5, 1778, to Lord George Germaine. Records of the British Colonial Office, class 5, part 1, Westward Expansion, 1700–1784, microfilm reel 7. Frederick, MD: University Publications of America.

Thornton, Russell. 1990. The Cherokees: A Population History. Lincoln: University of Nebraska Press.

Williams, Joseph. 1776. Letter dated November 6, 1776, to president of the Provincial Congress of North Carolina. In The Colonial Records of North Carolina, edited by William L. Saunders, 10:892. Raleigh, NC: P. M. Hale, Printer to the State, 1886. Documenting the American South, http://docsouth.unc.edu/csr/index.html/document/csr10-0424 (accessed January 15, 2013). University of North Carolina, Chapel Hill.

Williams, Samuel C., ed. 1925. Colonel Joseph Williams' battalion in Christian's campaign. Tennessee Historical Magazine 9:102–14.

Wood, Peter. 1987. The impact of smallpox on the Native population of the 18th
    century South. New York State Journal of Medicine 87:30–36.
———. 1989. The changing population of the colonial South: An overview by
    race and region. *In* Powhatan's Mantle: Indians in the Colonial Southeast,
    edited by Peter H. Wood, Gregory A. Waselkov, and M. Thomas Hatley,
    35–103. Lincoln: University of Nebraska Press.

# 9

# Quality of Life

## Native Communities Within and Beyond the Bounds of Colonial Institutions in California

*Kathleen L. Hull*

In 1986, a delegation of Yosemite Indians visiting the Smithsonian Institution National Museum of Natural History was confronted with a disturbing exhibit that proclaimed the extinction of their group more than one hundred years earlier (Rose 1990). Were it not for the profound social and political implications of such an error, one might be reminded of Mark Twain's famous quip that "the report of my death was an exaggeration." Instead, this event—and no doubt many similar experiences of other Native people in North America in recent decades—highlights the failure of scholars, museums, and public institutions to fully appreciate and adequately communicate both the process and the outcome of indigenous encounters with non-Native disease during the colonial era. While mass mortality and the loss of traditional lifeways in the wake of introduced diseases is the master narrative in many public venues—and such simplistic stories have captured the imagination of the public (e.g., Diamond 1997; Mann 2005), sometimes encouraged by the injudicious language of an earlier generation of anthropologists (see Leventhal et al. 1994)—the issues of health and survival are much more complex than we are often led to believe. It is a disservice to both descendant communities and our collective heritage and history to ignore the myriad factors that contributed to when and how Native peoples confronted such challenges to survival and how groups, if not many individuals, often endured.

This interpretive shortcoming may lie, in part, in the fact that discussion of indigenous health in the wake of colonial-era lethal epidemics has often entailed one of two extreme analytical approaches—either qualitative concern for individual experience of illness and suffering, or quantitative focus on population vulnerability and demographic impacts. Within the diverse contexts of Native and non-Native peoples, places, practices, and pathogens in which indigenous people of the Americas engaged with European colonialism, however, the community may form a better locus for considering this process with respect to both biological and social health. Neither too personal nor too large, *community* captures both the relevant scale of Native experience and the dynamic environment in which options with health implications were assessed and exercised. Equally important, it is this sociopolitical core that often dictates recognition of contemporary indigenous groups under federal law in the United States—that is, if and how such communities were sustained contributes significantly to the acknowledgment of their sovereignty as nations today (see Lightfoot 2006; Lightfoot et al. 2013).

Thus, this chapter takes the community as an analytical frame to explore both qualitative and quantitative data regarding how community factored into Native experience and response, how Native communities may have reconstituted themselves in the aftermath of mass mortality, and how decision making in the wake of disease may have led to the vital communities that exist today. To accomplish this task, I first consider what is meant by *community* and what measures of a "healthy community" might have been affected by disease-induced catastrophic mortality. Next, I apply these concepts to colonial California, exploring case studies of the different communal experiences of Native people in the interior—beyond direct interaction with non-Native people but nonetheless dealing with the consequences of this foreign presence—and other Native people on the coast who were incorporated into Spanish colonial institutions and economies, as we typically envisage colonial encounters. Such comparisons highlight the importance of community processes to the outcomes of colonial entanglements. Community is especially germane to California, where small-scale Native groups were embedded in webs of interconnection within and beyond their villages. Ethnohistoric and archaeological data reveal both similarities and differences in the sustainability and quality of life of Native communities in coastal Spanish colonial institutional settings and those in the distant interior beyond the direct effects of European colonization. Such differences in community, rather than simply distance from or proximity to colonizers or exposure to disease, had profound implications for Native people and, thus, how we should understand Native health outcomes.

## Life of the Community

*Community* has been variously defined, understood, and debated by anthropologists, archaeologists, and other social scientists for more than one hundred years, in part because the term enjoys widespread use both within and beyond the academy (Brint 2001; Yaeger and Canuto 2012). While there is a common public perception of community that connotes shared location, knowledge, interests, identity, and social solidarity, scholars recognize that communities are rarely so bounded and cohesive. In addition, application of the term to geographically unconstrained cyber, virtual, or "imagined" (Anderson 2006) communities has further complicated the concept. There is now relatively little consensus on whether, and which, qualities are essential to *community* in such diverse applications. Still, many researchers contend that the concept is relevant in sociological, anthropological, and archaeological studies, "in part . . . [because of] an awareness of the community's importance in larger social processes" (Yaeger and Canuto 2012:4; see also Brint 2001; Pauketat 2012:19).

Rather than defining community by a list of traits—or, worse yet, simply equating "community" with "site," as has been common in archaeological research (Yaeger and Canuto 2012:3)—recent scholarship has moved to a process-oriented, emic understanding in which community is conceived "as a dynamic socially constituted institution that is contingent upon human agency for its creation and continued existence" (Yaeger and Canuto 2012:5). That is, *community* refers to a particular locus of interactions in which "a sense of belonging is . . . promoted by gratifying experiences, reassuring narrative, and expectations of future nurturing, but it is also promoted by desires and intentions, negative as well as positive. What counts is expression of belonging, in ways that are socially apparent" (Isbell 2012:249). This perspective on community resonates with the concept of *gemeinschaft* employed by sociologist Ferdinand Tönnies (2001) in the late nineteenth century to distinguish community from society (*gesellschaft*) but eschews the implicit notion that communities are "natural" or uncontested. Rather, communities are produced and reproduced through human agency in historically contingent contexts and ways, consistent with Pierre Bourdieu's (1977) notion of practice. Moreover, as an "ephemeral and ever-emergent" entity constantly in the process of becoming through actions and intent (Yaeger and Canuto 2012:8), community has properties of a "living organism," subject to growth, change, and perhaps decline, transcending individuals as "the parts are dependent on and conditioned by that whole, so that the whole itself possesses intrinsic reality and substance" (Tönnies 2001:21).

Following this emic perspective, community served "to successfully reproduce organism, society, and culture" (Isbell 2012: 243) and thus is a reasonable approximation of the way many indigenous groups in North America both understood and lived lives of mutual dependency and benefit at the time of European (and later American) colonization. Such peoples, whether small-scale agriculturalists or hunter-gatherer-fisherfolk, freely associated from birth within groups of several hundred people that were, in turn, embedded within larger social networks of no more than perhaps two thousand total individuals—all or some of whom may have come together only once or twice a year, effectively expanding "community" beyond the bounds of everyday interaction for at least a brief time in practice rather than simply in spirit. Economic activities, access to resources, authority, decision making, and affinity were based at the local level and often involved communal consent and action. The basis of relationships lay in mutual support, cooperation, and reciprocity, contributing to a spirit of fellowship and shared identity. These characteristics are consistent with what have been termed bands or tribes (Service 1962).

Such organization was clearly the case in most, if not all, of Native California, for example. As noted by Alfred Kroeber (1925:832), "[T]he California Indian . . . always gives the impression of being attached first to a spot, or at most a few miles of stream or valley, and to his blood kindred or a small group of lifelong associates and intimates" (see also Lightfoot 2006:64). While some diversity of sociopolitical organization and scale has been noted across California between different ethnolinguistic groups—which are themselves constructs of ethnographers rather than entities recognized by Native people in everyday life—large polities and complex sociopolitical organization were largely absent.

In addition, archaeological evidence spanning thousands of years substantiates this assessment and indicates a long tradition of local, direct interaction and, presumably, shared identity and practice (e.g., Bennyhoff and Fredrickson 1994). Such a small scale likely necessitated both physical and social dependency, while facilitating a sense of community. Community was a living entity in its own right, nurturing its members and, in turn, nurtured through ritual and daily practices even as individuals came and went over the course of a lifetime.

Kroeber referred to these Native California entities as tribelets, "village communities" that existed as "sovereign though miniature political unit[s], which . . . [were] land-owning and maintained . . . frontiers against unauthorized trespass. The population size might run as low as 100, or as high as 500–600" (Kroeber 1955:307). Moreover, "'village' in this connection must be understood as implying a tract of land rather than a settlement as such" (Kroeber 1925:831); in fact, there were often shifts in the location of the primary tribelet village seasonally or over the longer term. Given the basis of tribelet identity around land rather than a specific village, group names often referenced place and were maintained regardless of the specific location of the major village at any given time. Exogamy or other forms of intergroup marriage, which were typical of many traditional California Native peoples, underscored the sense of difference yet connection within a broader regional network. As noted by Randall Milliken (1995:24), however, intermarriage tended to be between individuals from adjacent or nearby groups, and "long-distance intermarriage was limited in part because of the commitment people felt to their home territory and to their own way of doing things. The unfamiliar was disturbing and seemed dangerous."

Elsewhere in North America, indigenous identity—and presumably, community, as used herein—also resided at local level even when within a superstructural "society" tied together by religious beliefs, exchange, and hierarchy. This is suggested, for example, by Native tribal names in the Southeast, which were maintained even as groups relocated during the colonial era from the place to which the name originally referred (Waselkov and Smith 2000). This likely also pertained prior to the colonial era, although at that time such southeastern groups may have been larger polities that were, in turn, part of the Mississippian interaction sphere (Blitz 1999). As in California, groups elsewhere in North America likely found their origin in extended kin relations; shared economic orientation, tasks, language, and worldview; and had a common identity that was intentionally or unintentionally reinforced through daily practices. In building and maintaining mutual support and belonging, community in Native North America was integral to the social, political, spiritual, and economic life of indigenous peoples.

As these data suggest, the notion of community as a living organism provides a useful metaphor for considering the implications of community on biological and social health outcomes attributable to direct or indirect encounters with Euro-American colonialism. Likewise, this perspective allows us to assess what a "healthy community" might entail. Beyond the practical necessity of individual aid when in the grip of potentially fatal illness, as a living entity itself, a healthy community must both support and be supported by its members to endure through periodic challenges. In fact, the notion of a healthy community has found traction in scholarship and policy making in recent decades, as contemporary municipalities seek to both preserve and enhance the well-being of their residents. In this modern context, two general categories of community health have been identified: sustainability and quality of life. Each plays out over a different temporal span, with the former related to "long-term health and vitality—cultural, economic, environmental, and social" (Belseme and Mullin 1997:47), while indicators of the latter "focus on a more immediate time frame and make fewer linkages across issue areas" of physical and social health (Belseme and Mullin 1997:48).

Sustainability in contemporary thinking generally refers to continued development "without compromising the ability of future generations to meet their own needs" (Belseme and Mullin 1997:47). For the current argument, it is appropriate to focus primarily on cultural rather than natural resources in terms of needs, although both were certainly intertwined for Native people. Thus, sustainability is equated herein with perseverance of a shared identity and mutual support through maintenance of an unbroken trajectory of beliefs and values—if not all specific material and religious practices—that are the lifeblood of a living community. Importantly, sustainable communities persist despite the fact that individuals may not interact on a daily basis and even as population shifts with births and deaths.

Whereas sustainability relates to long-term survival, quality of life is perceived and assessed on a daily basis via the priorities of a particular community. Therefore, such priorities, as well as the measures of success related to each, vary from group to group but typically encompass physical, emotional, and social needs made possible by access to resources, interaction with others, individual agency, and other factors. So, not only does a healthy community endure over the long term as a collective entity (that is, sustainability), but also individuals within the community gauge satisfaction in the short term on diverse issues by whatever measures are appropriate to (and dictated by) the time, place, and people.

In the event of colonial-era lethal epidemics, both quality of life and sustainability of indigenous communities were threatened, although sustainability—perhaps ultimately dictated by the cumulative effects of quality of life in the wake of colonialism—is what had the most profound implications for the sovereignty of contemporary Native groups. The introduction of non-Native disease had the potential to undermine the foundations of Native community within and beyond the bounds of colonial institutions in several ways, as groups responded to such crises. As discussed in detail elsewhere (Hull 2009), archaeological and ethnohistoric evidence from across North America reveal social, cultural, and demographic consequences of substantial, rapid population decline due to fatal epidemics. These include population aggregation, perhaps of disparate groups with different practices and identities; emigration to areas outside traditional territories; shifts in external relations and regional interaction; decreasing cultural diversity as a result of the founder effect; despecialization in particular practices or roles; simplification of social structure; blending of different practices and beliefs through creolization; and perhaps even ethnogenesis (that is, the establishment of a new communal identity) as a result of group blending or simply in response to the trauma of an event. One or more of these effects may also have prompted or forced survivors to enter missions or other colonial institutions, effectively dissolving community as known up to that point. In addition, there may have been psychological or emotional effects, although these are most germane to individuals rather than communities.

Importantly, consequences such as "emigration, creolization, ethnogenesis, and despecialization . . . relate to decisions of the survivors in the face of challenging circumstances" rather than simply stochastic processes, and "these changes involve perception, needs, and actions" (Hull 2009:170). That is, the outcomes of catastrophic depopulation were neither inevitable nor free from the individual or collective agency of the people involved. Disease was not simply about qualitative individual suffering or quantitative demographic impact; instead, epidemics presented a series of challenges to daily life, identity, fraternity, and dependency that defined community. In light of these observations, it is clear that health and survival were not just about individual bodies or whole population numbers but rather about long-term sustainability of communities and short-term decisions related to quality of life.

## The Cultural Landscape of Colonial California

In contrast to some regions of North America where European colonialism was both early and pervasive, non-Native incursions into California were relatively late and largely restricted to the coastal area in the southern two-thirds of the state. While there were periodic encounters between Native people and European seafarers as early as Juan Rodríguez Cabrillo's voyage of 1542, settlement by non-Natives did not occur until the initiation of the Spanish mission system in Alta California in 1769 (Starr 2005). By 1823, twenty-one missions, each placed about one day's travel from the next; four presidios, each overseeing a military district surrounding several missions; and four secular pueblos were established between San Diego in the south and Sonoma, north of San Francisco Bay (figure 9.1). Presidio commanders and pueblo alcaldes also had the authority to grant land within their jurisdiction to private citizens, and approximately thirty such grants for ranchos were approved during the Spanish colonial era (Perez 1982). Many of these grants were also in the coastal region, although some were located in the adjacent interior.

Russian incursion followed the initial Spanish settlement in Alta California but was limited to the establishment of Colony Ross by the Russian-American Company in 1812 on the coast northwest of the Sonoma mission. In contrast to the religious intent of the Spaniards, the Ross settlement was a mercantile operation largely focused on otter and seal hunting for the Pacific fur trade. This operation brought together Russian administrators and merchants, Native Alaskan men who

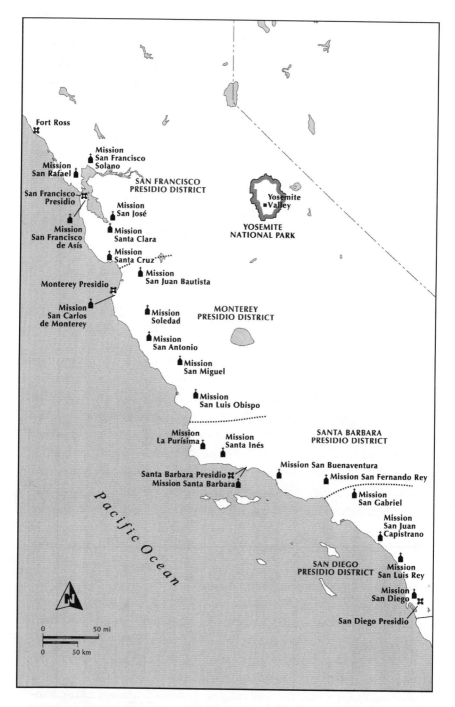

**Figure 9.1.** Map of Spanish and Russian colonial interests in California circa 1815. (After Hull 2009:17.)

hunted for the company, and Native Californians who either worked on one of the three ranches that supported the operation or established multiethnic households with Native Alaskan, or to a lesser extent Russian, men within the colony (Lightfoot 2006).

No Euro-American presence was established on the northwest coast, in the Cascades of northeastern California, in the Central Valley and adjacent Sierra Nevada, or in southeastern deserts until California was ceded to the United States by Mexico in 1848. The most substantial influx of non-Native people after the United States gained control occurred in the central Sierra Nevada foothills with the gold rush of 1849. This significant demographic shift brought about dramatic and pervasive change for indigenous people, as genocide, deliberate removal, and widespread resource degradation took the place of introduced diseases and institutional hardships as the primary vehicles through which Native populations were reduced.

Despite the contention of some scholars that fatal non-Native disease may have been introduced into Alta California prior to Spanish colonization (e.g., Erlandson and Bartoy 1995; Preston 1996), it seems unlikely that sporadic contacts with sailors who had been at sea for some time would have resulted in transmission of deadly pathogens and epidemics within indigenous groups. Likewise, there is no evidence to suggest that Native people associated with the Russian presence at Colony Ross were exposed to non-Native disease to such an extent that epidemics and catastrophic depopulation resulted. The relative isolation of Colony Ross from interaction with other Russian or Spanish colonial settlements, the freedom of Native Californians to come and go as they chose, and the maintenance of Native villages separate from (although near to) Russian outposts likely contributed to such outcomes (Lightfoot 2006). In contrast, Spanish colonization, institutionalization of large numbers of Native people within missions, and the close living conditions in such settings did contribute to mass mortality of indigenous people during the colonial era (see Cook 1976). Thus, this chapter focuses on the era of Spanish colonialism from entry in 1769 to the shift to Mexican control in 1821.

Fortunately, the relatively late and geographically limited European incursion into California also resulted in an exceptionally rich ethnographic record for the state. Therefore, we have a very good picture of Native life and organization at the time of European colonization. Such ethnographic bounty is especially fortuitous given the ethnic, linguistic, and cultural diversity in Native California, as well as the community organization that prevailed. The bulk of such ethnographic data, collected in the early 1900s by faculty and students affiliated with the University of California, represents "memory culture" elicited from elders with knowledge of traditional lifeways. Ethnohistoric information, often gleaned from Spanish mission records, has added important data to this corpus in more-recent years and speaks especially to the nature and extent of landholding units. For example, Milliken (2010) has documented more than 660 such groups in the western two-thirds of California based on mission records and other data (figure 9.2), with some of these territories only "some eight to twelve miles across" (Milliken 1995:2). Overall, both ethnographic and ethnohistoric data reveal a dense mosaic of small tribelets of hunter-gatherer-fisherfolk typically living in resource-rich environments who often practiced some form of residential or logistical settlement mobility and relied on material culture of stone, bone, and vegetal materials. Archaeological data are consistent with this picture of daily life, and both archaeological and ethnographic data reveal extralocal religious practices and widespread exchange (see Jones and Klar 2007; Jones and Perry 2012), which served to link tribelets together in both social and economic ways.

As one might expect, incorporation of Native people into Spanish missions of Alta California often occurred as a result of the complex interplay of individual tribelet, intertribal, and colonial actions, since so many groups were ultimately involved, local circumstances (including exposure to disease) varied, and the process unfolded over more than thirty years. In some cases, violence or coercion was employed by the Spanish; in other instances, Native people joined willingly either individually or en masse, although sometimes doing so only when options to remain outside the system were becoming increasingly limited. Milliken (1995; see also Hackel 2005) provides a detailed discussion of this process for the three missions in the San Francisco Bay area—Mission San Francisco de Asís (founded in 1776), Mission Santa Clara de Asís (founded in 1777), and Mission San José (founded in 1797)—based on Spanish ecclesiastical records and military accounts, and this analysis serves as a useful outline for the process in general. In this region, interactions between Spaniards and Native people often quickly shifted

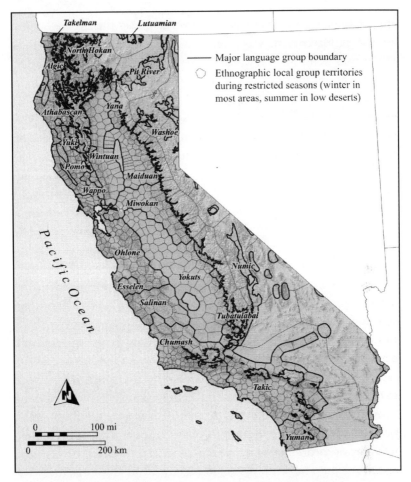

**Figure 9.2.** Map of California Native landholding units. (After Milliken 2010:21, courtesy Far Western Anthropological Research Group, Inc.)

between amicable exchange intended to draw Native people into the missions, periodic tensions, and outright hostility. Still, missionaries were able to gradually expand their recruitment out from each mission, first seeking converts within the territory where the mission was located and, over time, taking in ever more distant peoples, in part because of high neophyte mortality.

Unlike Mission San Francisco, the missions at Santa Clara and San Jose were not on an isolated peninsula. Therefore, the geographic scope of recruitment at the latter mission, in particular, ultimately spread well beyond the Bay Area into the adjoining coast range, the Sacramento–San Joaquin delta, and the northern San Joaquin Valley. As a result, like several other missions in the chain, Mission San Jose hosted culturally and linguistically diverse peoples over the course of its operation. Early recruitment at Mission Santa Clara also differed somewhat from Mission San Francisco because the nearby pueblo of San Jose provided an alternative path for Native people to acquire European goods, forgoing the religious commitment required of the missions. Some local groups initially forged economic connections with the pueblo rather than the mission and thus were able to maintain their villages for a time (Milliken 1995). Similar residential autonomy prevailed for many people affiliated with Mission San Luis Rey and Mission San Diego in southern California, although this accommodation was because of local mission authority, Native sociopolitics, and resources rather than pueblo competition (Lightfoot 2006:65) and persisted for the entire span of mission operation, unlike at Mission Santa Clara.

Life for Native neophytes in the missions was strictly regulated and required religious devotion and practice; labor in the fields or mission grounds; and restrictions on interpersonal relations imposed through access and corporal punishment. For example, single women were housed in separate dormitories to which they were confined under lock and key at night, and strict reporting requirements were required even for married couples (Lightfoot 2006:62). In effect, the mission system sought to create a pious, obedient peasant class of Native people within the highly structured *casta* society. As detailed by Edward Castillo (1978; see also Lightfoot 2006), sometimes harsh treatment by the missionaries or military enforcers contributed to poor health and even death of neophytes, as did close living conditions that promoted the spread of communicable diseases. At times, the number of individuals suffering from illness reached epidemic proportions, but even in nonepidemic years (for example, between 1780 and 1784 at the San Francisco Bay missions) "death rates . . . were nearly double that which one would expect in a native village" (Milliken 1995:90). Milliken (1995) documented five epidemics at one or more of the missions of the San Francisco Bay area between 1777 and 1806, although the specific pathogen is often unclear. The 1806 epidemic was measles, however, and Milliken (1995) reports that other, nonepidemic diseases affecting Native people likely included diphtheria, scarlet fever, tuberculosis, typhus, and syphilis.

Given the living conditions, physical punishment, and ravages of disease, neophyte escape from missions was common. Unfortunately, this provided opportunities for some deadly pathogens to spread beyond the confines of Spanish colonial settlements into interior California. There may be archaeological evidence for such transmission in the form of multiple or mass burials at some sites in central California (e.g., CA-CCo-138, see Atchley 1994:19, 62), and there is also some ethnohistoric evidence of such events in other regions. Smallpox and measles were probably most suited to such long-distance transmission. Thus, Native individuals and communities not participating in colonial institutions or even ever interacting with non-Native people were vulnerable to the effects of introduced pathogens and evidently suffered significant population loss as a result.

## In the Hinterlands: The Case of Yosemite Indians

One such inland area was Yosemite Valley in the central Sierra Nevada, more than 250 kilometers from the nearest Spanish mission in Alta California (see figure 9.1). Here, a combination of archaeological, dendrochronological, and ethnohistoric evidence points to catastrophic population decline owing to introduced disease approximately fifty years before non-Native people entered the area (Hull 2009). The Native Miwok-speaking inhabitants occupied various portions of the Merced and Tuolumne River watersheds throughout the year, relying especially on deer and acorns for subsistence and interacting with neighboring groups to the east and west to acquire materials such as obsidian and to forge relationships through exchange and marriage (Levy 1978). The gold rush brought an influx of Euro-American miners into the foothills west of Yosemite after 1849, but it was not until 1851 that non-Native people entered Yosemite Valley. At that time, growing tensions as a result of non-Native encroachment into traditional territories downstream and Native raids on miners' camps and trading posts led to the formation of the Mariposa Battalion, a volunteer unit charged with removing Native people from the middle reaches of the Merced River and relocating them to a reservation on the Fresno River in the San Joaquin Valley (Russell 1992).

The most detailed account of this expedition was written about thirty years after the fact by Lafayette Bunnell (1990 [1911]), one of the battalion members, who had both medical training and a keen interest in Native people dating back to his childhood in Michigan (Kelly 1921). As a result, once the Mariposa Battalion entered Yosemite Valley, Bunnell took pains to elicit cultural and historical information from Tenaya, the leader of the Native group. Among other things, Tenaya noted that in the time of his father "nearly all [his people] had been destroyed" by a "black sickness" (likely smallpox or measles [Bunnell 1990 (1911):64–65], although there are no data to confirm this diagnosis), which was probably transmitted into Yosemite Valley from one or more individuals who had recently resided in or near a mission in the San Francisco Bay area. This illness decimated the Awahnichi—the people of Awahnee, as the valley was then known—and the survivors relocated to Mono Paiute territory on the eastern side of the Sierra Nevada for one generation.

The displaced Awahnichi intermarried with the local Paiute people, intensifying what had probably been an existing, if less frequent, tradition. For example, there is abundant archaeological evidence for interaction between people of the eastern and western Sierra in the form of obsidian artifacts (Hull and Moratto 1999) and also ethnographic information on trans-Sierra trade and trails (e.g., Davis 1961). Tenaya was the product of one of these unions, born to a Mono Paiute woman married to an Awahnichi leader. When Tenaya was of age, sometime after his father's death, he was persuaded by an aged Awahnichi medicine man to lead his people back to settle again permanently in Yosemite Valley. Dendrochronological data on aboriginal burning, archaeological settlement data, and Tenaya's genealogy indicate that the black sickness struck sometime between 1785 and 1800, while the return of Tenaya and the other descendants occurred no earlier than 1805 and perhaps as late as 1820 (Hull 2009:62–65).

Two covarying proxy measures of population size (debitage quantity and site frequency adjusted for site size) derived from a random sample of archaeological sites in Yosemite Valley—and thoroughly evaluated to demonstrate the demographic basis of the temporal trends despite potentially confounding site formation processes (see Hull 2009:119–34)—reveal the magnitude of this demographic event and also place it in a long-term context spanning nearly 5,500 years of Native occupation (Hull 2009). These data indicate that the colonial-era epidemic resulted in a minimum 25 percent decline in population. Equally important, this event came on the heels of an even more significant decline—which began more than 1,400 years earlier and unfolded over several hundred years—that saw the population reduced to the lowest level since the initial occupation of Yosemite Valley (Hull 2009:136). While the causes of this earlier population decline remain to be thoroughly explored, Native oral tradition indicates that environmental factors such as drought may have been partly responsible (Hull 2009:152), and regional archaeological data also suggest increased violence at this time (see Hull and Moratto 1999). Thus, the Awahnichi community was especially vulnerable to significant demographic impact given its small size, although previous experience with population decline may have informed the Awahnichi response. These long-term quantitative demographic data provide important insight into community sustainability and quality of life that likely affected the decision making of Native people in the wake of colonial-era population loss.

Population estimates calculated using an estimated founding population size and the population growth rates derived from the archaeological population proxies suggest that the Awahnichi numbered only around 300 individuals at the time the disease struck (Hull 2009:146). The population was only just beginning to rebound following the population nadir from either death or emigration approximately 400 years earlier. These same methods indicate that fewer than 200 individuals survived the black sickness. Such a small population size was particularly critical, because proxy population measures indicate that growth rates were no greater than 1.6 persons per 1,000 individuals per year. Therefore, it would have taken 200 years for the population to recover to the predisease size (based on a doubling rate of 400 years), assuming that such a small population was even viable. And this latter assumption is dubious; computer simulations of demographic recovery given such slow growth rates and probable marriage practices reveal that a population of this size was unlikely to survive more than four hundred years under such circumstances (Hull 2009:150; see also Wobst 1974).

That is, stochastic fluctuations typical of small populations would have periodically reduced the growth rate and stymied population recovery. While changes in marriage practices (such as relaxing incest taboos, re-marriage proscriptions, and age at first marriage) might have alleviated or forestalled population collapse, the survivors appear to have opted not to compromise their traditional values (Hull 2012). Therefore, the Awahnichi decision to relocate to the eastern Sierra and intermarry with Mono Paiutes—people with whom they had likely formed some unions in the past—was critical to both the biological and the cultural sustainability of their community.

The ethnohistoric information also suggests that the Awahnichi did not simply integrate into Paiute life on the eastern side of the Sierra, and this is the second significant observation pertaining to community sustainability in the wake of disease. Partial evidence for this comes from Bunnell's (1990 [1911]:179) observation that Tenaya spoke both Awahnichi (Miwok) and Paiute. That is, despite years of living among the Paiutes, "the Miwok language was still sufficiently intact in the Yosemite area to be used by Tenaya when speaking to . . . interpreters and to be later recorded by ethnographers" (Hull 2009:164). In addition, physical segregation of groups seems to have been the norm when people from Yosemite sojourned in Mono Basin. Recounting events from the early 1850s, Bunnell (1990 [1911]:265; emphasis added) noted that "according to the custom of these mountaineers [that is, the Mono Paiutes], *a portion of the territory was given* to . . . [Tenaya and his followers] *for their occupancy* by the consent of the tribe. . . . Ten-ie-ya staid [*sic*] with the Monos until late in the summer or early autumn of 1853, when he and his people suddenly left *the locality that had been assigned to them* and returned to their haunts in the Yosemite Valley." Thus, it may be that fifty years earlier, the surviving Awahnichi similarly maintained a separate village and affinity, despite intermarrying with local Paiute people. No doubt this also contributed to the maintenance of community cohesion and identity. Notably, a similar arrangement may have pertained for a displaced Iroquoian-speaking community within a larger multiethnic settlement in Mohawk territory of the interior northeastern United States during the colonial era (Snow 1996), suggesting a similar strategy to preserve community identity despite relocation.

Tenaya's story of the medicine man also provides a third important clue regarding how the community sustained itself and continued to rebuild after the Awahnichi returned to Yosemite Valley: "Not long before the death of this patriarch, as if endowed with prophetic wisdom, he assured Ten-ie-ya that while he retained possession of Ah-wah-ne his band would increase in numbers and become powerful. *That if he befriended those who sought his protection*, no other tribe would come to the valley to make war upon him, or attempt to drive him from it" (Bunnell 1990 [1911]:71; emphasis added).

That is, Tenaya and the other Awahnichi descendants grew their community by welcoming outsiders. As Bunnell (1990 [1911]:71) noted, Tenaya's group was joined by "the descendants from the Ah-wah-ne-chees" who had found refuge with people other than the Paiutes "and by others who had fled from their own tribes to avoid summary Indian justice," building a community of survivors and "outlaws" (Bunnell 1990 [1911]:64) in the decades immediately prior to the gold rush. Such growth likely helped sustain the group when threatened by violence in the early years of the gold rush, including "wars" with neighboring Native groups (Perlot 1985) that may have erupted as incursions of non-Native miners precluded access to resources in the foothills to the west. The inclusion of new members with no previous ties to Yosemite Valley is further confirmed by the sudden appearance of serrate Desert Side-Notched projectile points at this time in the archaeological record of the Yosemite region. These artifacts evidently reflect the blending of a local point style with a nonlocal embellishment that originated centuries earlier in the Sacramento–San Joaquin delta region, perhaps as a marker of cultural identity (Hull 2004). Therefore, Native people with roots in the northern San Joaquin Valley, at least, appear to have moved east into the Sierra Nevada, perhaps to avoid the expanding sphere of Spanish influence and the threat of missionization. Ethnographic data indicate that the reconstituted group in Yosemite Valley minimally included individuals who could trace their descent to Miwok, Paiute, and/or Yokuts people.

Finally, in addition to welcoming Native outsiders and maintaining language and traditions through what was no doubt a turbulent time, Tenaya and his followers also made a conscious effort to reform their identity in their new circumstances, perhaps in recognition of the more diverse people they had become. They became the Yosemite rather than the Awahnichi, although the transition was sufficiently recent that many individuals, including Tenaya, still recalled this previous identity. Given the timing of this transition—decades before non-Native people entered the area—ethnogenesis in this case was not a reaction to colonialism or some form of resistance (Hull 2007). Rather, it was a proactive, internal decision that undoubtedly contributed to a sense of community even though not all individuals had been together since birth and, at least initially, few had been born in Awahnee. Bunnell (1990 [1911]:65) specifically commented on this shift in identity: "[F]rom my knowledge of Indian customs, I am aware that it is not uncommon for them to change the names of persons or localities after some remarkable event in the history of either. It would not, therefore, appear strange that Ten-ie-ya should have adopted another name for his band."

In summary, the ethnohistoric and archaeological data suggest both a desire and a remarkable ability to maintain their community despite the ravages of introduced disease and consequent significant population loss. The Awahnichi did not discard traditions or lose identity, but they did adapt, making conscious decisions to either maintain or revitalize their community in ways that had implications for both quality of life in the moment and sustainability in the long term. As the "living organism" that community represents, it was both sustaining and sustained—the community transformed but did not disappear, with people returning to the valley that was their home time and again, even when forcibly removed on more than one occasion to the Fresno reservation. And this appears to have been an ongoing, generative process even years after non-Native people finally settled in Yosemite Valley. Yosemite Indians were integrated into the local economy, but they maintained their own villages at some distance from both American settlers, for whom they often worked, and occasional seasonal occupations by Mono Paiutes. The latter is suggested by comparison of a historic map that depicts the location of native Miwok villages (Bunnell 1880) and a set of photographs of a Paiute camp by Eadweard Muybridge from 1873 (Bradley and Rolufson 1873). The location of the latter does not appear on the map and was, in fact, in a place that would have been habitable only during times of low water in the Merced River.

## In the Colonized Zone: From San Diego
## to the San Francisco Bay Area

As a point of comparison to the Yosemite story, it is instructive to consider the experiences of Native Californians living within the range of the Spanish missions with respect to community sustainability and quality of life. In this zone, the health of numerous tribelets was threatened by seizure of lands, loss of resources, physical removal or relocation (that is, *reducción*), and potential exposure to multiple epidemics of lethal disease. While many of these factors ultimately also pertained to inland areas that never witnessed Spanish colonization—as the Yosemite case demonstrates, although most were delayed until the gold rush—Native decision making in colonized areas was much more limited, given the profound changes in which indigenous groups were enmeshed. It was indeed "a time of little choice" (Milliken 1995). The entanglement of Native people in missions, ranchos, or pueblos also undermined community identity, as autonomy was lost to Spanish overseers.

Several scholars (e.g., Hurtado 1988; Lightfoot 2006; Shipek 1978) have considered whether and how the experience of integration into Spanish colonial, and later Mexican, occupation impacted Native community sustainability and quality of life in Alta California, although not expressing their arguments in exactly these terms. For example, many neophytes associated with Mission San Luis Rey and Mission San Diego in southern California were allowed to live outside the mission compound in traditional villages. Not only did this lessen potential for exposure to deadly pathogens, but also these "neophytes incorporated changes into [the] preexisting structure of political hierarchies and social relations. The identities of Luiseno- and Diegueno-speaking peoples remained . . . rooted to the individual polities and villages where they were born" (Lightfoot 2006:203). In contrast, the experience of Native people brought into the missions of the San Francisco Bay area and elsewhere in northern California was very different—tribelet identity was undermined, mortality was high, and authority and traditions were lost. Lightfoot (2006) also compared the experiences of neophytes of the northern and southern California missions with those of the Kashaya Pomo people, whose interaction with non-Native people was limited to the Russians at Colony Ross. As one would expect, Lightfoot found that these Native people were able to withstand potential challenges to the biological and social health of their communities much better than those Native people relocated to the missions.

As the Mission San Luis Rey and Mission San Diego cases suggest, the challenges to maintaining Native community biological and social health within the missions were not simply because of proximity to missions, regular interaction with Spaniards, or even exposure to disease. This is underscored by data from baptismal and death records from Mission San Jose, for example, which reveal that some neophytes survived more than ten years after integration into the missions, although the average life expectancy after baptism was less than five years. That is, there may have been sufficient continuity in community membership to maintain tribelet, or forge a new collective, identity similar to the path followed by Tenaya, but there is no evidence that this was the case for those people who took up residence within missions.

Demographic data presented by Phillip Walker and John Johnson (1994) suggest one reason for the dissolution of community and identity within missions—sex and age distributions in Native populations were radically altered by missionization, likely undermining community structure and practices that contributed to sustainability and quality of life. The Spanish practice of bringing together Native peoples of disparate cultural affiliation also likely worked against such cohesion, as Lightfoot (2006:64) notes that "this policy of *reducción* involved the aggregation of people from many small polities, often with different languages and dialects, in large, crowded neophyte communities. . . . [T]his process went against the innate centripetal tendency of most native Californians, who enjoyed highly dispersed and fluid settlement patterns." No doubt the surveillance and restrictions imposed by missionaries (see Lightfoot 2006:63; Young 1987), especially with respect to traditional ritual (see Douglass et al. 2013:7.12), also precluded meaningful community building. Alternatively, Sarah Peelo (2011) has suggested that ceramic vessel production practices—largely introduced into Native California by the Spanish—created "communities of practice" that could have formed the basis for a new common identity and community as defined herein. She was unable to find any evidence that such new identities were created, however, and also noted that "ceramic production . . . created arenas for social distinction within indigenous communities" (Peelo 2011:642) that may have undermined community. Instead of substituting for traditional community life, the structure of and interactions within mission communities dictated by the padres rather than Native neophytes represented a different process of community formation and maintenance that did not affirm shared identity and purpose—the neophytes were not ultimately responsible for sustaining this strange way of life and so were not sustained by it.

It is also important to note that Native community or individual decision making in coastal areas regarding forms of entanglement with Spanish colonialism affected sustainability and quality of life. The most fundamental decision in this regard was determining whether and when to enter into relations with one or more of the institutional options with which they were presented. John Douglass and his colleagues (2013) provide a detailed example of just such decision making in their study of Gabrielino/Tongva villages of the Los Angeles basin based on mission records. Their study reveals four alternatives that were exercised by Native individuals: (1) be baptized and relocate to a mission, abandoning one's Native village; (2) remain in one's Native village but labor at a nearby rancho; (3) remain in one's own or an adopted Native village and labor in a nearby pueblo; or (4) "reject all aspects of the new colonial structure as much as possible, and either stay in their village of origin or move to a more remote area and join a refuge community" (Douglass et al. 2013:7.25). Given that more than one option was available, dispersal of community members was almost inevitable. While such decisions may have been made earlier, the establishment of ranchos within traditional Native territories in the early 1800s seems to be the critical point when decisions could no longer be delayed. As Douglass and his colleagues (2013:7.25) note, "[W]ithin just a few years of the establishment of ranchos, native villages often disintegrated. It is likely that some of these native inhabitants left their villages to live on the ranchos themselves as workers, but it appears that a large number left their native villages for the missions, probably never to return." The catalyst was probably degradation of traditional resources by livestock and cultivation, factors that did not pertain to interior areas such as Yosemite Valley.

## The Community as a Strategy for Survival

While support of the physical health of individuals was certainly important to Native people during and in the immediate aftermath of lethal disease events, so too was short-term quality of life and long-term sustainability of the "living organism" of community to which they belonged. Without the sense of shared responsibility and commitment that community entailed, individuals likely found themselves without support beyond that of their immediate family and lacking the ability to acquire, defend, and perhaps even access necessary subsistence resources. Equally important, however, if daily practice, ritual, belief, and identity did not endure in some form through the concerted efforts of the survivors, the community itself faded in fact for those individuals during their lifetime. By maintaining community outside of colonial institutions, Native people were able to establish their own priorities for quality of life and achieve sustainability on their own terms.

Ultimately, it is neither the suffering of individuals nor the number of survivors of introduced fatal diseases—that is, the two scales at which the question is often examined—that should determine how colonial-era Native mortality is understood by the public and, too, whether a tribe is granted recognition from the federal government as a sovereign nation. Rather, the quality of life and sustainability of the communities to which Native individuals belonged are critical to such understanding, and strategies for community survival were ongoing and evidently flexible as circumstances and perceptions of community health demanded. Study of the colonial-era experience of indigenous groups in the hinterlands and colonized zones of Alta California with respect to community brings such processes and outcomes into stark relief. Such a perspective prompts us to more thoroughly consider and recognize the diversity of experiences of various Native groups. Although Native people in both contexts were exposed to lethal pathogens that resulted in catastrophic mortality, Native groups beyond the bounds of colonial institutions, free to rebuild their communities in the wake of disease, clearly made numerous decisions over many years that supported this goal. The scale of Native sociopolitical organization in California likely makes such stories especially visible with respect to Native engagement with the Spanish, but the same Native decision-making process likely played out for larger polities elsewhere in North America that interacted with the Spanish, English, French, or Dutch. Even there, Native affinity at the local level probably factored into experience and survival.

# References

Anderson, Benedict R. O'G. 2006. Imagined Communities: Reflections on the Origin and Spread of Nationalism. New York: Verso.

Atchley, Sara M. 1994. A Burial Analysis of the Hotchkiss Site (CA-CCO-138). Master's thesis, Cultural Resources Management Program, Sonoma State University, Rohnert Park, CA.

Belseme, Kate, and Megan Mullin. 1997. Community indicators and healthy communities. National Civic Review 86(1):43–52.

Bennyhoff, James A., and David A. Fredrickson. 1994. A proposed integrative taxonomic system for central California. In Toward a New Taxonomic Framework for Central California Archaeology: Essays by James A. Bennyhoff and David A. Fredrickson, edited by Richard E. Hughes, 15–24. Contributions of the University of California Archaeological Research Facility 52. Berkeley: University of California Press.

Blitz, John H. 1999. Mississippian chiefdoms and the fission-fusion process. American Antiquity 64:577–92.

Bourdieu, Pierre. 1977. Outline of a Theory of Practice. Cambridge: Cambridge University Press.

Bradley, Henry William, and William Herman Rulofson. 1873. The Indians of California. Illustrated by Muybridge. San Francisco: Bradley and Rulofson. [Lone Mountain College Collection of Stereographs by Eadweard Muybridge, 1867–1880, Bancroft Library, BANC PIC 1971.055—STER, ALB, PIC, AX, B.]

Brint, Steven. 2001. Gemeinschaft revisited: A critique and reconstruction of the community concept. Sociological Theory 19(1):1–23.

Bunnell, Lafayette. 1880. Discovery of the Yosemite, and the Indian War of 1851, Which Led to That Event. Chicago: Fleming H. Revell.

———. 1990 [1911]. Discovery of the Yosemite, and the Indian War of 1851, Which Led to That Event. High Sierra Classics Series. Yosemite National Park: Yosemite Association. Reprint of 4th ed., orig. pub. Los Angeles: G. W. Gerlacher.

Castillo, Edward D. 1978. The impact of Euro-American exploration and settlement. In Handbook of North American Indians, vol. 8: California, edited by Robert F. Heizer, 99–127. Washington, DC: Smithsonian Institution.

Cook, Sherburne. 1976. The Conflict Between the California Indians and White Civilization. Berkeley: University of California Press.

Davis, James T. 1961. Trade routes and economic exchange among the Indians of California. University of California Archaeological Survey Reports 54. Berkeley: University of California Press.

Diamond, Jared. 1997. Guns, Germs and Steel: The Fates of Human Societies. New York: W. W. Norton.

Douglass, John G., Seetha N. Reddy, Richard Ciolek-Torrello, and Donn R. Grenda, eds. 2013. People in a Changing Land: The Archaeology of History of the Ballona in Los Angeles, California. Vol. 5, Gabrielino/Tongva Origins and Development: A View from Guaspet. Draft manuscript. Tucson, AZ: Statistical Research.

Erlandson, Jon M., and Kevin Bartoy. 1995. Cabrillo, the Chumash, and Old World diseases. Journal of California and Great Basin Anthropology 17(2):153–73.

Hackel, Steven W. 2005. Children of Coyote, Missionaries of Saint Francis: Indian-Spanish Relations in Colonial California, 1769–1850. Chapel Hill: University of North Carolina Press.

Hull, Kathleen L. 2004. Emergent cultural traditions in the central Sierra Nevada foothills. Society for California Archaeology Proceedings 17:113–18.

———. 2007. Defining identity in interior colonial California: A view from the Sierra Nevada. Paper presented at the 72nd Annual Meeting of the Society for American Archaeology, Austin, TX.

———. 2009. Pestilence and Persistence: Yosemite Indian Demography and Culture in Colonial California. Berkeley: University of California Press.

———. 2012. Death and sex: Procreation in the wake of fatal epidemics within indigenous communities. In The Archaeology of Colonialism: Intimate Encounters and Sexual Effects, edited by Barbara L. Voss and Eleanor Conlin Casella, 122–37. Cambridge: Cambridge University Press.

Hull, Kathleen L., and Michael J. Moratto. 1999. Archaeological Synthesis and Research Design, Yosemite National Park, California. Yosemite National Research Center Publications in Anthropology 21. Yosemite National Park: U.S. Department of the Interior National Park Service.

Hurtado, Albert L. 1988. Indian Survival on the California Frontier. New Haven, CT: Yale University Press.

Isbell, William H. 2012. What we should be studying: The "imagined community" and the "natural community." In Archaeology of Communities: A New World Perspective, edited by Jason Yaeger and Marcello A. Canuto, 243–66. Hoboken, NJ: Taylor and Francis.

Jones, Terry L., and Kathryn Klar, eds. 2007. California Prehistory: Colonization, Culture, and Complexity. Walnut Creek, CA: AltaMira Press.

Jones, Terry L., and Jennifer E. Perry, eds. 2012. Contemporary Issues in California Archaeology. Walnut Creek, CA: Left Coast Press.

Kelly, Howard A. 1921. Lafayette Houghton Bunnell, M.D., discoverer of the Yosemite. Annals of Medical History 3:2.

Kroeber, Alfred L. 1925. Handbook of the Indians of California. Bureau of Ameri-
    can Ethnology Bulletin 78. Washington, DC. Reprint, New York: Dover
    Publications, 1976.
————. 1955. Nature of the land-holding group. Ethnohistory 2:303–14.
Leventhal, Alan, Les Field, Hank Alvarez, and Rosemary Cambra. 1994. The
    Ohlone back from extinction. In The Ohlone Past and Present: Native
    Americans of the San Francisco Bay Area Region, edited by Lowell J. Bean,
    297–336. Anthropological Papers 42. Menlo Park, CA: Ballena Press.
Levy, Richard. 1978. Eastern Miwok. In Handbook of North American Indians,
    vol. 8: California, edited by Robert F. Heizer, 398–413. Washington, DC:
    Smithsonian Institution.
Lightfoot, Kent G. 2006. Indians, Missionaries, and Merchants: The Legacy of
    Colonial Encounters on the California Frontiers. Berkeley: University of
    California Press.
Lightfoot, Kent G., Lee M. Panich, Tsim D. Schneider, Sara L. Gonzalez, Matthew
    A. Russell, Darren Modzelewski, Theresa Molino, and Elliot H. Blair. 2013.
    The study of indigenous political economies and colonialism in Native
    California: Implications for contemporary tribal groups and federal recog-
    nition. American Antiquity 78(1):89–103.
Mann, Charles. 2005. 1491: New Revelations About the Americas Before Colum-
    bus. New York: Alfred A. Knopf.
Milliken, Randall. 1995. A Time of Little Choice: The Disintegration of Tribal
    Culture in the San Francisco Bay Area, 1769–1810. Anthropological Papers
    43. Menlo Park, CA: Ballena Press.
————. 2010. Contact-Period Native California Community Distribution Model:
    A Dynamic Atlas and Wiki Encyclopedia. Vol. 1, Introduction. Davis, CA:
    Far Western Anthropological Research Group.
Pauketat, Timothy R. 2012. Politicization and community in the pre-Columbian
    Mississippi valley. In Archaeology of Communities: A New World Perspec-
    tive, edited by Jason Yaeger and Marcello A. Canuto, 16–43. Hoboken, NJ:
    Taylor and Francis.
Peelo, Sarah. 2011. Pottery-making in Spanish California: Creating multi-scalar
    social identity through daily practice. American Antiquity 76(4):642–66.
Perez, Cris. 1982. Grants of Land in California Made by Spanish or Mexican Au-
    thorities. Sacramento, CA: State Lands Commission, Boundary Determi-
    nation Office, Boundary Investigation Unit. Available at http://www.slc.
    ca.gov/reports/grants_of_land/part_1.pdf.
Perlot, Jean-Nicholas. 1985. Gold Seeker: Adventures of a Belgian Argonaut During
    the Gold Rush Years. Translated by Helen Harding Bretnor. New Haven,
    CT: Yale University Press.
Preston, William L. 1996. Serpent in Eden: Dispersal of foreign diseases into pre-
    mission California. Journal of California and Great Basin Anthropology
    18(1):2–37.

Rose, Gene. 1990. Indians long for tribal identity: Claim to Yosemite never relinquished. Fresno Bee, May 27, 1990.

Russell, Carl Parcher. 1992. One Hundred Years in Yosemite: The Story of a Great Park and Its Friends. Yosemite National Park: Yosemite Association.

Service, Elman R. 1962. Primitive Social Organization: An Evolutionary Perspective. Boston: Random House.

Shipek, Florence C. 1978. History of southern California mission Indians. *In* Handbook of North American Indians, vol. 8: California, edited by Robert F. Heizer, 610–18. Washington, DC: Smithsonian Institution.

Snow, Dean R. 1996. Mohawk demography and the effects of exogenous epidemics on American Indian populations. Journal of Anthropological Archaeology 15:160–82.

Starr, Kevin. 2005. California: A History. New York: Modern Library.

Tönnies, Ferdinand. 2001. Community and Civil Society. Cambridge: Cambridge University Press.

Walker, Phillip L., and John R. Johnson. 1994. The decline of the Chumash Indian population. *In* In the Wake of Contact: Biological Responses to Conquest, edited by Clark Spencer Larsen and George R. Milner, 109–20. New York: Wiley-Liss.

Waselkov, Gregory A., and Marvin T. Smith. 2000. Upper Creek archaeology. *In* Indians of the Greater Southeast: Historical Archaeology and Ethnohistory, edited by Bonnie G. McEwan, 242–64. Gainesville: University of Florida Press.

Wobst, Martin H. 1974. Boundary conditions for Paleolithic social systems: A simulation approach. American Antiquity 39(2):147–78.

Yaeger, Jason, and Marcello A. Canuto. 2012. Introducing the archaeology of communities. *In* Archaeology of Communities: A New World Perspective, edited by Jason Yaeger and Marcello A. Canuto, 1–15. Hoboken, NJ: Taylor and Francis.

Young, Mary. 1987. Pagans, converts, and backsliders, all: A secular view of the metaphysics of Indian-white relationships. *In* The American Indian and the Problem of History, edited by Calvin Martin, 75–83. New York: Oxford University Press.

# 10

# The Pestilent Serpent

## Colonialism, Health, and Indigenous Demographics

*James F. Brooks*

Deep in the summer of 1989, I found myself at On-a-Slant Village, a reconstructed Mandan earth lodge settlement in Fort Lincoln State Park near Mandan, North Dakota, at the junction of the Missouri and Heart Rivers. Founded around AD 1575 by Mandan families who had hived off from three nearby villages—responding to population increase and the need for new cultivation fields in the Missouri River bottom-lands—On-a-Slant now hosted "living history" and cultural talks for local schoolchildren and the occasional (usually European) tourist. This day, a graduate school colleague and I had come to film a public story-telling afternoon offered by "Marie," one of only a handful of surviving fluent Mandan speakers and a custodian of tribal history.

Thunderheads built over the western bluffs, and the afternoon grew increasingly humid. Marie sat in a folding lawn chair in the shade of a massive cottonwood, a worn star quilt over her lap, despite the heat. Most of her tales were Coyote stories, trickster tales filled with humor, details of the natural world, and not-so-subtle life lessons to pass along moral and behavioral norms. But as the shadows grew long and lis-teners drifted away, she paused, took a slow drink of iced tea, and transitioned into what emerged as her version of the narrative underly-ing the Mandan Snow Owl Bundle Society and its ceremonies. Snow Owl Bundle owners held arrow-making knowledge (and the exclusive right to craft and sell arrows) and, with those, bison-calling powers. The main bundle owner held exclusive rights to these bison-calling rites and could be solicited to perform the bison-calling ceremony, which normally took place in late winter (December–March) to draw bison down into the river bottoms, where they could be slain more easily than on the frigid snow-blown uplands. The Snow Owl Bundle constituted just one among a complex of some twenty bundle rituals noted by ethnographers in the early twentieth century (Bowers 1950: 20, 283–95).

Startled to hear what would normally be a story told only in winter months unfolding before us, I switched off the (then cumbersome and unreliable) video camera and pointed its lens skyward, in the hope that Marie would understand that I recognized the sensitivity of what she was doing and could thus perhaps gain her trust in the days and months ahead.

Her narrative began in terms somewhat familiar to me from earlier publications (Beckwith 1938:149–54; Bowers 1950: 283–95). During eagle-trapping season, ancient Mandans had resettled to seasonal dwellings on creek branches north of their winter villages, where men like Black Wolf dug pits atop the high buttes and, from those hidden traps, seized eagles that dove down to take the bait rabbits. This warm afternoon as he lay in his eagle-trapping pit, Black Wolf fell asleep, and when he awoke found himself trapped by a huge stone that had covered the pit mouth. Eventually working his way out from the pit, Black Wolf discovered himself a prisoner in unfamiliar country.

Black Wolf turned out to be the captive of an elderly arrow maker, Big Man, and his blond-haired "dwarf" assistant, fair-complected and yellow-haired Little Man. The arrow maker set a challenge to Black Wolf—to hunt a large white elk that lived in a lake to the north—the pursuit of which was assisted by a series of "grandmothers" in the form of earth-lodge-dwelling mice and moles. The moles eventually tunneled far beneath the earth and provided Black Wolf with the opportunity to surprise and kill the white elk from below, while it slept. Although his captor, Big Man, enjoyed three meals from the elk, he soon ordered another trial—the capture of Four Stripes, a man who lived far to the west, near the ocean.

Black Wolf assumed the form of a raven in order to more quickly reach the seashore. With the help of White Tailed Deer Woman, who molded his body with her hands to transform him into a comely human woman to better attract his quarry, Black Wolf Woman began strolling the beach in search of Four Stripes. From the ocean, however, crawled snakes that slyly offered assistance in hopes of making him their prey. These he overcame one by one until the fourth, a massive creature whose body was covered in bloody sores and oozing pustules, crawled from the sea. It came for Black Wolf with mouth agape, trapping Black Wolf Woman between the waves and the forest. "Finally, Black Wolf Woman jumped inside that serpent's mouth," said Marie, "and once inside used her flint knife to cut her way outside again. That is how Black Wolf conquered the monsters of the beach and was able to take Four Stripes' head, which he carried back to Big Man."

Big Man, thrilled with the gift, assumed his spirit animal form, that of the snow owl, and gifted his arrow-making tools (a shaft straightener, a sanding hide, a grapevine rope for bending bows, paints, and a large feather from his wing), as well as his arrow-making knowledge, to Black Wolf, with orders that the medicine be curated in the Snow Owl Bundle (Brooks, Fort Berthold field notes, July 27, 1989).

Although the "snakes on the beach" scene was familiar to me from published versions of the Snow Owl ceremony, the precise rendering of Marie's "Monstrous Snake" scene struck me as noteworthy and has stayed with me through the more than twenty-five years that have elapsed since that day. My fieldwork that season resulted in an essay in which I avoided this incident entirely. I did, however, make an effort to argue that historians take oral sources seriously for their ability to enrich Native American history (Brooks 1995). Not until the editors of this book invited me to offer some forward-looking remarks to this volume did the afternoon at On-a-Slant village came back to me.

Why, I wondered, does a pox-ridden monster suddenly appear in an oft-told tale about the founding of an important medicine bundle? Given the oddness of Marie's desire to share this story during the summer months, I shied away from asking her about this version's origins—although nothing about her presentation suggested that she was "winging it" on her own inspiration. One likely impulse, it seems to me, lay in our venue, On-a-Slant village. As one of a cluster of nine densely populated (an estimated 15,000 persons) and vital Mandan villages around the Heart/Missouri confluence, On-a-Slant probably hosted Pierre Gaultier de Varennes, sieur de La Vérendry, and his son Louis-Joseph in 1738 on their explorations from French outposts in Canada toward the Rocky Mountains, in search of the "River of the West" that would span the continent. The Vérendry family would pass through again in 1742, on a journey that would demonstrate that horse, gun, and slave trading indeed spanned the Rockies, with animals and humans transported as far as the Pacific coast (Smith 1980 [1951]). In the middle years of the eighteenth century, On-a-Slant was just one of a powerful complex of villages that lay "at the heart of the world" (Fenn 2014).

Yet Mandan supremacy in the center of the northern plains would disintegrate within a single lifetime. Decimated by the continental smallpox epidemic of 1775–82 (Fenn 2001:209, 217–20), in 1781 a few remaining families took their household goods and medicine bundles and joined other such refugees—Mandans and Hidatsas both—to establish a new mixed-tribal settlement of five villages (two Mandan and three Hidatsa) at the junction of the Knife and Missouri Rivers. Meriwether Lewis and George Rogers Clark would settle in with them there over the winter of 1804–5.

However idiosyncratic, Marie's version of the narrative now strikes me as a bridge into key themes and issues that guided the organizers of the Amerind seminar and the contributors to this book. Her story featured common motifs—a hero undertaking challenges that would, should he succeed in overcoming them, benefit all of his people—and a plotting that moves Black Wolf from the upper Missouri River to the shores of the Pacific (presumably). That dentalia shell trade beads from the Pacific appear in river village sites dating to the precontact era (prior to 1738) signals the extent of economic networks, if not face-to-face trade by itinerant traders. That a snake monster could manifest the physical symptoms of an array of diseases (bubonic plague, measles, and smallpox among them) in Marie's narrative also alerts us to the enduring tragedy of how the 1780 and 1837 epidemics of that disease very nearly obliterated the Mandans, as well as their neighboring allies the Hidatsas and Arikaras. Provocative to me was the possibility in her tale that the variola virus might have traveled *eastward* from the Northwest Coast to at least some interior peoples, rather than to the northern plains via Great Basin Shoshone who had acquired the pestilence when trading with the Spanish colony in New Mexico, who then passed the microbes along to the Crows, frequent raiding and trading partners of the river village tribes (Fenn 2001: 222). The latter argument proved an important counternarrative to the popular assumption that it arrived via flatboats moving up the Missouri yet leaves open the possibility of introduction from the Puget Sound and Columbia River contact zones.

Marie's version of the Snow Owl narrative makes one wonder whether the disease moved in three directions at once, a pincer of death that ravaged the peoples caught between. Robert Boyd identifies small-pox outbreaks in the Puget Sound area as early as 1770, allowing a full decade through which the microorganisms could travel down the line into the interior. The disease struck even more virulently in 1784, as the waves of death that had begun on the East Coast worked their way around Cape Horn or across the Pacific. And Native peoples incorpo-rated that trauma into oral tradition, considering the plague a conse-quence of their incessant feuds and small wars, a punishment for moral wickedness, or the consequence of eating salmon that carried the disease (Boyd 1999:54–55). We should admit to imagination, however, the pos-sibility that a heretofore-unknown virulent autochthonous disease, en-tirely distinct from Old World pathogens, may be hinted at in her Snow Owl narrative, given the temporal depth of the story, which contains no other flags of "historic"-era origin like those I worked with in my article on factionalism and the origin of the Crow nation (Brooks 1995).

Whatever the precise dating and vectors of the tragedy, On-a-Slant lay empty by 1781, its abandonment doubtless attended by similar efforts to make sense of the trauma within Mandan custom; in this case, the presence of the monstrous pox-ridden snake signals a harbinger of sor-row. Yet there also exists in Black Wolf's story the aspect of surmount-ing the disease. This, too, echoes in the Mandan (and Hidatsa and Arikara) story, one of repeated assaults on life, culture, and sovereignty and equally repeated strategies for overcoming those assaults. In 1837, of course, the Knife River villages suffered a second wave of smallpox, reducing the three tribes' population by more than 50 percent—the Mandans numbered only 125 souls when the ravages passed, Arikaras but 300, and Hidatsas (who were sojourning on the plains) around 500. With this larger context, like that provided by this volume, we can see in the Snow Owl story at once the local effects and the larger, regional, processes of epidemic and cultural response.

In the case of Black Wolf, at least, it was a successful response, as he destroyed the pestilent serpent. Although many indigenous people van-ished beneath the cluster-bomb devastation of microbes, enslavement, deracination, and deculturation, others did not. Despite the relent-less assault that Mandans, Hidatsas, and Arikaras suffered from Sioux and Assiniboine enemies, from the smallpox plagues of 1780, 1837, and yet another in 1856—after which the new mixed settlement at Like-a-Fishhook village was established—forced relocation in the 1950s by the Army Corps of Engineers with the construction of the Garrison Dam, and today, the overwhelming social challenges attendant to the fracking boom in North Dakota, these peoples persist in asserting land and sovereignty rights within the limits of federal law (ProPublica 2013). And in that triumph may lie the rebirth of Indian nations.

This volume, with its continental sweep, disciplinary range, and array of case studies, does much to clear away the simple-minded determinism that has come to predominate the public mind (and education— my own teenagers read *Guns, Germs and Steel* for their independent school history classes). The archaeologists, biological anthropologists, and historians collected herein present a new vision and sense of scholarly duty. From early contact–era (1513–1704) La Florida to the archaeology of the proto to historic Eastern Woodlands, from the racially marginalizing "social violence" of colonial Mexico and the bioarchaeology of "structural violence" in contact zones to contending memories of colonial and Cherokee peoples' descriptions of smallpox effects in the eighteenth-century Southeast, from the socially and culturally devastating impacts of captive-taking and slave raids across the continent as the Atlantic economy intersected with indigenous networks to variations in community structures and responses to colonial-era destabilizations in the periphery of Spanish Alta California, and finally to a long view of Native adjustments—and persistence—over two centuries in New England, we now comprehend a fully three-dimensional view of the issue. As the editors make clear in their introduction, the inevitable and accidental nature of the trauma visited upon the indigenous peoples of Turtle Island by the dispersal of invisible and unpremeditated microbial broadcasting can no longer relieve the heirs of colonialism from moral responsibility: "We may never know the full extent of Native depopulation, given the notoriously slim and problematic evidence that is available for indigenous communities during the colonial period, but what is certain is that a generation of scholars has significantly overemphasized disease as the cause of depopulation, downplaying the active role of Europeans in inciting wars, destroying livelihoods, and erasing identities."

Yet throughout, we see that the indigenous peoples of North America, even in the midst of catastrophic population declines from the cluster bombs, found ways to reconstitute families, clans, tribes, and nations toward cultural survival. This noteworthy phenomenon was perhaps first announced by James H. Merrell in his 1989 book, *The Indians' New World: Catawbas and Their Neighbors from European Contact Through the Era of Removal*, in which he shows over two long centuries the social creativity and strength through which Native nations of the Carolinas and Virginia engaged the "three intrusions"— alien microbes, Atlantic economy traders, and colonial settlers—that shattered precontact tribes. The Catawbas, like so many precontact sociopolitical units, remade themselves to accommodate new members from refugee communities: Enos, Occaneechees, Waterees, Keyauwees, Cheraws, and others found shelter and new life in the Catawba nation. Merrell captured well both the success of this survival strategy and the hardship on peoples who evacuated traditional lands with little more than their immediate possessions. As they "rewove the social fabric into new designs," language, ceremonial life, kinship, and descent systems, as well as economic activities, were remade to allow continuation of indigenous life.

The chapters in this volume follow Merrell with fresh cases of Native reconstitution, ranging from New England to the removal-era Southeast to the valleys of the Sierra Nevada. In doing so, they remind us that the notion of "community" takes many forms, some of which proved more able to negotiate cultural difference than others and therefore shaped capacity for cultural persistence.

Yet these cases take up their story generally with the advent of Europeans and Africans on the shores of the Americas. As much as I profited by the new knowledge contained therein, I also found myself wondering about the temporal depth of this remarkable adaptive capacity. I questioned whether we should not look into the "deep history" of the indigenous Americas to see whether demographic traumas in the precontact eras might have prepared many Native peoples with some of the very tools they would use to survive colonialism. I argued recently that in the precolonial Southwest, Ancestral Puebloan people had experienced "cycles of evangelism" in the form of powerful numinous movements like the Chaco phenomenon (circa AD 800–1150) and the katsina religion (circa 1300–1500) that shaped their variegated responses to the arrival of Franciscan missionaries in the seventeenth century (Brooks 2013).

George Milner's contribution to the volume (chapter 2) addresses this issue in important ways. His treatment of the precontact "Vacant Quarter" debates confirms that between AD 1300 and 1500 vast expanses of the Mississippian cultural world lay empty, apparently the consequence of disintegrating sociopolitical systems, widespread intergroup warfare, and morbidity associated with the deleterious consequences to public health of intensified agriculture and densely aggregated "urban" settlements like Cahokia, Kincaid, Angel, and Aztalan. Depopulation required innovations in the ability of communities to reform themselves, well before the first Spanish intrusions. New marriage systems may have allowed the integration of "outsider" women (or men), and the widespread patterns of captive raiding and adoption detailed in Catherine Cameron's essay (chapter 7) may have been redeployed from the purpose of garnering sacrificial victims for satisfaction of the gods (Alt 2008) to the augmentation of living communities. These creative adjustments are illustrated in the historic period in Alan Swedlund's discussion of New England tribes (chapter 6) and given fine-grain elucidation—in either their failures or their successes—in Kathleen Hull's comparison of Spanish mission–associated Indians with those of the Yosemite Valley (chapter 9). Thus, precolonial trauma led to the crafting of solutions employed during the colonial era.

Similar depopulations seem to have occurred simultaneously in the American Southwest and perhaps inspired similar social experimentation. A robust population of some 20,000 "Hohokam" peoples in the Phoenix and Tucson Basins in the early AD 1300s had declined precipitously by the time Jesuit missionaries arrived in the late seventeenth century, and little evidence exists of outmigration to new areas. Other regions in the Southwest, especially the Colorado Plateau, show marked, if not complete, loss of population during the same period, with estimates for the northern region showing approximately 100,000 residents in AD 1400 declining to some 65,000 by the arrival of Francisco de Coronado in 1540. Students of the mystery have identified warfare, nutritional stress, and unhealthy living conditions that lowered fertility rates and/or increased mortality as likely causes. Strong empirical data make it clear that "population decline began well before

European diseases could have been a causal factor" (Hill et al. 2004).
The "general health situation before people left parts of the Southwest,"
according to the latest synthesis, "included problems associated with
inadequate protein, illnesses associated with weaning, and a continuing
low level of infectious disease" (Cordell and McBrinn 2012: 234). Again,
intensified agriculture and dense settlement lay at the heart of the crisis:
"It seems that children at *all* sites and at *all* times after the advent of
agriculture suffered ill health, chronic malnutrition, and high infectious
disease rates that seemed to function in synergistic interaction" (Sobolik
2002; emphasis in original).

Even small changes in fertility and life expectancy, argue these
scholars, "can result in a slow contraction of population, slow enough
that people might not be aware of the trend." But under such circumstances, "total populations decrease remarkably quickly" (Cordell and
McBrinn 2012:234). In a wider analysis of demographic health across
the continent, evidence for tuberculosis has grown steadily, suggesting
that tuberculosis was widespread through the Americas before European contact and was concentrated in populations with high densities and lifestyles conducive to the spread of the disease (Wilbur and
Buikstra 2006).

Depopulation of whole regions, of course, does not necessarily signal complete population loss, and we know from the Southwest, at
least, that some of its own "vacant quarters" were the consequence of
community-level emigration to new locations. This seems to account
for the lesser decline in relative population between the Phoenix/Tucson
Basins and that of the Colorado Plateau, as at least some of the former
residents of the plateau likely resettled in the upper Rio Grande valleys
(Ortman 2012). Such migrations likely prefigured some of the adaptive
strategies we witness later among the Pueblo peoples of the Southwest
once they were forced to deal with even greater perils associated with
the colonial cluster bombs of Spanish settler-colonialism, strategies that
are now reflected in the essential identity of Pueblo peoples.

Among today's citizens of Santa Clara Pueblo (Posongeh Owingeh)
is Tessie Naranjo, director of the Northern Pueblos Institute at Northern
New Mexico Community College in nearby Española. Naranjo often
describes the essence of Tewa history and culture in a single, potent
metaphor, "life as movement": "This includes physical movement from

one place to another, the movement that was so fundamental to Pueblo peoples' way of life in the past. But it is also movement that character-izes life itself, the constant movement of changing circumstances. This metaphor, and others embedded in Tewa stories, shapes who we are as Pueblo people and provides a foundation for our community life" (Naranjo 2008).

Tewa migrations are not unlike those called out in Merrell's treatment of the Catawbas in the colonial era: wholesale relocations of communi-ties born of the imperative for preservation that would, in time, become aspects of essential Indian identity. Once we recognize this fundamental reality, the histories of the region's Puebloan peoples and the histories of migrants like Apaches, Navajos, Utes, and Comanches begin to inter-sect in fascinating ways. If we set aside outdated notions of "sedentary" peoples versus their "nomadic" neighbors and recognize that ecological fluctuation, epidemic disease, cultural tension, and innovation—as well as the simple human disposition toward restlessness—shaped the lives and decisions of all peoples in the Southwest, we begin to discern a mo-saic of movement, culture contact, exchange, conflict, and accommoda-tion that moves us closer to understanding the sweep of Indian history and experience across the American continent more broadly.

The evacuations of the Colorado Plateau, the Vacant Quarter, and perhaps other regions in precontact North America not only alert us to demographic dislocations that predate those discussed in this volume but also ask us to think in deeper terms about the ways in which in-digenous Americans managed their way through these traumas in ways that transcend conventional chronology. Marie's Mandan ancestors and their Arikara neighbors—likely descendants of those peoples flung out-ward by the centrifugal explosion of the Cahokian world—were the product of new community creation in the centuries after AD 1400. Tessie Naranjo's Tewa kinspeople are likewise the continuation of com-munities that left the Colorado Plateau as crop failures, malnutrition, infant mortality, eruptions of intra- and intercommunity warfare, and loss of confidence in their spiritual leaders spurred them to look for new lands and renewed life in the Rio Grande valley.

The Cherokees, whose depth of experience may have allowed them to avoid recontagion with smallpox in 1780, as proposed by Paul Kelton (chapter 8, this volume), today number well over 300,000 citizens, more than the total U.S. Indian population at its late nineteenth-century nadir of 250,000. Their endurance seems the consequence of reconstitution of the nation by the absorption of other southeastern Native peoples as well as African and European affines. The Navajo Nation exceeds 300,000 citizens as well. Their case presents a particular puzzle, in that no documentary records exist for epidemic disease among the Navajos in the colonial era—their population grew, according to Spanish, Mexican, and American censuses, from some 4,000 in the eighteenth century to 9,000 in 1868 to 18,000 in 1892. Even cholera and other illnesses associated with the crowded conditions and poor sanitation of the Navajos at Bosque Redondo seem not to have afflicted them as severely as many other Indian groups. Only the influenza epidemic of 1918–19 wrought severe declines among the Navajos, as it did without discretion among most poor Americans unable to receive medical assistance. It may be that the long tradition of integrating adoptees (whether voluntary or forcible) into the tribe insulated Navajos from the decimation suffered by neighboring Puebloan peoples (Bailey and Bailey 1986:19, 73, 119).

This reader, at least, not only gained critical new knowledge of the complex forces endured by indigenous peoples with the conquest of the Americas, treated so thoroughly in this collection, but also gained an appreciation for the palette of survival skills among North American indigenes who escaped obliteration under colonialism and the expansion of the American empire. As David Arnold wrote not long ago, "[C]hanging settlement patterns, the rise of syncretic revivalistic religions, and Native acceptance of Christianity and capitalism, suggest not only cultural destruction (which they do), but they also speak to the ways that Native Americans actively responded to such calamitous events and began to remake their lives, reassign meaning to their world, and reconstruct their cultures" (Arnold 2000:2). That creative impulse may have, as I argue above, drawn upon what Cherokee author Christopher Teuton has called "deep waters" of experience (Teuton 2010). As David Jones (chapter 1, this volume) argues in concluding his comprehensive and convincing overview of the "determinists" versus the "contingents" school of analysis, "Scholars must continue to do their part to find valuable data that have not yet been found." The path forward seems clear, and this book lies at its entrance.

# References

Alt, Susan. 2008. Unwilling immigrants: Culture, change, and the "other" in Mississippian societies. *In* Invisible Citizens: Captives and Their Consequences, edited by Catherine M. Cameron, 205–22. Salt Lake City: University of Utah Press.

Arnold, David H. 2000. Plagues and peoples on the Northwest Coast. Review of The Coming of the Spirit of Pestilence, by Robert Boyd. H-Net Reviews in the Humanities and Social Sciences. Electronic document, http://www2.h-net.msu.edu/reviews/showpdf.php?id=4547.

Bailey, Garrick, and Roberta Glenn Bailey. 1986. A History of the Navajos: The Reservation Years. Santa Fe, NM: SAR Press.

Beckwith, Martha Warren. 1938. Mandan-Hidatsa Myths and Ceremonies. Memoirs of the American Folklore Society 32. Boston: Houghton Mifflin.

Bowers, Alfred W. 1950. Mandan Social and Ceremonial Organization. Chicago: University of Chicago Press.

Boyd, Robert. 1999. The Coming of the Spirit of Pestilence: Introduced Infectious Diseases and Population Decline Among Northwest Coast Indians, 1774–1874. Vancouver: University of British Columbia Press.

Brooks, James F. 1995. Sing away the buffalo: Faction and fission on the northern plains. *In* Beyond Subsistence: Plains Archaeology and the Postprocessual Critique, edited by Philip Duke and Michael C. Wilson, 143–68. Tuscaloosa: University of Alabama Press.

———. 2013. Women, men, and cycles of evangelism in the Southwest Borderlands, AD 750 to 1750. American Historical Review 118(3):738–64.

Buikstra, Jane E., and Lyle W. Konigsberg. 1985. Paleodemography: Critiques and controversies. American Anthropologist 87(2):316–33.

Cordell, Linda S., and Maxine E. McBrinn. 2012. Archaeology of the Southwest. 3rd ed. Walnut Creek, CA: Left Coast Press.

Fenn, Elizabeth A. 2001. Pox Americana: The Great Smallpox Epidemic of 1775–82. New York: Hill and Wang.

———. 2014. Encounters at the Heart of the World: A History of the Mandan People. New York: Hill and Wang.

Hill, J. Brett, Jeffery J. Clarke, William H. Doelle, and Patrick D. Lyons. 2004. Prehistoric demography in the Southwest: Migration, coalescence, and Hohokam population decline. American Antiquity 69(4):689–716.

Merrell, James H. 1989. The Indians' New World: Catawbas and Their Neighbors from European Contact Through the Era of Removal. Chapel Hill: University of North Carolina Press.

Naranjo, Tessie. 2008. Life as movement: A Tewa view of community and identity. *In* The Social Construction of Communities: Agency, Structure, and Identity in the Ancient Southwest, edited by Mark D. Varien and James M. Potter, 251–62. Lanham, MD: AltaMira Press.

Ortman, Scott. 2012. Winds from the North: Tewa Origins and Historical Anthropology. Salt Lake City: University of Utah Press.

Palkovich, Anne M. 1983. The Arroyo Hondo Skeletal Remains. Santa Fe, NM: SAR Press.

ProPublica. 2013. Land grab cheats North Dakota tribes out of $1 billion, suits allege. http://www.propublica.org/article/land-grab-cheats-north-dakota-tribes -out-of-1-billion-suits-allege. Accessed November 10, 2013.

Smith, G. Hubert. 1980 [1951]. The Explorations of the La Vérendryes in the Northern Plains, 1738–43. Edited by W. Raymond Smith. Lincoln: University of Nebraska Press.

Sobolik, Kristin D. 2002. Children's health in the prehistoric Southwest. In Children in the Prehistoric Puebloan Southwest, edited by Kathryn A. Kamp, 125–51. Salt Lake City: University of Utah Press.

Teuton, Christopher. 2010. Deep Waters: The Textual Continuum in American Indian Literature. Lincoln: University of Nebraska Press.

Wilbur, Alicia K., and Jane Ellen Buikstra. 2006. Patterns of tuberculosis in the Americas—How can modern biomedicine inform the ancient past? Memórias do Instituto Oswaldo Cruz 101:59–66.

# CONTRIBUTORS

An interdisciplinary scholar of the indigenous and colonial past, JAMES F. BROOKS is a professor of history and anthropology at the University of California–Santa Barbara. He has held professorial appointments at the University of Maryland and UC–Berkeley, as well as fellowships at the Institute for Advanced Study in Princeton and at the School for Advanced Research in Santa Fe, New Mexico. In 2002 he became the director of SAR Press, and between 2005 and 2013 he served as the president of SAR. He currently serves as the chair of the board of directors of the Western National Parks Association, which supports research, preservation, and education in sixty-six national parks and monuments, including Bandelier National Monument, Chaco Culture National Historical Park, and Channel Islands National Park. Brooks is the recipient of numerous awards for scholarly excellence. His 2002 book *Captives and Cousins: Slavery, Kinship and Community in the Southwest Borderlands* focuses on the traffic in women and children across New Mexico as expressions of intercultural violence and accommodation. His publications also include the edited volumes *Confounding the Color Line: The Indian-Black Experience in North America* (2002), *Women and Gender in the American West* (2004), *Small Worlds: Method, Meaning, and Narrative in Microhistory* (2008), and *Keystone Nations: Indigenous Peoples and Salmon in the North Pacific* (2012). His book in progress, *Mesa of Sorrows: Archaeology, Prophecy, and the Ghosts of Awat'ovi Pueblo*, seeks to understand a massacre that occurred among the Hopis in the year 1700.

CATHERINE M. CAMERON is a professor in the Department of Anthropology at the University of Colorado. She works in the northern part of the American Southwest, focusing especially on the Chaco and post-Chaco eras (AD 900–1300). Her research interests include prehistoric demography, the evolution of complex societies, and processes of cultural transmission. She has worked in southeastern Utah at the Bluff

Great House, a Chacoan site, and in nearby Comb Wash, publishing a monograph on this research in 2009 (*Chaco and After in the Northern San Juan*, University of Arizona Press). She also studies captives in prehistory, especially their role in cultural transmission. She edited a volume on this topic in 2008 (*Invisible Citizens: Captives and Their Consequences*, University of Utah Press). Articles in *Current Anthropology* ("Captives and Culture Change: Implications for Archaeology," 2011) and *American Anthropologist* ("How People Moved Among Ancient Societies: Broadening the View," 2013) continue this theme. She has been a coeditor of the *Journal of Archaeological Method and Theory* since 2000.

GERARDO GUTIÉRREZ is an assistant professor of anthropology of the University of Colorado–Boulder. He received a PhD in anthropological archaeology in 2002 from the Pennsylvania State University, an MA in urban studies from El Colegio de México, and a *licenciatura* (BA) in archaeology from the Escuela Nacional de Antropología e Historia. He has done archaeological and ethnohistorical investigations in many areas of Mexico, including the southern Huaxtec region; the Zapotec, Mixe, and Chinantec regions of northern Oaxaca; the Mixtec-Tlapanec-Nahua-Amuzgo region of eastern Guerrero; and the Soconusco coast. His current primary research focus is the archaeology and ethnohistory of Guerrero, in particular the Postclassic Tlapa-Tlachinollan Kingdom. He is the senior author of *Codex Humboldt Fragment 1 (Ms. Amer. 2) and Codex Azoyú 2 Reverse: The Tribute Record of Tlapa to the Aztec Empire* (bilingual English-Spanish edition), *El Códice Azoyú 2: Política y territorio en el señorío de Tlapa-Tlachinollan*, and *Toponimia náhuatl de los Códices Azoyú 1 y 2: Un estudio crítico*.

KATHLEEN L. HULL is an associate professor of anthropology and a faculty affiliate of the Sierra Nevada Research Institute at the University of California–Merced. Her archaeological and ethnohistoric research interests include analysis of the interplay of demography and culture, ethnogenesis, and the assertion of identity through material culture in small-scale societies of the American West. For example, she has explored impacts of European colonialism on indigenous communities in her book *Pestilence and Persistence: Yosemite Indian Demography and Culture in Colonial California* (University of California Press, 2009) and has recently examined the practice and significance of communal ritual within ancient Native groups of the greater Los Angeles area. Her research has been published in several edited volumes and a variety of professional journals, including the *Journal of Anthropological Archaeology*, *Journal of Archaeological Science*, *Journal of California and Great Basin Anthropology*, *World Archaeology*, *California Archaeology*, and *American Antiquity*.

DAVID S. JONES is the A. Bernard Ackerman Professor of the Culture of Medicine at Harvard University. His initial research focused on epidemics among American Indians, resulting in a book, *Rationalizing Epidemics: Meanings and Uses of American Indian Mortality Since 1600* (Harvard University Press, 2004), and several articles. His current research explores the history of decision making in cardiac therapeutics, attempting to understand how cardiologists and cardiac surgeons implement new technologies of cardiac revascularization. The first book from this work, *Broken Hearts: The Tangled History of Cardiac Care* (Johns Hopkins University Press, 2013), examines why it can be so difficult for physicians to determine the efficacy and safety of their treatments. He is now at work on two follow-up books. One, *On the Origins of Therapies*, traces the evolution of coronary artery bypass surgery. The other examines the history of heart disease and cardiac therapeutics in India.

PAUL KELTON is a professor of history and a member of the executive board of the Indigenous Studies Program at the University of Kansas. His book *Epidemics and Enslavement: Biological Catastrophe in the Native Southeast, 1492–1715* (University of Nebraska Press, 2007) linked major outbreaks of novel diseases to the Native slave trade, while his latest book, *Cherokee Medicine, Colonial Germs: An Indigenous Nation's Fight Against Smallpox, 1518–1824* (University of Oklahoma Press, 2015), focuses on Native efforts to combat disease and colonialism's interference with that fight. Kelton received his PhD in history from the University of Oklahoma in 1998.

CLARK SPENCER LARSEN is the Distinguished Professor of Social and Behavioral Sciences and the chair of the Department of Anthropology at the Ohio State University. He received his BA from Kansas State

University and his MA and PhD from the University of Michigan. He is a former chair of the Section on Anthropology, American Association for the Advancement of Science, vice-president and president of the American Association of Physical Anthropologists, and editor in chief of the *American Journal of Physical Anthropology*. He was elected Fellow of the AAAS in 2006. Larsen's research is primarily focused on biocultural adaptation in the past 10,000 years of human evolution, with particular emphasis on the history of health, well-being, and lifestyle. He has directed the La Florida Bioarchaeology Project since 1982. Larsen is also a codirector of the Global History of Health Project, an international collaboration involved in the study of ancient skeletons from all continents to track health changes since the late Paleolithic, as well as bioarchaeological research programs in Turkey (Çatalhöyük) and Italy (Badia Pozzeveri). He is the author of numerous scientific articles and has authored or edited thirty books and monographs, including *Bioarchaeology: Interpreting Behavior from the Human Skeleton* (Cambridge University Press, 2nd ed., 2015), *Skeletons in Our Closet: Revealing Our Past Through Bioarchaeology* (Princeton University Press, 2000), *Bioarchaeology of Spanish Florida: The Impact of Colonialism* (University Press of Florida, 2001), and *Our Origins: Discovering Physical Anthropology* (W. W. Norton, 3rd ed., 2014).

DEBRA L. MARTIN is the Lincy Professor of Biological Anthropology at the University of Nevada–Las Vegas, and she has research interests in the areas of nonlethal violence and inequality, gender differences and disease, and the bioarchaeology of human experience, with a focus on groups living in marginalized and challenging environments. She is the editor for the Bioarchaeology and Social Theory Series (Springer), a coeditor of the *International Journal of Osteoarchaeology*, and an associate editor for the *Yearbook of Physical Anthropology*. Her recent books include *Bioarchaeology of Violence* (coeditor; University Press of Florida, 2013) and *Bioarchaeological and Forensic Perspectives on Violence* (coeditor; Cambridge University Press, 2014), as well as *Bioarchaeology: An Integrated Approach to Working with Human Remains* (coauthor; Springer, 2013) and *Bioarchaeology of Climate Change and Violence* (coauthor; Springer, 2014). Active in the American Association of Anthropology, she has been the secretary of AAA (2009–12), on the AAA Nominations Committee (2003–5), and on the AAA Executive Board (2005–8).

GEORGE R. MILNER received his PhD from Northwestern University and is currently a professor of anthropology at the Pennsylvania State University. His work covers two fields, archaeology and human osteology, with much of it focusing on the late prehistoric peoples of the American Midwest and Southeast, although he has also undertaken excavations in Egypt and Micronesia. Current areas of active research include, among others, identifying and explaining temporal and spatial variability in warfare in late prehistoric eastern North America, measuring the effect of trauma in medieval Danish populations, and refining skeletal age-estimation procedures for rigorous paleodemographic analyses. Among his many publications are *The Cahokia Chiefdom* (Smithsonian Institution Press, 1998) and *The Moundbuilders* (Thames and Hudson, 2004), both of which examine prehistoric societies in eastern North America.

ALAN C. SWEDLUND is a professor emeritus and a former chair of anthropology at the University of Massachusetts–Amherst. His primary research interests are in historical demography and epidemiology of the United States, particularly New England. Recent publications and research interests have focused on mortality in late nineteenth- and early twentieth-century America, population dynamics in the precontact and historical American Southwest, and the discourses of health reformers, eugenicists, and statisticians during the late Victorian and Progressive eras. He coedited the books *Human Biologists in the Archives* (Cambridge University Press, 2003) and *Plagues and Epidemics: Infected Spaces Past and Present* (Berg, 2010) and authored the book *Shadows in the Valley: A Cultural History of Illness, Death and Loss in New England, 1840–1916* (University of Massachusetts Press, 2010).

# INDEX

# AMERIND STUDIES IN ANTHROPOLOGY

## SERIES EDITOR JOHN WARE

*Trincheras Sites in Time, Space, and Society*
Edited by Suzanne K. Fish, Paul R. Fish, and M. Elisa Villalpando

*Collaborating at the Trowel's Edge: Teaching and Learning in Indigenous Archaeology*
Edited by Stephen W. Silliman

*Warfare in Cultural Context: Practice, Agency, and the Archaeology of Violence*
Edited by Axel E. Nielsen and William H. Walker

*Across a Great Divide: Continuity and Change in Native North American Societies, 1400–1900*
Edited by Laura L. Scheiber and Mark D. Mitchell

*Leaving Mesa Verde: Peril and Change in the Thirteenth-Century Southwest*
Edited by Timothy A. Kohler, Mark D. Varien, and Aaron M. Wright

*Becoming Villagers: Comparing Early Village Societies*
Edited by Matthew S. Bandy and Jake R. Fox

*Hunter-Gatherer Archaeology as Historical Process*
Edited by Kenneth E. Sassaman and Donald H. Holly Jr.

*Religious Transformation in the Late Pre-Hispanic Pueblo World*
Edited by Donna M. Glowacki and Scott Van Keuren

*Crow-Omaha: New Light on a Classic Problem of Kinship Analysis*
Edited by Thomas R. Trautmann and Peter M. Whiteley

*Native and Spanish New Worlds: Sixteenth-Century Entradas in the American Southwest and Southeast*
Edited by Clay Mathers, Jeffrey M. Mitchem, and Charles M. Haecker

*Transformation by Fire: The Archaeology of Cremation in Cultural Context*
Edited by Ian Kuijt, Colin P. Quinn, and Gabriel Cooney

*Chaco Revisited: New Research on the Prehistory of Chaco Canyon*
Edited by Carrie Heitman and Steve Plog

*Ancient Paquimé and the Casas Grandes World*
Edited by Paul E. Minnis and Michael E. Whalen

*Beyond Germs: Native Depopulation in North America*
Edited by Catherine M. Cameron, Paul Kelton, and Alan C. Swedlund